The Inner Building Blocks

The Inner Building Blocks

A Novel to Apply Lean-Agile and Design Thinking for Digital Transformation

Abhishek Rai

BEP

BUSINESS EXPERT PRESS

Leader in applied, concise business books

The Inner Building Blocks: A Novel to Apply Lean-Agile and Design Thinking for Digital Transformation

Copyright © Abhishek Rai, 2022.

Cover design by Rabia Sikandar

Edited by Michelle Shay

Illustration by Dede Setiawan

Interior design by Exeter Premedia Services Private Ltd., Chennai, India

First published in 2022 by
Business Expert Press, LLC
222 East 46th Street, New York, NY 10017
www.businessexpertpress.com

ISBN-13: 978-1-63742-219-9 (paperback)
ISBN-13: 978-1-63742-220-5 (e-book)

Business Expert Press Portfolio and Project Management Collection

First edition: 2022

10 9 8 7 6 5 4 3 2 1

Embrace the change as an ally

Description

Agile is the ability to quickly and naturally adapt to respond to changes. **Most companies are inherently fragile and not agile**—when they are hit by new developments, shifting consumer behavior or fast-moving competition, they struggle, falter and even cease to exist!

Inner Building Blocks is a novel about Neil Frost, a Director of Digital Transformation and Agile Centre of Excellence at Walkers Mart. The company is already grappling with a failing transformation and on the verge of bankruptcy when COVID-19 strikes!

Sid, the Coach instils constructive discomfort through a series of probing questions to:

- **Rethink agility** and **reimagine the future of work** with *hybrid operating models for remote teams.*
- **Launch a series of experiments** to reinvent the *Building Blocks* (e.g., strategy, talent, culture, structures, practices and digital technologies).
- **Discover twenty-six solutions** to *embrace lean-agile mindset for strategic agility.*

Could the company survive amid the global pandemic and ensuing supply chain challenges?

A compelling storytelling approach and provocative dialogues provide relatable context to adopt the concepts. The principles and techniques are delicately camouflaged within the underlying characters, their conversations and situations.

Keywords

lean, agile, digital transformation, hybrid model, talent, design thinking,
scaling framework, scrum, backlog, scrum master, product owner, sprint,
project management, culture, mindset, Kaizen, culture change, program
manager, portfolio funding, DevOps, DevSecOps, MVP, SAFe, LeSS

Contents

Introduction

Why This Book and Why as a Novel? Who Is It for?

Why This Book?

The need and purpose

Most companies are inherently fragile and *not agile*—When they are hit by new developments due to changing consumer behavior or fast-moving competition, they struggle and even cease to exist!

Lean is all about delivering the right product, in the right amount, in the right quality, at the right time, and at the right price to the customer!

Agile is an ability to quickly and seamlessly change course to respond to evolving customer preferences and needs of dynamic business environment and latest digital trends.

Design Thinking is a human-centric problem-solving process grounded in deeply understanding customer's needs, rapid prototyping, and generating creative solutions.

Enterprise agility encompasses the principles and mindsets of lean, agile, and design thinking. Embracing a well-rounded systems view of enterprise agility accelerates the success of digital transformations.

From the time agile manifesto was written in 2001, a significantly large number of organizations have initiated multiyear transformation programs with varying levels of commitments and rigor in their adoptions. Additionally, during the past six to eight years, multiple scaling agile frameworks are becoming popular as a means to "standardize" agile methodologies: scrum, Kanban, and XP. The notion of agile is continuously growing from a software development methodology to a lightweight substitute to project management.

However, a relatively smaller percentage of organizations implementing and/or scaling agile can genuinely claim to have sustained enterprise-wide agility leading to meaningful impact, tangible outcomes, and measurable financial results.

This is because we have restricted our understanding of agility to a limited subset of agile methods and scaling frameworks. While the methods and practices such as stand-ups, scrum ceremonies, and backlog management are important, it could easily mislead us by creating a charade of doing agile without genuinely transforming companies into vibrant, flexible, and nimble entities.

The significant proportion of the organizations deploying agile continue to suffer from silos of teams, sluggish processes, and stalled product releases due to continued traditional mindset, cultural paralysis, and other remnants of the past. A few everyday examples are (i) technical glitches and unstable portals leading to fire fighting and finger pointing; (ii) only a handful of people dominate conversations due to their hierarchical power instead of bringing customers to the core; (iii) excessive process adherence and maintaining status quo stifle creativity, resourcefulness, and innovation; and (iv) meetings are either too rigidly controlled or highly unstructured wasting time and efforts.

If not done right, any enterprise-wide digital and agile transformation could easily become directionless and chaotic. The disruptions, changing consumer behavior, fast-evolving digital trends, and other changes in business environment continually test the flexibility of the companies. The fast-paced disruptions in an industry do not yield to the multiyear transformations of companies. There is a clear need to rethink transformation strategies, roadmaps, and timelines.

The COVID-19 pandemic, turmoil in international supply chains, invasion of Ukraine, and ensuing instability in global business environment coupled with talent shortage have reaffirmed that the survival of a company depends on its adaptability. These recent events are tragic and unprecedented but also unlocks opportunity to be avant-garde in rethinking the importance of agility and in redefining the future of work.

Perfunctory and cursory adjustments to operating models and processes without strengthening the foundational pillars could be counterproductive, expensive, and time-consuming, leading to destruction of business value in the longer term.

Just like strength of our biological Building Blocks, that is, our cells define our fight against infections, viruses, or uncontrollable growth, we need to fundamentally and regularly rejuvenate organizations as living organisms and rebuild from the lens of the organizational Building Blocks, to sustain and grow in volatile times.

Instead of a new agile model or a scaling framework, this book outlines the basic changes to the internal fabric of an organization. When an organization holistically reimagines its *Inner Building Blocks* (e.g., strategy, talent, structures, culture and mindset, processes, and digital technologies), then it manifests in sustained organization-wide agility, which could not only help to respond to external changes but also allows to proactively create those changes to innovate and disrupt the industry. The companies must recalibrate the strategy, revitalize team structures, simplify processes, and rewire talent to be successful in a hybrid-remote model to profitably serve customers.

The Inner Building Blocks is a novel on applying lean–agile and design thinking in digital transformation. The book describes a set of 20 problems (Writings on the WALL) and provides 26 solutions (Building Blocks) numbered from a to z grounded in lean-agile and design thinking.

The story revolves around Neil Frost, a Director of Digital Transformation and Agile Center of Excellence, at Walkers Mart, a leading American retail chain. The plot is set at an *intersection of recent events* like the closure of many businesses amidst the pandemic, continuously evolving consumer behavior, profound life experiences, and resilience in the face of personal setbacks. The company launches a series of experiments to rediscover agility and the future of work to stay afloat.

Further to the introductory chapter, *the book is organized with four sprints.* The sprints are iterative and short timeboxes which are typically two to four weeks in duration.

Each *sprint comprises of three to four chapters.* The underlying chapters are organized using the Kanban principle to visualize core concepts starting with Chapter 2. This mode of using *Kanban board* helps to envisage key problems affecting agility at the opening of the chapter and the solutions are embedded in the body of the respective chapters.

Why as a Novel?

And not as an academic textbook

What gets us into trouble is not what we don't know. It's what we know for sure that just ain't so.

—Mark Twain

Our academic institutions, training firms, and corporate learning departments continue to disproportionately focus on content heavy and theoretical learning. The descriptive content, lengthy presentations, and decks make learning abstract, perfunctory, and superficial.

We cannot continue to assume that the learners and students are passive recipients of information. People are smart, and just providing additional content to mature learners and experienced professionals does not translate to practical wisdom, adoption, and success.

An organization must be viewed as a living entity comprising of people. People work in specific contexts with other people using social routines, collaboration practices, and interaction norms. Certain individuals, functions, departments, and groups wield more power and influence than others in vast majority of organizations. The efforts to truly transform an organization need to consider, contextualize, and meaningfully alter these underlying and apparently sacrosanct power equations.

However, a significant number of professionals and practitioners think of agile, lean, and design thinking narrowly within the constraints of concepts, terminologies, and processes. They try to apply it without appreciating the overall work environment, hierarchical structures, and the boarder system.

This book is an attempt to change that by providing the relatable background and relevant context for applying the concepts using the format of a novel.

Most textbooks have two dimensions: concepts and the underlying content. A business novel is three-dimensional with content, concepts, and context. It lays out concepts and interweaves applicable content within the backdrop of relevant context.

It emphasizes the importance of a rational problem-solving approach tailored for situations and developments. Common observations and events around us reveal simpler ways to learn and solve our problems.

Using the characters and situations, we illustrate an empirical and disciplined thought process focused on asking probing questions to look beyond the obvious into the boarder set of systemic patterns. The chapters revolve around a slew of incisive questions to create the *constructive discomfort*. The answers to the questions are identified with the deductive and logical reasoning approach. This process is related to the Socratic method named after the Greek philosopher, Socrates.

Agility is both science and art. The principles and concepts must strongly relate to the work we do. Instead of content and concept-driven learning, the principles of enterprise agility are illustrated better using the *context-driven learning*. The dialogues, illustrations, and visuals in this book describe how influence, decision making, and speed of execution work within organizations and how it gets shaped by the silos of matrix organizations.

A compelling storytelling approach, day-to-day conversations, and provocative dialogues are deliberate to illustrate the relevance of work environment in the adoption of principles. The conversations are deeply embedded into the work situations, concerns, and challenges within a company. It depicts the significance of exploring the dynamics and circumstances before we jump to an answer or prematurely conclude that there is only one answer. We have presented examples of applying lean and agile thinking in unique environments like a hospital and a mall.

In place of "Push" of more content, frameworks, and methodologies, the novel is meant to encourage "Pull" of *just-enough* concepts—a modular approach to adopt suitable techniques.

A stronger integration of models with context improves the execution along with the end results. The intent is to enable readers to apply easy-to-remember techniques and methods pragmatically to achieve the desired outcomes.

Who Is It for?

The intended audience

We have extensively focused to make this book useful for a broad category of audience by introducing complex concepts in an easy-to-understand, intuitive, and interactive storytelling approach.

The book is perfect for *business leaders, executives, program and project managers, IT and digital professionals, lean–agile practitioners, and management students* to understand lean, agile, and digital with a backdrop of a compelling story inspired by actual events. The learning topics include:

- Expanding *agile to strategic agility* by staying nimble in near term and abundantly open to newer possibilities in longer term
- A simple but powerful approach to bring customer at the core with the *Customer Wall,* Visual Customer Support, and customer-centric OKRs (Objective and Key Results).
- A fundamental construct of Common-minimum Lean–Agile Practices (CLAP), which could be adopted across functions, departments, organizations, and all types of work
- Illustration of a shift from vertical top-down to a flatter organizational structure with a *truly horizontal organization, Flow-to-work, and construct of Chapters*
- Developing the *best-in-class* T-shaped talent pool with *Dojo* and *Continuous Talent* for rapid learning and accelerated implementation
- Zen philosophy for *inner agility, mindfulness, and cultural renewal* to embrace change
- *Hybrid operating model* with an optimum combination of remote and in-person work
- Reduce internal wastes using a visual and collaborative space or a big room, *Obeya*
- *Platform as a strategy* to build business ecosystem and market-place using reusable interactions and shared infrastructure

The *design, product, sales, and marketing professionals,* will additionally learn:

- Profound connection of our minds with the ways we think and behave in our lives
- Advanced methods of Design Thinking, Design *Re*Thinking with seven Zen design principles for improving design of everything—processes, products, and experiences!
- Enriching total experience (i.e., experience of customers, people, and suppliers) by establishing feedback loops with the digital technologies

Acknowledgments

The book is a product of the range of events and cultures I have observed when working with professionals globally. I acknowledge my mentors, co-workers, professionals, students, and trainees whose perspectives and challenges gave me the strength to write this book. Many former colleagues have influenced the thought process, characters, and dialogues. This is also a testimony to the brave souls who show poise, dignity, and endurance every single day to move forward with strength, despite of frustrations of working in traditional, hierarchical, and matrixed organizations.

Thank you, *Business Expert Press*—our publishers: Scott Isenberg for believing in this bold experiment and Tim Kloppenborg and Kam Jugdev for gently but methodically pushing the limits with their pragmatic guidance and encouragement.

A note of thanks to our editors Michelle and Ami and designer Dede who are part of a self-organized, committed teamwork spread across three continents. I convey my gratitude to reviewers Nerida Youngwith and Shweta Bisarya for providing valuable feedbacks.

I am grateful to my thoughtful father, my mother, a true fighter being a cancer survivor, and my sister Richa, who personifies servant leadership. The book is dedicated to my family who continue to sacrifice many weekends when I am working. The storytelling format of the book is inspired by my supportive wife Megha and our chirpy children Ariv and Ami.

Glory to the brave People of Ukraine! for righteous *Obligation to WAR*. They personify the meaning of *Inner Building Blocks*.

Prologue

Context-Based Learning With Characters, Situations, and Conversations

The novel is based on the central belief that principles, model, and techniques need to closely relate to the work we do. In place of abstract competencies, theories, and content, the endeavor of *The Inner Building Blocks* is context-driven, applied, and concise learning by means of the story of a retail company, Walkers Mart.

The characters, developments, and interactions in this book are *intentional and not coincidental*. The plot, considerations, and underlying dialogues are not by chance but are developed to echo the challenges in organizations with lean–agile and digital ambitions. The colloquial tone underpin the attitudes, actions, and mindsets of the individuals and their positions in the company.

The principles and concepts of lean–agile and design thinking are delicately camouflaged within the underlying characters, their conversations, and situations.

The key players in the company and the informal style of conversations between them spin around aspirations for becoming digital and agile. The exchanges and questions are designed to stimulate critical thinking and to draw out ideas to advance our understanding of principles.

The storytelling approach of a novel is designed to establish a bridge between the concepts and where they get applied, that is, at the *Gemba*, a Japanese word meaning "the place of real work."

Readers, who may not intend to read this book as a novel, could flexibly navigate this like a textbook, using the following structure:

Sprint, goal at the beginning and review and retrospective at the end of each sprint.

Kanban board, at the beginning and end of chapters (Chapters 2–16)

Problems, Writings on the WALL numbered from 1 to 20 (WALL#).

Solutions, Building Blocks, numbered with alphabets from a to z (BB).

Problem–Solution Matrix, by which problems are clearly mapped to their solutions (refer Figures 17.3-1 and 17.3-2).

Summary, in the final chapter abridging the key concepts and experiments (Chapter 17).

Key Characters and Their Impact

These characters and the underlying interactions help to answer the fundamental question:

"How leadership style, mindsets, behaviors, culture, and practices impact agility and digital transformation of companies?" For example:

- Why Neil is *failing to steer* the lean–agile and digital transformation of the company?
- How does Sid, the coach, foster *productive discomfort* with his incisive questions?
- How Richie, the CIO, represents the power that leaders wield in *perpetuating the status quo* in organizations?
- How Gus, the VP of IT operations and infrastructure, with his *command-and-control style and micromanagement* impacts culture and team engagement?
- Why Tim's insistence on PMO *status reporting, documentation, and presentation decks* leads to bureaucracy and red-tape?
- Why Saira, a project manager, and Seth, a scrum master, get caught between the two *worlds of project management and agile*?
- Why Daisy, an assertive business leader, struggles to increase the E-Commerce revenues?

Important Situations and Consequences

- How the COVID-19 crisis reveals that companies are inherently *fragile and not agile*?
- Why does *changing behaviors due to the pandemic* requires a new digital mindset?

- What are the *IT challenges* in migrating customers and workforce to digital routines?
- Why *uncontrolled spread of frameworks, processes, tools, and roles* in organizations is as damaging as the abnormal growth of cells in organisms, causing cancer?
- How unforeseen changes in the external business environment expose the *rigidity of internal processes* in funding, product development, and talent mobilization?
- What could we learn about *customer collaboration from a lemonade* stand?

Vital Conversations and the Underlying Lessons

- What is agility? And why is genuine agility so hard to institutionalize and sustain?
- How office politics, rigid culture, *hierarchy, and wasteful practices destroy agility?*
- How could the company processes and structures hide a *whopping 30 percent waste?*
- What forecasting of weather teaches us about confidence levels in *predictability of changes* in short term and long term?
- What could our cell, *the basic Building Blocks*, explain about having strong foundations for sustaining agility, resilience, and growth?
- How stairs, escalator, and elevators demonstrate the *different methods in flow of value?*

Characters

Primary Characters (and Their Fun Facts)

- *Neil* Frost, Director, Digital Transformation and Agile CoE
  "I am coffee connoisseur and could distinguish 42 flavors"
- *Sid* Bose, The Coach
  "I am fluent in seven languages"
- *Gustavo* Perez (Gus-the-Pus), Head IT Operations and Infrastructure
  "I am fluent in seven languages (swear words only)"
- *Richard* Parker (Riche), CIO
  "I am an avid golfer and start my days with golf"
- *Tim* Woods, Head, PMO
  "I have been archiving shopping receipts for last 20 years"
- *Daisy* Love, E-Commerce and Operations Leader
  "I own a light-sport aircraft and a boat"
- *Hana* Saito, Sr. Manager Governance, Compliance and Risks (GRC)
  "Hmm … let me think!"
- *Seth,* Senior Scrum Master
  "I am carbon neutral for last three years!"
- *Keisha* Thomas, Product Owner
  "I was a miss Jamaica contestant in 2006"
- *Saira* Ahmed, Project Manager
  "I started meet-ups on graphic design in three cities"
- *Paris* Fey, HR Director
  "My childhood nickname was 'book of geography'"
- *Neil's family*
  "We always like donuts as frosted just like our last name"
- *Dr. Anu*
  "I could teach you 33 yoga asanas"

Guest Appearances

- Charlie, the CEO
- The GOD, Guru of Design
- Bobby Hanks, IT Director, DevSecOps
- Prof. Nussbaum, Behavioral Scientist
- Doug Dicky, Head of Lean CoE
- Bart, Acting CFO

Figure 0.1 Characters

CHAPTER 1

The Discovery

Background, Key Players, and Situations

Thursday, January 23, 2020

It's 6 a.m. on another cold and foggy morning in Spring Green, a small Midwestern town in Wisconsin. I stretch my right arm out across the satin beige sheets to grab my phone and snooze the alarm. I decide to take a sneak peek at the texts sitting on my home screen, after hearing multiple dings. *Could it be Richie this early*, I think.

Sure enough, it is Richard Parker, my boss and our CIO. I quickly open the messages, thinking it's unusual for Richie to start the day so early in the morning. Half awake, I struggle to read with half-open and blurry eyes. I bring the phone close to my face as I read the text messages.

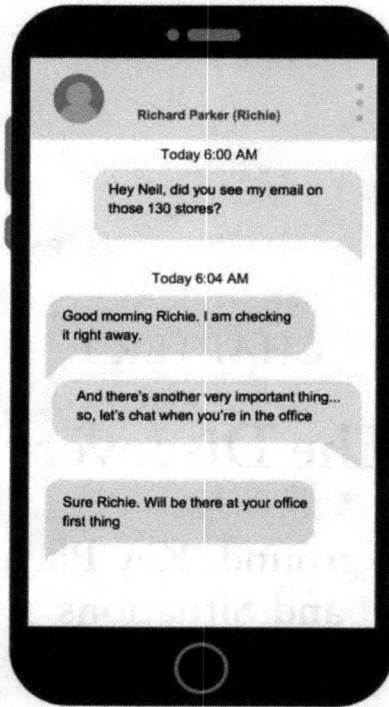

Richard Parker (Richie)

Today 6:00 AM

Hey Neil, did you see my email on those 130 stores?

Today 6:04 AM

Good morning Richie. I am checking it right away.

And there's another very important thing... so, let's chat when you're in the office

Sure Richie. Will be there at your office first thing

Figure 1.1 Text—Richie and Neil

I look at my inbox with an influx of e-mails coming in on my phone. I notice 50 more unread e-mails since I had last checked around 7:15 p.m. I recall having wrapped up earlier than usual in the office, and I didn't check my e-mails as our little one Tina was down with the fever.

While it is common to see a dozen of those e-mails each morning in my role as Director of Digital Transformation at Walkers Mart Corp, where I work closely with various global teams in India, Philippines, Poland, and the United States, looking at the sheer number gives me goosebumps.

Damn, I sigh and quickly slip on my glasses. I start reading them, and many of them are short two liners on our international supply chain issues being driven by coronavirus-related challenges. I am copied in along with five to six other leaders.

Lately, I have been more attentive and sensitive to e-mails where Richie is copied in, and as I scroll down, I see he is indeed copied in most of these. *Something critical was going on.*

Although the Walkers Mart conglomerate is an established and diversified global retail group, it is no secret that our retail chain, which was once one of the leading corporates with high market capitalization, is struggling like never before. Our finance division is considering options like restructuring our debt or cutting back on costs to meet our long-term financial obligations. It seems like we are on the brink of potential bankruptcy if things do not improve soon, especially with significant fluctuations in the market value of the firm. The customers are scaling back on new orders and international suppliers are lately changing their terms of delivery due to red tape in our supply chain processes. This is coming much sooner and much faster.

In the last few years, we have had a monumental ambition for enterprise-wide digital transformations focusing on e-commerce, enhancing online shopping experiences with seamless home deliveries of our products, and embracing newer ways of working and leveraging agile. But we haven't been so lucky when it comes to delivering our ambition.

As I continue to scroll through my e-mails, I find the e-mail from Richie. It was sent just minutes after I went offline, when Tina wasn't feeling too good.

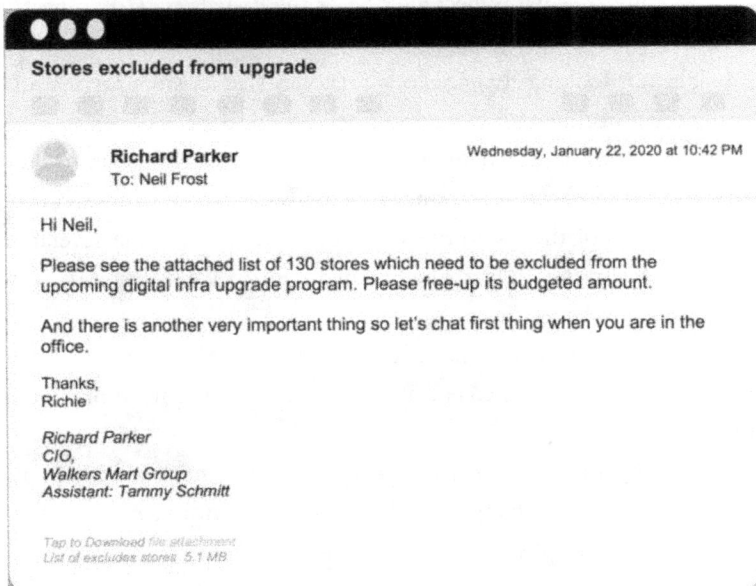

Stores excluded from upgrade

Richard Parker   Wednesday, January 22, 2020 at 10:42 PM
To: Neil Frost

Hi Neil,

Please see the attached list of 130 stores which need to be excluded from the upcoming digital infra upgrade program. Please free-up its budgeted amount.

And there is another very important thing so let's chat first thing when you are in the office.

Thanks,
Richie

Richard Parker
CIO,
Walkers Mart Group
Assistant: Tammy Schmitt

Tap to Download file attachment
List of excludes stores 5.1 MB

Figure 1.2 E-mail—upgrade

I mutter to myself "the writing is on the wall." And these stores too will shut down for good. *Now we have shut our doors at 200 locations out of 406!*

As I mentally add up numbers while recalling the 70 stores that were closed earlier in the summer, I start to wonder which stores had made it to that list.

I have been with Walkers for the past 15 years, who used to be among the top five largest retail groups in the country. I had been doing reasonably well in my previous position as the Senior Manager of Corporate Information Technology before I got promoted to a new role as Director of Digital Transformation with enterprise-wide agile adoption responsibilities. To think of it, that was almost three years ago now that I reflect back on the journey. Essentially, I was asked to spearhead the largest transformation in the company's history, to re-invent the customers' digital experience.

However, last summer, soon after the initial wave of store closures, for the first time in 65 years of monumental history, the company has initiated massive layoffs across the board, especially in the Merchandizing and Store operations group.

The Digital group was not in the initial wave of those impacted by the last layoffs, although deep down I fear that it is only a matter of time when we could inevitably become one of the casualties. *Here comes the second wave of store closures.*

I sigh, not looking forward to what today had in store for me after starting my morning with that sort of news to digest.

I pull myself out of bed and start brushing my teeth. I begin to think about how I could have done things differently. I was one of the architects and champions of the enterprise-wide digital transformation leveraging agile ways of working. In fact, I had named it FA@ST which stood for the "Framework for Agile@Scale Techniques."

Although Walkers Mart has been transitioning to digital and online sales, it still has over 80 percent of its revenues coming from brick-and-mortar stores.

I rinse my mouth, frantically weighing different scenarios in my head. I look at my reflection in the mirror, reminding myself of the greater goal ahead.

After wrapping up reading and responding to other critical and time sensitive e-mails, many of them from Gus, my old boss and our Head

IT Operations and Infrastructure, I take a brief shower thinking about what Richie has in mind and urgently wants to talk about. The steam building up in the shower eases my mind and brings me back to a state of calmness.

I make it downstairs to the kitchen in our four-bedroom home on Green street and join my wife Cindy and our two daughters Ami and Tina over the breakfast bar. I pretend as if it was a usual workday like any other and put a brave smile on my face, trying my best to look cheerful.

"Good morning dad."

I see Tina is giggling and cheerful about something. I kiss her cheek, giving her all my attention.

"Dad I have my story telling contest today. I am going to tell a curious monkey story," she mentions while having her favorite Frosties cereal.

I touch Tina's forehead and try to make eye contact with Cindy.

"She looks totally fine, *right*?" I worry.

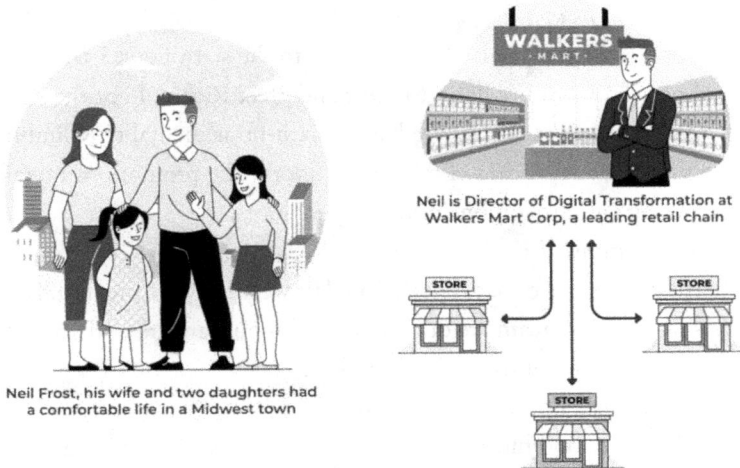

Neil Frost, his wife and two daughters had a comfortable life in a Midwest town

Neil is Director of Digital Transformation at Walkers Mart Corp, a leading retail chain

Figure 1.3 Neil's introduction

I sigh thinking about how today will be another long day after checking my e-mails.

"Hey Cindy, it seems like there's going to be some action today at work."

I explain, frantically scrolling through my work phone as the influx of e-mail notifications pop up.

"I think I'll stay at the office late today, is that ok?" I apologetically look at her.

Cindy looks at me, with a surprising look that reminds me of her follow-up doctor's appointment today that I completely forgot about.

She has been avoiding going to the doctors for a year after seeing abnormal changes to her body with unusual symptoms, but last week she finally went after much persuasion from our family and friends.

I look at my calendar on my phone for a reminder.

Ah, it seems like Becky, my assistant, did not update my calendar. I sigh, mentally shifting my schedule around. I will have to come back home early.

I look at our two beautiful daughters having Frosties for breakfast.

I laugh out loud when Tina cheers me, "Dad you know why I like Frosties, because they have our last name!"

"Bye Tina and Ami, I love you girls." I blow them kisses before leaving.

As I approach the parking lot, I can see the Pearl Green Lexus, which is Richie's car. Richie is early today and has even skipped his golf hours. *Something must be up.*

As soon as I enter the building straight to the sixth floor, I take a left instead of heading to my floor, to meet and greet Richie. I got the sixth-floor office over a year back. We have a sixth-floor mentality. Climbing the corporate ladder means climbing the floors. The promotions literally mean getting an office on one of the higher floors.

"Hello Tammy," I meet his assistant.

She is filing a pile of paperwork from last week's divestiture deal. Legal experts from Hana's team are due to meet with our lawyers to discuss the future terms of our contractual agreements.

"Is Richie in?" I peep at her calendar.

"Yeah Neil. Good morning to you too." She says with an attitude.

"Sorry, that was rude of me, good morning." I apologize with speed.

She smiles, accepting my apology.

"He is inside, feel free to walk in. He canceled his usual meeting with the consulting folks." She mentions, taking a sip of her green smoothie.

The consulting folks are the PMAG team or more formally the Prized Management Advisory Group, who are our consultants for a wide range of programs and projects in the company. They have been supporting my teams as well in Digital by staffing project managers, developers, scrum masters, and agile coaches.

"Hey, good morning Richie."

I walk into his office with confidence, trying to mask my curiosity about what is going on.

"Hey." Richie replies rather tersely while looking at his monitor.

He cuts straight to the chase, as if he knows what I am about to ask.

"So, you saw my message, we are very close to deciding on the dates for those 130 stores, the board is aligned on that."

I watch him closely as he leans back in his chair and puts his hands together. The million dollars' worth of a watch on his wrist glistens as he points at me.

"You know the drill. We don't want to spend any more money on those stores and at the same time, you know we are letting people go at our Chicago office." He continues.

I stand still, uneasy about this.

"I also want to share by EoD, how much we will save by not upgrading those stores and cutting down our work force."

"Yeah, I got that." I reply, trying to pretend as if things were normal.

"So, is there anything else you wanted to talk about?"

The room got tense.

"Yeah." Richie pauses for a few seconds, taking a deep breath.

He looks directly at me.

"So, Neil how is FA@ST going? I know we have had our troubles and tussles, and challenges but I think that is our last bet, which is failing. We are not far from a dismal failure and being a laughingstock pretty soon."

A light laugh escapes his lips.

"Do we know what is going wrong? Our apps take longer to hit market and our guys keep fixing broken stuff rather than building new ones. There are escalations on a daily basis due to outages, teams seem to falter in delivering upgrades, releases get pushed by weeks if not months, we have too much glitches and production defects."

"I continue to hear poor feedbacks about FA@ST."

At this point, I don't know if I am supposed to feel angry or disappointed. He leans back in his leather chair, bringing his hands together.

"FA@ST is part of the problem, I am told, so we need to fix it. And need to fix it now, please! We are running out of options!" He exclaims, catching me off guard.

"Let's not even talk about our extreme budget constraints given the latest business outlook, which by now we all very well understand. Don't we?" He further adds.

"As you will see in the e-mails from this morning, the virus-related supply chain disruption could be bigger than we think." He sighs.

"And for your information, Sid Bose is coming in today."

He swings his tablet device toward me to read the e-mail.

Sid is a Transformation Coach engaged in the corporate department last quarter by Charlie, our CEO. Charlie and Sid have a mutual connection, who recommended him to Charlie over dinner at The Ritz in London with our key international stakeholders from the European markets.

I bring my attention back to Richie speaking.

"I listened to you when you asked for more time to turnaround FA@ST all by yourself, now it's critical we get him actively involved on the ground to get some independent expertise!"

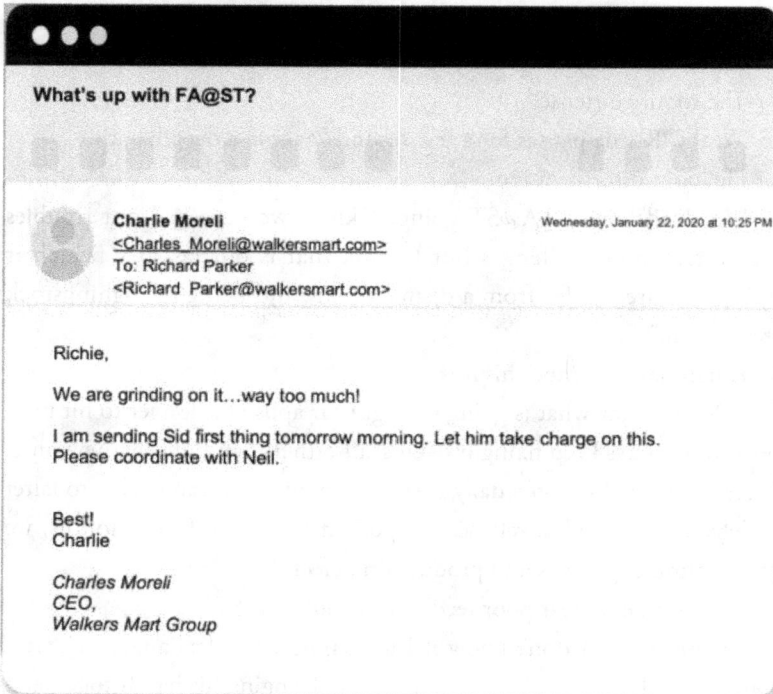

What's up with FA@ST?

Charlie Moreli
<Charles_Moreli@walkersmart.com>
To: Richard Parker
<Richard_Parker@walkersmart.com>

Wednesday, January 22, 2020 at 10:25 PM

Richie,

We are grinding on it...way too much!

I am sending Sid first thing tomorrow morning. Let him take charge on this. Please coordinate with Neil.

Best!
Charlie

Charles Moreli
CEO,
Walkers Mart Group

Figure 1.4 E-mail—FA@ST

This guy, Sid is known in the industry for his deep expertise to "transform transformations" especially those which are struggling pretty much like ours.

Richie bends his head to look at the ding on his phone, hinting that this conversation is over.

"We will meet him and coordinate it," I reply and start to make my way out of his office.

There was no other civilized way Richie could have said this. I guess I will be forced to hand over my own job to someone like him if I can't figure out a way to collaboratively work with him. I feel insecure with the thought.

In the last three years, Walkers has been trying in some ad hoc ways to respond to changing customer preferences by piggybacking on our digital programs, which some colleagues used to refer to as lean–agile transformation.

We have been using digital and agile interchangeably in the company. I have both the responsibilities, and in tough meetings, I frequently use the chicken and egg analogy, asking our leaders whether they could be digital without being agile, or the way around. I know I use some of the semantics more often than I should to avoid the elephant in the room. But somehow, it seems like we have confused ourselves way too much in the process.

In the middle of my thoughts, I see Daisy walking toward me. She always means business.

"We are behind our e-commerce revenue target which makes my work more challenging in the current ambiguous business environment."

She sighs, muttering her regrets.

"Ship-to-store features are getting delayed further and further. What do you know about it? And do you really care?" She folds her arms, looking at me.

"I absolutely do Daisy," I say with some level of embarrassment.

Daisy is in a full venting mode and rightly so, I reassure her.

"Are they still waiting for someone's blessing?" Her tone changes.

"I know, I know all that." I say in a hurry to calm her down.

She speaks over me as she waves her hands about in the air.

"Gus actually says he doesn't care what customers say and his responsibility is narrowly limited just to ensure the stability of his IT systems."

"GRC folks wanted another two full weeks of compliance reviews, and as expected, Hana concurs with her team. I realize as per our process that we need an exceptional approval from our CIO to get the release done."

"I had e-mailed Richie precisely as you asked me last week. But it appears that he didn't read his e-mails. So, you tell me, what am I supposed to do?" She leans back against the wall in the hallway.

"I know I sound upset, but I feel like our processes and release timelines are getting crazier day by day."

Daisy clearly feels that her e-commerce priorities are suffering due to our rigid processes.

I step forward, trying to reassure her again.

"I will look into it shortly."

She walks away without responding to my repeated assurances.

Daisy has been quite unhappy lately with project delays and the rising budgets of my teams. She is a straight talker and an assertive leader known for getting things done, even if it means having difficult and uncomfortable conversations.

Her tone comes from her clout and the significant influence she has at Walkers, much more than me by status and title. She is the senior VP and heads the entire e-commerce business portfolio, with Digital as one of her priorities, although I know it's a major headache.

Her digital projects, especially ones for omni channels and payment gateways projects, are frequently delayed in releasing newer upgrades, apps, and features. She is also my boss on the business side of the organization, so I am not about to let her down.

I quickly get distracted, as my phone begins to ring. It's my wife Cindy.

"Hey hun, the doctor's office just called. They want you to accompany me as they want to share the results."

"That's unusual but yeah sure. I will be happy to. I'll text our babysitter to keep an eye on the kids until we are back home." I mention, making a plan.

"One more thing, I wanted to let you know during my last visit, the doctor noticed some abnormalities from the ultrasound, so she took a sample for a biopsy too." She mentions.

"Is everything ok honey? What else did she say?" I come back to reality.

A part of my heart sinks, thinking the worst. I play with my fingers, trying to keep calm for my wife, but the possibility of it being anything cancerous dampens my hope. *I'm overthinking it's probably not a big deal.*

"You know I had my last annual checkup, so I thought they were being extra cautious. I did not want to bother you for nothing. You already have too much on your plate with all that's going on at work."

I respond to Cindy in a feeble voice.

"I, I don't even know what to say honey."

I am still processing the information and she lets the news sink in for the next few seconds. But soon after, she tries to rush the conversation and bring it to an end.

"I gotta go Neil, I love you!"

"Love you too." I manage to say, without releasing the full extent of my emotions. We exchange those words as we usually do but with a much deeper meaning this time.

I hang up and find myself speechless. I am in shock. My wife, the pillar of our family is being tested for cancer. Cindy is barely 40 years old. *How the hell is this happening?*

Walkers has kept me so preoccupied lately that I almost forgot about Cindy's lump that she mentioned a few days ago. It didn't look like a tumor, but I am no doctor.

I hurriedly create a reminder on my phone as we have the 4:15 p.m. appointment to discuss the results of Cindy's biopsy report.

As I reach my office, I notice someone already inside. A middle-aged stranger in a blue surfer t-shirt, a leather jacket, black sneakers, and jeans is in my office. His dress code makes him stand out as we are all invariably more formally dressed.

After multiple approvals, I had allowed smart casual dress codes in a few digital teams only on the last Fridays of the month. But the culture was still very much formal and didn't accept anything otherwise.

As soon as I enter my office, this man gets up and apologizes for not requesting to meet me formally via e-mail.

"I'm sorry to intrude, I just took some liberty to make myself comfortable. It's an aggressive timeline you know!" He blurts out loud, sensing that I was clueless about who he was.

"Sid Bose, pleasure to finally meet you, Neil."

He moves forward with his right hand out to shake mine. I don't show much thought or emotion as I am still recovering from my call with Cindy.

"Same here," I reply poignantly.

"How are you this morning?"

The guy looks hyperactive and wants to strike the conversation right away. He wants to sound friendly, but I am not interested. I was not expecting to see him in my office in this way and definitely not so soon.

So, I nod lightly, not willing to say much.

"As you already know by now, I'm Neil the Director of Digital and Agile," I make it clear, my position pointing at my silver nameplate on my desk.

"I noticed some of the posters and displays of FA@ST on my way to your office. I do have quite a high-level background, but would you care to fill me in?" He tries to get too comfortable not hiding his curiosity.

"So why are you doing agile or lean or FA@ST, or whatever you want to call it?"

"Yes, I could." I reply thinking what is his deal and what this guy really up to?

Deep down, I am thinking at the back of my mind, *do I really have a choice when it comes to working with this guy? And is he, my replacement?*

He scans my office with his eyes, eager to get to the bottom of it.

He reaches to the left side white board "Could we structure our session on the following points?"

- Why? *Purpose of the transformation*
- What? *The current scaling framework*
- Who? *Key stakeholders and their roles*
- How? *Approach to assess the challenges*
- When? *Timelines to transform the transformation*

And anything you want to add?

"This seems like a handful. I'm not sure I have all the time you are asking for."

"Better make it Neil, you know what is at stake." He almost intimidates me.

"Let me cancel my meetings for today so you can continue to interrogate me." I say rudely in a frustrated voice.

I soon try to zip it up before it's too late, discerning this guy has a mandate from none other than the CEO!

Why?

Purpose of the Transformation

"So, first item on the purpose is a great question. Unfortunately, the answer changes depending on whom you ask. I do have my own view too. Let us come back to this one toward the end as I want to share a boarder perspective with you not just mine."

I move on to the next point to avoid too much conversation on this difficult topic.

What?

The Current Scaling Framework

I try my best to stand tall with confidence, explaining to him on the whiteboard.

"So, we started the FA@ST program, which stands for Framework for Agile@Scale Techniques, about three years ago with a five-year road map. Technically, we are somewhere in the middle of it, but you know, the leadership feels we are not getting the right outcomes. In fact, Richie and perhaps some other people could argue FA@ST is meant to make us faster, but it has actually made us slower though I don't entirely agree."

"We have trained and certified many people too across the company." I try to defend my side of story.

"With budgets drying up we need to make some difficult choices and take hard decisions if we want to keep doing this transformation or if we want to put a lid on it forever."

"What are your thoughts and any questions for me?" I ask almost fleetingly.

Sid smiles, letting a laugh escape his mouth.

"I have plenty of questions, all I do is I ask questions and we will jointly find the answers. What do you say buddy?"

"Actually, we are going to go together. Let's go for some coffee, shall we?" Sid replies.

I pause to grab my cold iced quad latte and start to guzzle before continuing to the next item.

Who?

Key Stakeholders and Their Roles

After checking the door is closed, I list down main contacts on a notepad adding some color:

- *Richie* is the CIO. He is my boss and given our traditional and top-down culture I am not expected to criticize or challenge any of his decisions. Let's just leave it there.
- *Gus* is the VP of IT operations and infrastructure. He is known for his pushy management style and rather brazen way of talking to people.
- *Tim* is head of PMO. He is known for status reporting and long meetings.
- *Daisy* is a senior business leader and responsible to grow our e-commerce business. She is a straight-talker and widely known in the company for getting things done.
- *Seth* is a senior scrum master. He helps teams do agile in our *not-so-agile* company.
- *Keisha* is a seasoned expert from Daisy's team and represents product owners.
- *Saira* is a project manager. We reach out to her to make fancy presentation decks.
- *Hana* heads the Governance Risk and Compliance, while *Paris* is the HR director.

"What exactly does Tim do in PMO?" Sid asks with a smirk on his face.

"He is the boss of Project and Program Managers."

Sid rolls his eyes, "Yes, but what does he do?"

"Bosses do lots of things in this company. They attend meetings, make comments, review deliverables, receive status review reports, send nasty e-mails, allocate work, approve or decline expense reports, conduct performance appraisals, and give lengthy speeches in town halls."

"And they regularly ask you, 'how is it going?' ... without really meaning it. But don't quote me, or else you will get me fired." I gently warn him.

"Absolutely, I appreciate you being transparent and please know that our personal conversations are strictly confidential. You have my word." Sid assures me with a loud laugh.

"But to your question, I think Tim is the guy you could work with as well, especially on the PMO stuff."

"Yes, I will be very interested to meet Tim, perhaps tomorrow. The role of PMO and project managers in a lean–agile transformation is always intriguing and could be equally challenging too." Sid adds.

I need to introduce you to Gus and then Tim, who are two leaders who will dislike seeing a stranger walking and talking to their teams right in their territories.

"Program and project managers and some scrum masters report to Tim, while IT and some digital folks roll up to Gus ... with resources loaned to Tim and myself."

- Central Testing
- Enterprise Architecture
- Technology Services
- Infrastructure
- DevSecOps
- Release Management
- Environments
- Production Support

"And there is a layer between Business, Digital, and IT called Business Technology. You can say it is like information system (IS) some companies have a legacy from the last decade.

Our product departments are run by a VP who has a dotted or solid line reporting relationship with Daisy, who heads e-commerce. She has a mandate and aggressive targets for growing online business in each of the segments."

I jot down the product departments on the notepad.

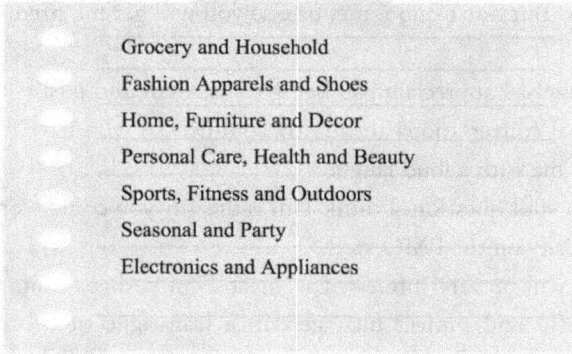

Grocery and Household

Fashion Apparels and Shoes

Home, Furniture and Decor

Personal Care, Health and Beauty

Sports, Fitness and Outdoors

Seasonal and Party

Electronics and Appliances

Figure 1.5 Product departments

I look at my phone it's already 12:15 p.m. *Where did my morning go? This jerk is taking the rest of it!*

We take a lunch break and then meet again after an hour on the next topic.

How?

Approach to Assess the Challenges

"So, what is your framework? Do you have a deck?" I point a finger to his closed laptop.

I am expecting him to show me another colorful and decorative PowerPoint with a swanky assessment model along with some consulting talk.

"None. We don't need a shiny new framework or a slew of abstract concepts." He surprises me.

"Really ... ? So, what's the deal? What do you think needs to be changed in our current framework?" I speak in a puzzling tone.

He responds in a pensive tone. "Neil, as we know people don't work alone. They work with other people, in groups and in contexts using a set of practices, norms, and interaction routines.

We need to understand *the relationships between people, concepts, and their work context."*

"But how exactly could we do that?" I inquire immediately in a perplexed tone.

"We must *go and see* to find what is going on around us and ask the right questions.

We need to walk around the office and talk to those who do the actual work. We need to adopt active listening, develop situational awareness, and respectfully ask inquisitive questions to each other and to everyone. In our constant quest to find answers, we don't ask enough questions and don't listen as much. As human beings we generally tend to rush toward solutions without clearly defining the problem, its context, root causes, and sources."

He pauses for a few seconds and then persists.

"We need to craft incisive and probing questions to build a deeper understanding of the situation. The questions need to be built to activate our reflection, analysis, and further research. They need to be designed much like the Socratic method to stimulate our critical thinking."

"We must define questions which we are trying to answer?" I try my own incisive question.

He strongly nods. "Exactly. There you go!"

"And you think this will help us to transform Walkers?" I say with a sarcastic pitch to convey my reluctance with his approach.

He continues to rationalize "The questions help us to analyze the root causes of our problems. It aids us to explore solutions to our problems that are specific, contextual, and firmly embedded into the real work.

We must carefully *learn lessons from our conversations, situations, and developments.* This aids us to recognize the *context of our problems by connecting with our current knowledge.* For example, our knowledge of agile and lean principles could help us to objectively assess the effect of rigid processes, broken systems, undue influence of certain individuals, and excessive hierarchical powers.

And the most important of all *how agile are we in serving the customers and how customers feel about their experience?*

"We will define a set of hypotheses and launch a set of experiments to test those hypotheses."

Sid further explains.

When?

Timelines to Transform-the-Transformation

"Instead of planning afresh for another reset of transformation for many more months, we will do it incrementally and iteratively." Sid starts writing on the right side of the whiteboard.

"We could have four sprints with a lightweight cadence so we have a structure and timebox to establish feedback loops with executive team, and stay truly lean and agile to *Transform-the-Transformation.*"

The cadence of four sprints will be:

- Sprint 1: Current state assessment: 2 weeks
- Sprint 2: Reflection and Reimagination: 2 weeks
- Sprint 3: Analysis and Improvements: 3 weeks
- Sprint 4: Rebuilding and Recovery: 4 weeks

Each Sprint needs to have the following events.

Sprint Planning

This is on the first day of sprint to plan, prioritize and commit to the backlog. The backlog includes the *sprint goal* and a list of work items to be achieved within the sprint.

Stand-Up

Fifteen minutes to communicate progress to each other and identify blockers. Standing up the team helps keep meetings short! No preparation is required and this is not status reporting.

Sprint Review

This is on the last day of sprint to demonstrate the current state of the product and receive feedbacks from the customers or a diverse set of stakeholders who represent customers.

Sprint Retrospective

This is on the last day of the sprint to reflect on what went well, what didn't go well, and prioritize improvement actions for the next sprint.

I ask with a stunned look at his proposed cadence and timeline, "I have never seen sprint cadence used to launch a bunch of experiments. And could we do this in 11 weeks?"

Sid tries to calm me down.

"This helps us to identify problems, prioritize, and actionize top improvements in PMO, IT, and digital within this timeframe and establishes a predictable rhythm. We can inspect and adapt our cadence a needed. If we get this right, we could absolutely see the effect of these improvements in the Walkers business performance."

"Is it not too ambitious?" I confront him again.

"Do we have a choice?" Sid replies succinctly.

I reluctantly agree to set up a lightweight cadence for our TTT, starting with stand-up and retrospective.

Sid continues. "We need a few working sessions for the next few weeks to define the tactical plan of action. I need key vision–mission statements and information on funding processes, product roadmaps, team structures, organization charts, and roles and responsibilities to simultaneously define our rules of engagement."

"And I propose we both jointly visualize all our *activities, meetings, agendas, and sessions* using a Kanban board. The Kanban method allows to visualize the flow of work and limit work in progress (WIP). The word Kanban has origins in Japanese and roughly translates as 'visual card'. A simple three columns updated at least once every 48 hours, with *To-do, In progress,* and *Done.*

This helps to understand the workload and if it is regularly *flowing to completion.* Let us put a limit of six for work in progress for us, meaning items in 'In Progress' column is less than six at any point of time. We could jointly update the Kanban board on key priorities but could you help set it up?" He is polite but really assertive.

"Let us use the Kanban board during our stand-ups." He affirms.

"Wow! That's a lot of information, documents, and things to do. It seems like I need to halt all of my work and give you what you need." I say with an overwhelmed voice.

"Can we get help from your assistant, Becky, to align our calendars with items of Kanban board and timely schedule meetings and block time for our conversations?" He asks.

I look at my watch. It's almost time to start driving for Cindy's appointment. "Let me see what I can do, but for now I have to leave for a personal appointment."

I am already suspecting by now that he's up to something wicked. He wants a Kanban board, runs sprints, and makes all our problems visual, out there in the open!

I feel like he is trying to publicly embarrass me and get me fired.

Cindy's Appointment

I hurriedly start driving back as soon as he gets out of my car.

As I park my car on my driveway in front of our home, Cindy is almost ready and stepping out to meet me. Our babysitter has just arrived too.

"Hey girls, seems like we are going to have some fun tonight?" The sitter smiles at the kids.

We arrive at the medical practice 20 minutes before Cindy's appointment.

The fear and the anxiety that we are both feeling is evident, and it's hard to mask. I hold Cindy's hand in mine, looking at the clock and struggling to keep it together.

I look at the practice, staring at the other patients in the waiting area, and after waiting for almost half an hour, a woman who looks like she is in her late 30s emerges from one of the rooms.

"Mr. and Mrs. Frost, hi my name is Dr. Anu. How are you today?" She smiles, opening up a calm and welcoming conversation to relax us both.

As we reach her office, Dr. Anu mentions that Cindy's regular doctor had referred to her for discussing the report.

We both take a seat, wishing we could get past this and put it behind us.

"Mr. and Mrs. Frost, I carefully looked at the biopsy reports from the tests."

I gulp, preparing to hear the news.

"After cautious consideration we concluded that Cindy has TNBC, what we call triple-negative breast cancer."

She yields for us to assimilate the news, and Cindy is quiet. I hold her hand to comfort her, but in the process, I am feeling overwhelmed.

"Sorry so TNB?" I stutter.

"TNBC," Dr. Anu gently corrects me patiently.

"And so, what does this TNBC mean again? What does it really mean?" I hear my own unsettled voice as I am speaking up.

"Is it treatable?" I blurt out.

"Yes, it is treatable." Dr. Anu nods, placing her hands on her desk.

"But I am afraid, this type of cancer is considered to be an aggressive type of cancer, with a poorer prognosis than other types of breast cancer. I am sorry to share the bad news." She adds.

At this point, I am flabbergasted with all the medical terms.

Dr. Anu suggests for Cindy to return in two days to decide and discuss her treatment plan and treatment options.

Our drive back is silent. I try extending my hand to touch her palm, but Cindy is in a state of denial and confusion. I see her vigorously searching websites on her phone about breast cancer survival rates.

I am also pondering on my own frightful day at work. *We can't lose my health insurance at this time*; I think in my own deep thoughts. Losing my job could now mean almost losing our health insurance as well. *How did we get here?*

I feel my stomach turn. Cindy's cancer diagnosis will be extremely terrifying for our family; an array of thoughts crosses my mind.

We get home just after 8:50 p.m. I am relieved to hear from the babysitter that both our girls are already asleep. I try to make some time to comfort Cindy as we have time to ourselves.

We barely eat our dinner with some leftovers of the Fork-Tender Pot Roast from last night. I could see tears in Cindy's eyes. We hug and I try to soothe her while controlling my own tears, staying strong for her sake.

As I lie on my bed in sorrow after a grueling and devastating day, I say a prayer in my head.

My life has just changed in ways I had never expected, both professionally and personally in less than 24 hours.

SPRINT 1

Current State Assessment

Sprint Goal

- Formulate a lean–agile approach to clearly define key problems in the company's transformation.
- Identify areas leading to the destruction of value across the company.
- Diagnose the root causes with Gemba Walks, value stream mapping, and waste analysis.

CHAPTER 2

Building the WALL

An Inclusive Approach to Define Problems

Friday, January 24, 2020

The news of Cindy's diagnosis is starting to sink in. Both of us get little sleep and wake up quite early in morning.

Our early morning spins around hugging, patting, and imaging yesterday's hospital visit and some intermittent conversations.

The silence of the predawn hours makes me anxious in anticipation of what the future holds. I wake up early and heed to Sid's advice and create a new Kanban board for key sessions, activities, and their preparations.

Given our conventional and hierarchical culture, I start with a restricted access of the board to Sid, myself, and my assistant. I could set up working sessions with scheduling help from Becky.

Table 2.1 Kanban board

To-do	In progress	Done
• Approach for enterprise-wide retrospective • Why? Purpose of the transformation • Introduction to Gus and his management style • Analyze Net Promoter Score (NPS) and voice of customers		

Transform-the-Transformation Kanban Board

I feel exhausted after staying up for most of the night, holding Cindy and comforting her.

We have another open and honest conversation about how we both feel about the news.

Our daughters wake up soon after with the beeping sound of the coffee machine. Cindy is still pretending to be normal with the girls, but I don't know how much longer we can keep this up.

I look at her eyes and clearly, she has not slept much. I didn't either. I take a sip of my cup of coffee, looking carefully at Cindy.

"Girls come on you can't eat and dance at the same time, table manners. C'mon, go and grab your lunch bags before the school bus arrives."

As I hit the road after breakfast, I continuously ruminate about Sid's question from the yesterday. *So, why do we need to do a transformation?*

I grab a cup of coffee on my way and open the door firmly.

"Good morning." I greet Sid, but I don't get an eager response. It's almost time for our first session on calendar.

Approach for Enterprise-wide Retrospective

As I unzip my laptop bag, I see Sid is busy on the whiteboard. "You know we need the Writing on the *WALL.*" He says out loud.

Sid gets up from his chair and starts looking around our office, checking out all the space and staring at our posters and walls for the next few minutes. I am not sure what he is up to. I am getting nervous.

"You know what?" Sid pauses, brushing his chin.

I stay silent almost avoiding him as I continue flicking through my phone, checking my latest notifications. Sid clicks his fingers in my face.

"Hey you listening?"

"Yes, sorry go ahead."

I try to pretend as if I have more important things to do on my phone. This was my small gesture and a way of telling him who is still the boss here!

"We need to create a space; you know a *WALL* for us somehow." He stresses on the WALL.

"What's that corner office? Looks like an amazing place for us to set a wall."

He points to the other side of the hall with glass doors.

"Who sits there?" He insists for a fast response.

"What WALL?" I almost sound frustrated by his many questions.

"Are you being serious right now or are you playing games with me?" I demand a clear answer.

At this point, I am no longer hiding my frustration, with a scowled look on my face making it clear that I am still perplexed by his pushy and strange behavior.

Suddenly, he is a bit composed and doesn't even bother looking at me. He gets up from the chair, imagining something in his head.

"Yes, we will create a *WALL*!" He exclaims in his own world.

He walks to the mini whiteboard on the right of my desk, picks a dry erase marker, and writes

WALL ... **W**alkers **A**gile–**L**ean **L**essons learned

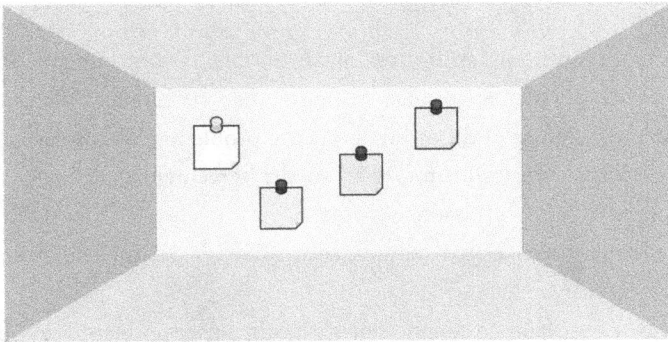

Figure 2.1 **WALL**

"Any technique is as good as our ability to remember it." Sid remarks insisting that we keep things intuitive by using terms which are easy to remember and quick to recall. He wants to be uber creative in making concepts unforgettable so that they can be evoked in a jiffy.

"This will be our space for everyone to come, enter, see, and write on, but let's keep it tidy and readable for us. And by *us,* I mean both of us." He adds.

"We will have this WALL, and everyone will write on it whatever they have learned and struggled with until now, essentially answering the questions we all want answers to, like why we are not truly transforming Walkers—what's working, and what's not working.

An enterprise-wide retrospection and observations on FA@ST all on a visual board, *the WALL!*"

He exclaims, stretching his arms out in emphasis. I try to visualize what he was trying to communicate.

"We will identify problem areas and make things visual on the Wall. We will surface up and irradiate our problems. We will jointly assess what's not working and further improve what is actually working. Everyone needs to contribute to this so it's a democratic, inclusive, and comprehensive exercise. We need diverse perspectives to define our problems. Everything needs to be on the table."

He continues.

"So, we will write our problems and the writing will be on the WALL! You know what I mean?" He looks at me for confirmation.

"Are you suggesting that we wash the dirty laundry in the public?" I confront him.

"Actually, we are going to make problems transparent, totally transparent, and visible to all! Nothing should be hidden. We need to be absolutely honest and candid about the problems. We are also doing this to sensitize leadership to get a broader agreement and buy-in!" He emphasizes bringing his hands together.

"So, could we take that space, it seems like it's vacant?" Sid points to a empty executive office.

I start to explain, "Actually that high office used to belong to Shawn Callaghen. He was a Senior VP of OSAP but ended up being a casualty in the last round of pink slips." I quickly realize that I am sounding quite sarcastic as I utter those words.

"Hang on, let me check with Paris, our HR Director. She oversees the HR and also the facilities department."

I scoot the office chair, and bash the keys on the keyboard, as I click and open our internal instant messaging chat window and start typing.

Sid continues to dig in, "So, what's the deal with OSAP?"

I begin to explain, "Shawn headed the Office of Strategic Alliances and Partnerships, or OSAP in short. Every ask coming out of OSAP was ASAP! They were involved in every major decision on the digital side of things too, though I considered Richie to be my boss based on the organization chart. The OSAP head who was SVP seemed to trump Richie often for reasons I could not understand, but clearly that is above my pay grade." I openly admit to Sid.

"No one really knows what his actual role, responsibilities, and exactly what he or his team did when he was around. He had a fancy office, lots of meetings, many external visitors in a day, and direct access to CEO. Yet still, he was fired in the end!"

"No kidding!" Sid exclaims.

I hear a ding from my chat window and Paris has responded quickly.

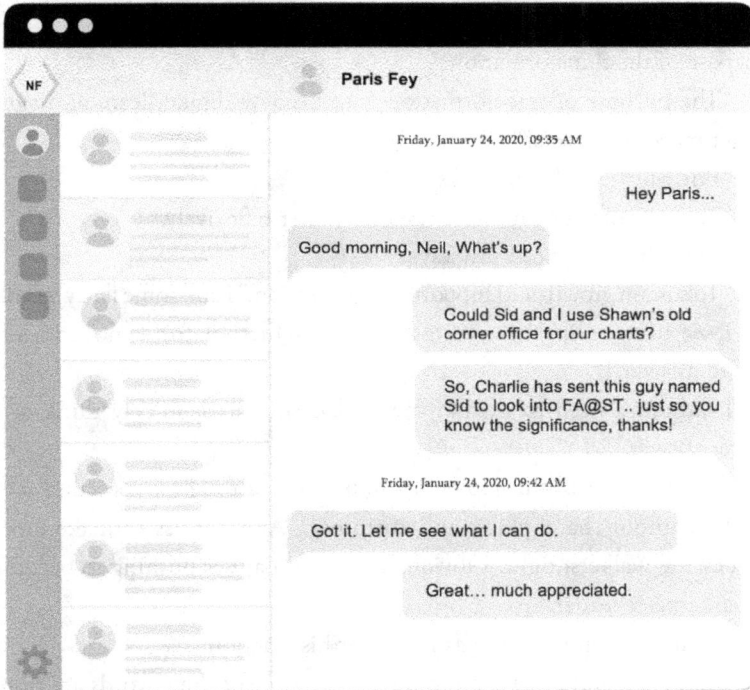

Figure 2.2 Chat—Paris and Neil

As a curious HR person, she walks into my office to meet this new guy sent by the CEO.

"Hey, I am Paris, I am HR head." She shakes Sid's hand.

"Let me guess from your name, where you born in Paris?" Sid jests.

"Yes, but not the Paris in France, but Paris, Texas. My maiden name was Paris Portugal and my classmates made fun of me, calling me names like *book of geography!*"

Finally, she turns to me.

"Hey Neil, we had planned to convert Shawn's vacant office to a large conference room. But our facilities budget got suspended recently. So, its vacant for now, you guys could use it."

I thank her as she walks out.

Sid nudges me, "So, any initial thoughts for our WALL?"

Why? Purpose of the Transformation

I did think about that question yesterday "Hmmm. So, what is the purpose of the transformation?"

"The purpose of transformation is to become digital, lean, and agile to get more customers."

"But why?" He further asks.

"To get more customers," I respond rather reflexively.

He is tilting his head sideways.

"To sustain growth and support wealth creation." I add some fancy words.

I see him rolling his eyes as he probes further for a more meaningful answer.

I fathom a need to expand my explanation, and quickly think of a better answer.

"We are transforming to compete better in a tough market and naturally help our shareholders and customers. And I guess to make more money for Walkers, right? Obviously, the company is pushing to become a marketplace leader."

I hear my own rambling as I wait for his reaction.

"I know I sound like I'm rambling, but some of these words are from our company's mission statement." I admit.

"Could I see it? I'm curious, were you part of building it?" He asks.

"Honestly, no I was not part of it. It was created by our top management team in a ski resort up in the mountains about four years ago. We don't really pay much attention to it. We take new employees through the mission statement during their orientation and occasionally display it at our corporate events, town halls."

We look at my screen where I pull up the mission statement from the intranet.

Walkers' primary objective to transform is to maximize shareholder value and attain undisputed marketplace leadership with aggressive business growth and best quality through dedication of our employees.

He ponders for the next few minutes.

"Are we missing something?"

"What do you mean?" I quickly ask a reverse question.

"Where is the customer in this statement?"

"The primary focus is on shareholders and being a market leader not customer? The employees are asked for their dedication and commitment, but they are not involved in building the statement. Most employees on ground I bet may not be aware of this." He is almost denigrating our mission statement.

"Well, you have a point. It's not mentioned but 'quality' wording is partially for customers. Never mind, I agree it's not distinctive and inspiring." I say giving up any defense.

"Our company culture has a top-down execution, the kind where no questions are asked. You don't question your superiors you just do it. I know I didn't contribute much in communicating either, but they kept me occupied almost every day due to so-called other priorities, firefighting almost on a daily basis to navigate the complex and siloed organization, while managing Richie's leadership meetings, reports, and satisfying Tim's PMO expectations."

How could we blame our frontlines and the boots on the ground of their oblivion? They are regularly told not to ask too many questions about transformation … just do it. The company has continued years of transformation with little change on the ground. The initiatives have restarted and pivoted multiple times and we continue to struggle.

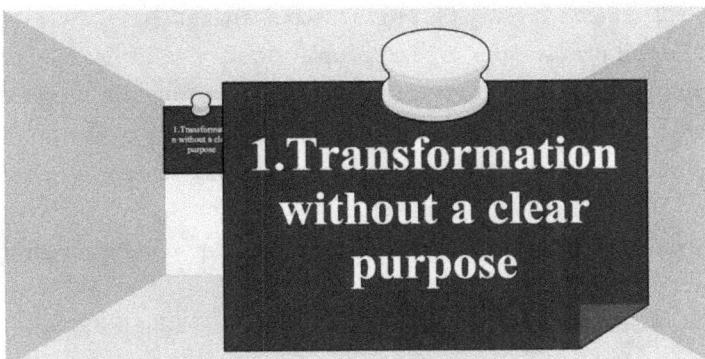

Figure 2.3 WALL No. 1

Table 2.2 The Writing on the WALL No. 1

1. Transformation without a clear purpose	
What does it mean?	• A common motive of companies launching multiyear transformations is to follow their competitors or other companies without a concrete purpose or clearly defined outcomes • There is no clear and consistent way to objectively measure results and make regular course corrections, when needed
What are its effects?	• Diminishing return on multiyear investments • Opportunity costs of not focusing on immediate outcomes • Lack of excitement and clear direction for workforce

"That's spot-on Neil. The transformation as the word suggests is about fundamentally shifting the ways of working. However, most of the organizations have started to adopt agile without making the required changes in their structures, cultures, and mindset."

He grabs another pen to add another point while reviewing our business strategy and product documentation.

Soon after, we walk and sit on a corner table.

"Hey man, I could sense there has been some tension between us. Do you mind if we have a heart-to-heart conversation?" Sid suggests out of nowhere.

"Hmmm I have a busy calendar today." I frown.

"I know this is strange and a bit intimidating for someone external like me to come and tell you guys what to do. Isn't it? So, let me talk as straight and transparent as I can be. Hear me out." He still opens up.

"I get that you are anxious, insecure, and somewhat defeated from the recent pressure. I am not here to cast aspersions or criticize anyone, but together we can help Walkers succeed. And we will! I don't intend to be your replacement. Period." He sets the record straight.

"We will plan sessions to meet people and observe the current state. You will be driving this effort with my support from the rear seat so that you are not undermined in any way. Believe me or not, your success will be my success and we both know our success totally depends on turning around Walkers as soon as possible.

And for this, we need to form a focused core team—the special forces. Any thoughts?"

"Well Seth is our most talented scrum master whom we hired three years ago, despite him being fresh out of business school with no formal agile certification and with little agile experience. He stayed positive, receptive, and patient throughout our long and dysfunctional hiring process of 21 rounds of interview, which was the reason we knew he is a great agile talent, and he could fit in our not so agile culture, pun intended."

Sid: "No kidding, 21 rounds ... huh?"

"Keisha, a product owner, embodies a true servant leader style, someone who is inclusive, structured but at the same time assertive when the situation demanded."

What really still strikes me is their open mindset, and a polite yet bold styles. Let's hear from the horse's mouth. I invite them both shortly.

I introduce them. "This is Seth our seasoned scrum master in Digital, and Keisha is the product owner from business. She reports to Daisy." I make our reporting territories clear.

I explain the concept of WALL and ask them to engage their teams and spread the word around to invite colleagues to add to the WALL. Seth takes the action to announce it in whiteboards in the coffee corners. Keisha will help e-mail communications.

"So, Sid wants to meet and talk briefly to your teams."

"Have you introduced him to Gus?" Seth asks in an alarmed tone tilting his head.

"And to Tim?" Keisha also speaks up with some anxiety.

I pause and make eye contact with Sid. "You see, as I mentioned. They both are right!

It would be almost impossible for you to get access to the IT teams without them knowing you. Even the digital team had a good number of folks from IT teams which rolled up to Gus, though most of them just partially participated in agile team!"

Our culture does not permit anyone to be around the team areas without his permission.

IT teams are on ground floor. Gus like most other executives sits in the sixth floor. You see "higher you climb the corporate ladder ... the higher your office."

Introduction to Gus and His Management Style

I decide to take Sid to Gus. I bring Sid up to speed and make him aware about Gus.

"You see, Gus is the Vice President in IT. He is a real strong personality, opinionated and too upfront. I advise you to choose your words carefully. He heads IT operations and infrastructure, and he is the boss of over 1,000 people sitting in the ground floor of this building." I try to explain him euphemistically what an a**hole he is.

Sid smiles. "We will see!"

"So, would you mind being extra cautious of what you say in front of him?" I repeatedly warn him, reading his mind and body language.

I move close to him, with my mouth an inch from his left ear as I whisper in a low pitch.

"You know he is highly unpopular with his own IT folks, just inside info, they call him *Gus the Pus!*" I whisper in a very feeble voice.

Gus had met all the financial and cost cutting targets of his group by consecutively firing a number of people. His productivity numbers, *at least on paper*, and efficiency paid off well for him, as he got promoted last year despite concerns from many of his team members.

As soon as we reach the far end of the building, we can see Gus from outside glass windows. He is on a call. We camp for the next few minutes on a white round table and Gus is too loud to be ignored. Gus has a high-pitched voice and he frequently raises it.

"Ok. Let me then open the schedule provided by my team." We hear him speak.

"The dates need to be in mid-June and not May. The IT version of the project plan confirms it. Also, I looked at PMO's version of the project plan and this first major milestone for the IT schedule is even later. Could you ask the business to adjust their project plan?" His voice gets louder.

"I don't care if customers are complaining or confused, I want you to provide the report to Richie, our CIO. I want to review it and want a few other reviewers before it comes to me but be careful about who you invite to meetings."

He raises his index finger pointing upwards and then waves his hands in emphasis.

"Are you clear or not?" He elevates his voice again as a high-handed boss who has delivered his final verdict.

"I know agile is all about responding to changing needs, but changes lead to instability in, invariably impacting stability of production application. Am I lying here?" He queries in an aggressive tone.

Gus has always required for his team to report back to him and get approval for every change requested by Daisy. He always asks business to get his approval or rejection before even discussing any change.

He is discussing another application development team schedule.

"They can add any number of people, but they need to work on the changes I approve. Could you make it formal and ensure no one reaches out to product owner? They must reach out to me first? Period."

"Freaking f***." We both pretend to ignore as we hear a stream of foul language.

"Let them rascals know that I am the one who will approve the changes to that app and you also find out who works there in that team! And is he project manager or scrum master?"

"Actually, it doesn't matter. Can you get this person to work in the back-end team instead for the app team? The SDK team needs a project manager too. I will assign Saira." He adds.

"If they ask questions, let them know it's from me. You tell them immediately to talk to me directly if they have any concerns."

It sounds like he is getting some pushback.

"No, no, no. I don't want to control everything I just want to help. Everything needs to go through me as I don't like surprises. This will make your work easier for all of us."

He repeats again, "To be clear … I want to help you guys."

Sid and I look at each other and realize this is hardly any help, the way he is talking. This is pure command and control. This is micromanagement at its core. I knew Gus as an ex-boss, and I was not surprised.

Every executive and even manager in the company have defined their territories. Gus has made the bad situation worse by converting his IT territory into a *terror-tory.*

We walk into his office finally.

Gus is curt and his push back is mild "Hmmm I need to know the plan. Please do not sidetrack my teams. And Neil, you need to ensure that you keep me in loop."

Our introductions last a couple of minutes. Hana Saito is at his door for a risk management meeting. Hana does not like any interruption in her GRC meetings.

Gus is not a native English speaker and does not have the best of command over language, and this exacerbates his abrupt and impolite style of conversations.

"*Latino!*" Sid exclaims as we walk back.

"Excuse me?" I confront him, assuming he was making a racist remark.

He repeats, "I said *Latino.*"

He wastes no time to clarify, "LATINO stands for Lean Agile Transformation in Name Only."

"So, I see Walkers is actually into LATINO!"

"Yes, I agree to your interpretation. Indeed, its old-fashioned culture and perfunctory. It really could become a deception at times especially with some of the mindset and behavior of our senior management guys."

I sigh to express that I feel relieved that he was not trying to be racist with the selection of word.

"You see my sister-in-law is actually Latino and so is my one-year-old niece." He reassures me.

He opens his phone to show me his screensaver, an adorable picture of his niece in a Frozen Disney costume. For the next five minutes, Sid and I are warmly and affectionately exchange stories and memories of his niece and my two daughters, Ami and Tina.

I reflect that in the last few hours, I have started to work well together with this guy. I have come to realize that he is unlike our external consultants I have worked with. He shows a clear sense of urgency and desperation, and he wants the same from me.

Back at our Wall, we jointly make another addition, *we need to "deboss" this organization!*

I hear another ding on the chat. It's Tim asking me the status of the weekly status report.

Hana pings me too on another window.

"Hey Neil, you missed the yesterday deadlines for the weekly risk management report and the latest compliance report for the digital programs. Could you please send it ASAP?"

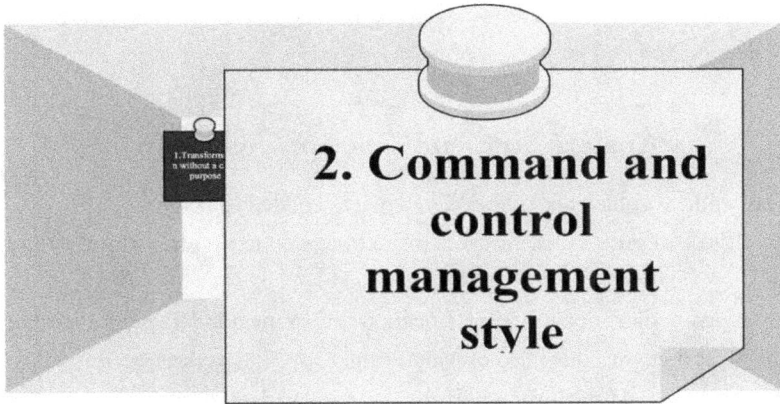

Figure 2.4 WALL No. 2

Table 2.3 The Writing on the WALL No. 2

2. Command and control management style	
What does it mean?	• Senior management and executives make everything about themselves to satisfy their own egos and appease their own bosses instead of prioritizing business outcomes • Micromanagement and excessive control of the work of juniors and subordinates by the bosses gets accepted as a norm
What are its effects?	• Demotivates workforce, crushes creativity, and stifles innovation • Emphasis shifts inwards drastically reducing customer centricity

I ask Sid for some time to focus on completing the reports for GRC and the PMO.

Sid looks surprised to see that in the midst of so many urgent things, I am now working on my reports and presentations deck. He doesn't hold back.

"That's crazy. I would need to meet them. And first meet your PMO guy, Tim, right?" He reminds me.

"Ok. I will ask Tim to join us on one of the days in our stand-ups or perhaps plan a short meeting soon." I assure him.

It's time for next session. I have invited business stakeholders to review NPS.

Analyze NPS and Voice of Customers

Daisy and Keisha walk to the WALL with scowled looks.

"Do you guys know how deep the hole we are digging for ourselves is?"

Daisy walks out soon after. Keisha walks to me and lets me know that they just met with our head of Marketing. Our NPS averages across product categories have hit rock bottom again in the last month.

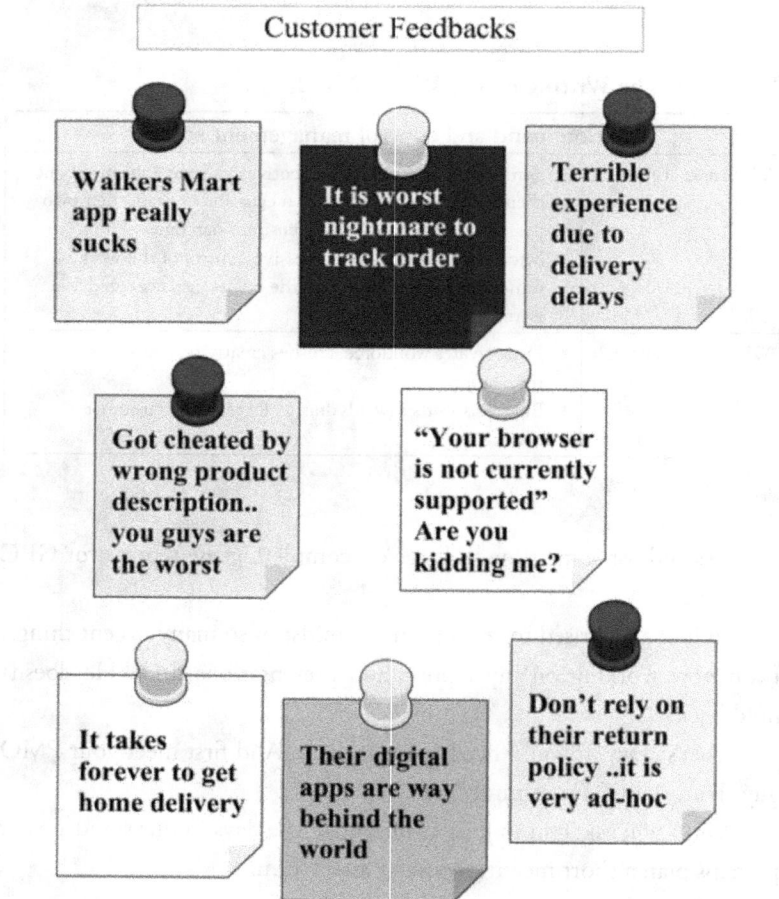

Figure 2.5 Voice of Customers

The NPS is the percentage of customers that would potentially recommend Walkers' products or services to their friends, relatives, or colleagues based on their own experience.

"Walkers Mart really sucks," Keisha reads out some of the customer reviews.

"Worst nightmare, terrible experience, I got cheated, never again." She continues.

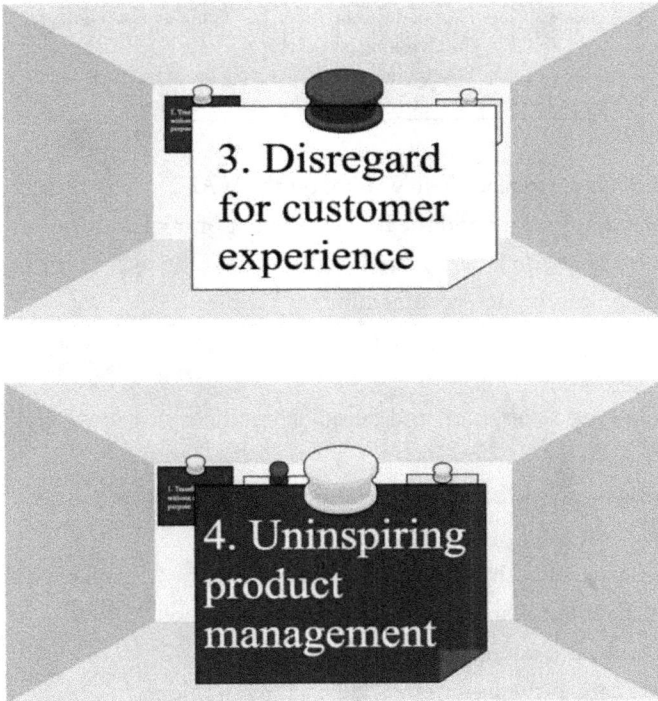

Figure 2.6 WALL No. 3 and 4

Table 2.4 The Writing on the WALL No. 3

3. Disregard for customer experience	
What does it mean?	• The emotional journey of customers across the product lifecycle and diverse touchpoints gets inconsistent, transactional and differs starkly across channels, locations and product portfolios • Customers get dissatisfied from inflexible policies, service levels, harsh attitude, and behaviors of service representatives. The dull, lackluster, and mediocre products and services disinterests customer
What are its effects?	• Greater effort for customers to consume products reducing sales • Harmful perception and negative publicity raise marketing budgets

Table 2.5 The Writing on the WALL No. 4

4. Uninspiring product management	
What does it mean?	• The voice of market is not steadily addressed due to lack of innovation and disintegrated product management processes across the life cycle of visioning, development, positioning, pricing, and marketing of the products • The product vision is far from state-of-art which does not create "wow" feelings and an emotional connect with the customers
What are its effects?	• Lack of differentiation due to dull, monotonous, and uninteresting products • Lukewarm and half-hearted interest from customers ultimately deterring business prospects

I walk closer to read their Writing on the WALL.

I look at my watch and the framed portrait of my family on my desk. It's almost 7 p.m. on a Friday and I start getting ready to pack my bag. Sid follows me, wanting to get something off his chest.

"Hey buddy, want to join me for dinner? Or do you have other plans?" He asks.

I take long to respond, and he quickly notices that something is up with me.

"Everything ok at home?" He looks at me with a degree of care and sincerity.

"Well, there is a situation on the personal front with my wife's health, but I'll talk about it another time." I quickly mention.

Sid nods, not asking any further questions.

"Take care in the meantime." He pats my shoulder.

I make a mental note in my head to pick up the bags of fresh fruit and other fresh groceries on my way back home, as Cindy has expressed her desire to change our eating habits.

As soon as I arrive home, Tina runs to me. I pick her up and kiss her on the cheek.

"Hey dad what is cancer?" She asks out of nowhere.

My face freezes. I struggle to answer her, as I have not spoken to them about Cindy's news up until now. I hadn't prepared myself for this.

I keep my laptop and grocery bags aside on the ground and walk with my girls to our living room.

"I heard mom on the phone with her doctor, and I heard the doctor say that mom has cancer."

I take a deep breath, preparing to explain to the girls.

"Come here." I hug and hold them close as I begin.

"Cancer is an abnormal growth of cells in our body. The cells start growing more than we need them to. The cells inside our bodies begin to divide without stopping and spread into other part of out of bodies."

They both nod, as I turn on their favorite quiz show on TV to occupy their minds.

During the weekend I continue to imagine scenarios if I lose my job sooner than I expect? I need my health insurance for my family more than ever.

Table 2.6 Kanban board

To-do	In progress	Done
	• Introduce Sid to Tim and the role of PMO	Approach for enterprise-wide retrospective using "The Writing on the WALL"
		The initial four Writings on the WALL: 1. Transformation without a clear purpose 2. Command and control management style 3. Disregard for customer experience 4. Uninspiring product management

The last few days have been excruciating and I feel a massive desire to take a break.

Despite the immense pressure at work and packed week with meetings, I still take the next two days off to take care of girls and more importantly help Cindy mentally prepare for the treatment.

Well, Cindy is sick. She is my first priority.

CHAPTER 3

Obligation to Waste Avoidance and Removal (WAR)

Relentless Focus on Value

Wednesday, January 29, 2020
6:30 a.m.

I check my calendar on the phone. Becky has scheduled multiple sessions and blocked time on my calendar. I connect the dots; Sid must have suggested her.

Table 3.1 Kanban board

To-do	In progress	Done
• Orientation: Eight lean wastes • Working session: What is agility? • Value-add and non-value-add • Reminder: PMO status reports (Neil partially out of office Monday–Tuesday) • Hospital appointments for Cindy	• Introduce Sid to Tim and the role of PMO	

I quickly send a text to Sid.

I finally put the phone down to focus on the family chitchat over breakfast. I decide to spend my morning with family, not giving in to my usual distractions with e-mails and text messages clouding my mind.

"Hey girls, where would you like to go for vacation once mom feels better?" I try to raise their spirits.

"The beach."

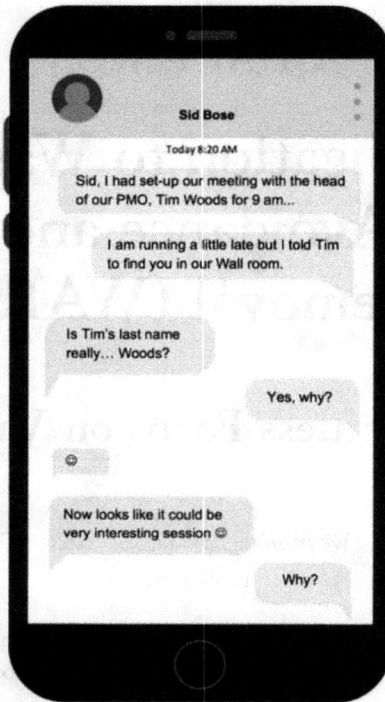

Figure 3.1 Text—Sid and Neil

"Can we go to Miami Beach? My friend, Dylan, always goes there." Tina raises up the idea of visiting the beach. I chuckle knowing I was going to give in and make plans for us to visit the beach soon.

After breakfast, I arrive at the office and head straight toward the WALL.

Orientation: Eight Lean Wastes

From a few feet away, I notice Sid standing next to a rolling whiteboard. As I approach the room, I hear Tim's voice.

"Is it WAR you say? Huh? I never heard of it." Tim says in a frustrated tone.

"What is WAR? and how do you wage a WAR?" He crosses his arms.

Tim Woods is sounding aggressive and hostile, firing a barrage of questions to Sid. Tim is a very firm believer of traditional project planning and making long-term plans. He is also one of the main critics of agile adoption in the organization.

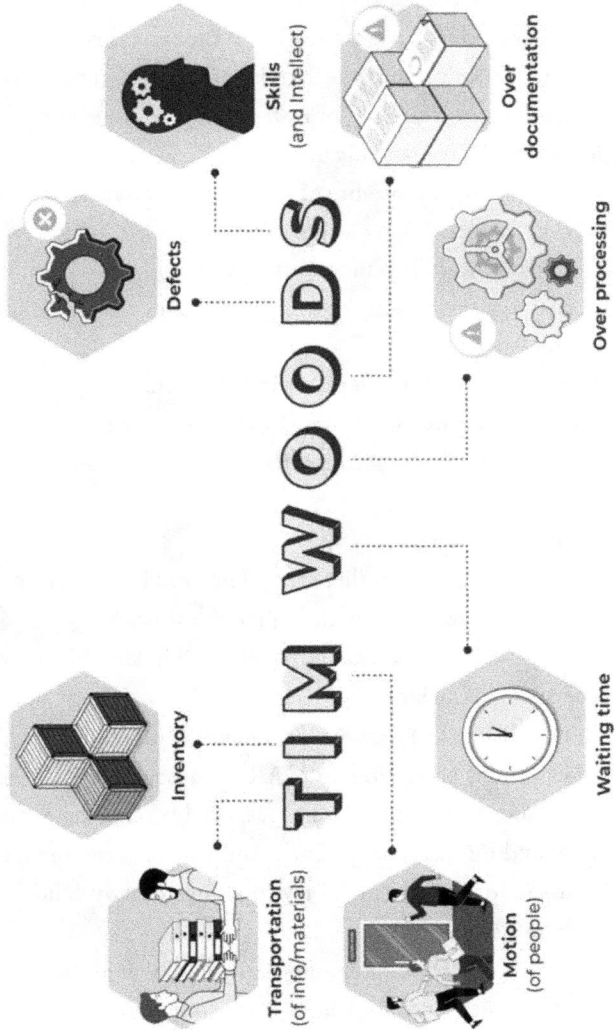

Figure 3.2 TIM WOODS

I am somewhat surprised by the heated exchange, as Tim is generally more diplomatic and shrewd in deciding the right battles to fight.

I enter the room and glance at the large screen displaying Tim's name.

"Oh, this term." I chuckle briefly.

I recall Tim Woods instantly being used by some lean practitioners to easily memorize the lean wastes. I never thought this term could be used in our context. Now, I get why Tim is sounding so upset and even as I sit down silently. I am thinking of how closer I am to solving Sid's mysterious puzzle from our texts this morning.

As I sit, there is a cease fire of sorts. Their conversation stops as I pull out a chair. They both look at me to modulate the heated exchange.

I decide to lower the temperature, exchanging pleasantries and talking about the weather and our morning commutes and some other stuff for the next few minutes.

But Sid confronts the elephant in the room.

"Tim, I know this sounds weird and I guess insulting to you, but actually I didn't realize that is your last name until this morning. Apologies for this coincidence."

Tim looks restless.

Sid continues in a friendlier tone "Tim, you had a really great question a while back, you asked, how to implement this?"

"Coming back to WAR, it's totally nonviolent but very effective if done right." Sid chuckles.

"The WAR means *Waste Avoidance and Removal of the waste*." He adds.

"I mentioned obligation to WAR because all of us need to wage a WAR. We need to identify and respectably challenge ourselves, our colleagues and our leadership for the purpose of waste reduction."

"That sounds interesting." I try to almost exactly echo Sid's words to show our new strength.

"So, all of us need to have an obligation to war all the time every day! Don't we?" He pauses to look at us all for our response.

"This is an obligation for completely *nonviolent* WAR. A waste reduction focused war which is meant to reduce and eliminate anything that is not adding much *business value!*"

This is my way of telling Tim about what he is doing to our organization with his colossal and bureaucratic PMO processes. I am gleeful deep inside myself to make Tim realize his contributions toward our company's red tape. He has created wastes!

Sid proposes to identify the wastes impacting our agility along with entire executive team, but I warn against a big bang approach to keep it informal. I suggest Seth, Keisha, and Saira Ali, the project manager from Tim's team, to represent program and project managers.

With some initial hesitation Tim also wants to join us and we decide to meet after lunch.

What Is Agility?

We start the session by writing down the most basic question we should be asking.

"What does agility mean?"

We start to get different answers, perspectives, and expectations and some of those are confusing enough for us to realize that we don't have a clarity and consensus.

"I am not as agile as you guys are." Tim interrupts.

Tim always had this "you guys" versus "I" mentality.

"So, I am not an expert on this stuff, but I think you need to have a really well-defined and detailed project plan.

Saira, why don't you show how carefully and deliberately we plan our projects?"

Tim steals the show with his stupid view of agile. Saira knows it's not agile but answers dutifully, pointing at the connected large screen.

"We do detailed plans until end of the project and we have RACI matrix for everyone. We see a Gantt chart with dependencies, predecessors, successors, and dates for next seven months including a finish-to-start task link by default, with first task, the predecessor, to be finished before the second task, a successor, could start."

I am thinking why Saira is thoughtlessly obeying her boss. *Her paychecks depend on* not *understanding certain things.* I discern the obvious.

I am restless with Tim and Saira talking about traditional project management, so I jump in.

"We make plans, but we all know that most of the time we don't stick to this plan, don't you agree?"

"Yes sure, we are agile and we replan every single time there is a change." Tim replies.

Sid interrupts forcefully.

"No, no, no. Tim, that is definitely not agile to plan for an entire project and then spend days changing it every time there is change. Does that even make sense to spend so much time and energy to plan something with such enormous details in the first place, which we all know will change frequently?

A project is defined as a temporary endeavor. It has a defined scope and resources. In traditional project management, you would continue to spend longer time and more money until you have completed all the tasks. This type of sequential approach creates mental and literal compartmentalization. It creates silos of work, departments, and minds."

Sid sketches his thoughts.

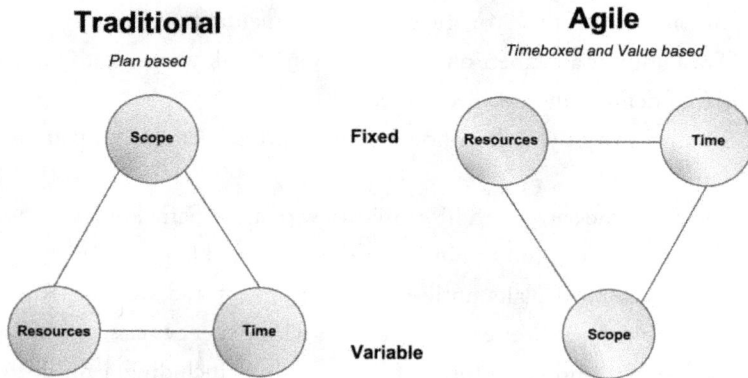

Figure 3.3 Traditional vs. agile
(Plan driven is a traditional approach | Value driven is an agile approach)

"In agile you fix cost and time and vary the scope of requirements in a project based on the prioritization for business value."

Tim looks perplexed. "But who decides what is business value? Is this not the management's role in a company?"

Seth scribbles on the whiteboard,

Business value = Something which a customer is willing to pay for.

- Who is the customer?
- What do our customers want and are willing to pay for?
- What is the most cost-effective and fastest way to deliver that value to customers?

After a while, we come back to the original question on the large screen. So, what is agility?

Seth promptly replies, "It's the ability to quickly respond to changes. Isn't it?"

"Yes, and more importantly the ability to proactively create changes by innovation and disruption in an industry," Sid adds.

"So *why is true agility so hard* to achieve and sustain?" I ask forcefully.

"Because we aspire to be agile without a wholehearted effort to stay lean!"

Saira: "Sid, can you articulate how is lean different?"

"Lean is all about maximizing value by delivering the right product, in the right amount, in the right quality, at the right time, and at the right price to the customer!

And because the non-value-adding activities and wastes reduce speed, frustrate people, and complicate efforts to change course for responding timely and effectively to customer needs." Sid illuminates us.

"For example, on a given day, let's go through the activities which many of us, especially managers and team leads, have to go through. They have a load of meetings, e-mails, reports, many of which actually are not really meant for any value-adding." I add.

Value-Add and Non-Value-Add Analysis

Table 3.2 *Value Adding and Nonvalue Adding*

Value-Adding activity or step	Non-Value-Adding-or wasteful activity
Definition: An activity which we know customer would be willing to pay for, e.g.:	Definition: An activity which customer does not want to pay for, e.g.:
• Interviewing customers and analyzing feedbacks • Redesign customer experience • Writing and improving lines of code • Building architectural foundations • Automation to improve speed and reduce manual errors • Resolving customer problem ticket	• Follow-up for information • Searching for right contact • Lengthy and effort intensive project plans • Excessive documentation and reporting • Too many reviews and approvals • Excessive documentation • non-value-adding meetings • More people than needed • Multiple partial project allocations • Excessive multitasking and context switching • Micromanaging or controlling teams

"What could be the underlying causes of this?"

Sid argues "Surely a combination of the ways the companies are structured, the mindset and behaviors of the people, complacency, job insecurity, the rigid policies and procedures, and the cultural stereotypes we are so afraid to break."

"Bottomline is that *Everyone has to have an obligation to WAR!*" He exclaims.

Toward, the end of our hour-long session, each one is invited to identify at least one report, process, tool, status review document, meeting, and practice which is adding no value to customers. We end up with much more than expected.

I close with a remark "Thanks all. This is a value-adding conversation on non-value-adding activities. As a next step may I please ask you all to consult relevant key stakeholders and plan to kill whatever is a waste. Let's demo it to Richie in the next few days."

As soon as I am back in my office, I get nervous to see another one of Daisy's requests.

Daisy gets straight to the point the minute she sees me.

Table 3.3 The eight lean wastes—TIM WOODS

Transporting something farther than necessary: • The stories and requirements modified multiple times during sprint • Acceptance of artifacts and deliverables after multiple stages of approval • Process of continuously and frequently assigning and reassigning work multiple times among different individuals or different teams, departments, vendors	*Inventory* due to supply in excess of immediate and reasonable demand: • Partially completed code waiting for improvement or release • Requests waiting for analysis or for closure • Unutilized licenses of software tools/IT applications • Unutilized features in software tools/IT applications
Moving people or equipment more than required to perform the processing: • Searching for the latest versions of processes, documents, standard operating procedure (SOP), tools, and templates • Toggling between screens while working on resolving an issue • Unplanned task switching	*Waiting* for the completion of a step to start the next step: • A completed program waiting for user acceptance • Waiting for inputs and clarifications from requester • Waiting for inputs from subject matter experts • Waiting for approval for closing or completing helpdesk tickets

Overprocessing to an extent that customer may not find valuable:
• Reviewing and inspecting a document multiple times
• Service-level agreement (SLA) more stringent than real business needs
  o Requests waiting for analysis or for closure
  o Unutilized licenses or features in tools/applications
	Overdocumentation or producing amounts/quantities more than required:
	• Lengthy project plans and scheduling for multiple months
	• Releasing multiple variants which was not asked for
	• Providing extra features in the software

Defects due to error, bug, or mistake that requires rework or redoing: • Repeat issues of the same type • Rework because of not completing the request correctly and completely • Failure to resolve the request • Incomplete or incorrect story description • Insufficient or daily changing acceptance criteria • A coding with bugs	*Skills and intellect* due to underutilization of the skill, expertise, and talent of people: • Skilled data scientists and programmers doing data entry • A system analyst doing simple coding • System architect or experienced developer doing helpdesk support work • Scrum master only scheduling meetings • Limited cross trained resources across different applications

"Given the fast-evolving virus situation, we need to urgently launch an upgrade to Ship-to-Store and we are planning a new feature in app for curbside pickup. It seems like we need at least two new digital teams to expedite. Do you agree?"

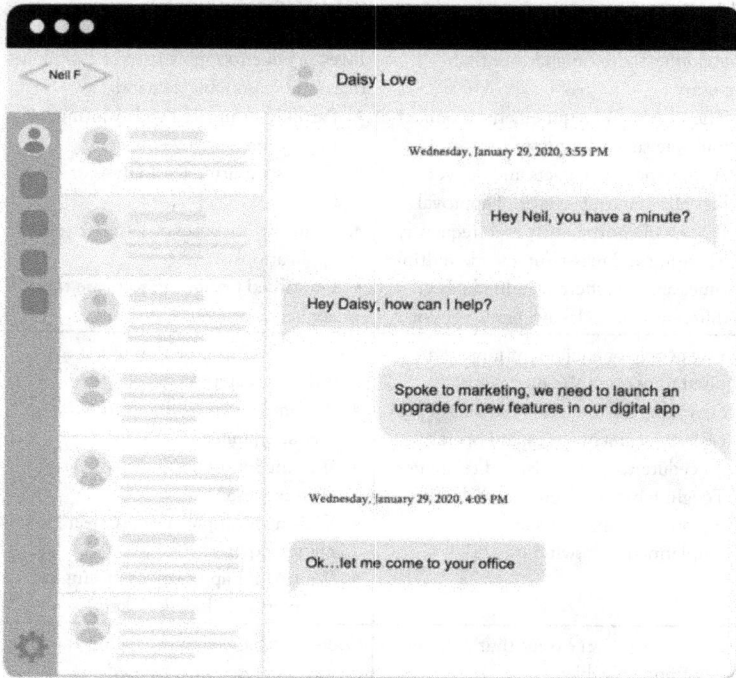

Figure 3.4 Chat—Daisy and Neil

She looks at me for a response.

I hesitate initially as launching any new team will need a new budget request, which will take three to four months and multiple approvals including direct approvals from multiple C-suite executives.

"Let me check if Seth's digital team could include the new features in their backlog."

I suggest, pulling out my phone from my pocket inside my suit jacket.

"I don't give a *damn* about what your dev teams backlog!" She exclaims, catching me by surprise.

"I want to get this stuff released for our customers to start using in next two to three weeks before they migrate to our competitors and we keep busy in our internal approvals. We need new digital features out of our freaking door, asap!"

"You run our digital shop, Neil. Make it happen please!"

"Let me try something soon." I assuage her with speed, noticing her raised voice.

Soon after, I knock at Richie's door for the budget for new teams.

"I wish I could help Neil. But you know how it is these days!"

As usual I don't get a clear answer.

The next morning, I meet with Sid to review the situation.

"So, what exactly stops you from creating new digital teams?" Sid examines.

"We need approvals and some other team releasing which has unused funds and then this team getting the funds. It's complicated to overwrite the rigid budgeting process and pretty time consuming too."

Sid poses a notable question.

"What is the value of unused funds and approved budgets from the customers standpoint?"

I think for a moment and utter in an undecided voice. "Zero?"

"Spot-on!" Sid walks away having triggered a thought with his incisive query.

I pick up the phone and call the VP in Finance who is acting CFO. Our CFO had quit just after two years. I heard he was highly frustrated with the Boards' expectation to micromanage budgets, analyze each and every expense, and cut costs mercilessly.

Someone picks up the phone and I hear a rough and raspy voice on the other hand.

"Bart here."

"Hey Bart, this is Neil, Director of Digital." I explain the situation as Bart listens.

"Hah hmmm ... and you want me to release funds for your digital team?" He asks.

Bart didn't sound convinced, perhaps he was thinking *who is this Director level person telling me what to do?*

"Sorry but it took months of negotiations and meetings after which we got the budget approved and I cannot just release funds right away. But I will keep you in mind." He resists.

"Bart, we need the funds now, this is from Daisy." I say with a sense of urgency.

"When do you think you could get back to me?" I am attempting to push him.

Bart pauses and suggests after next quarter. At this point, I am restless.

"What if we don't have the next quarter?" I suggest with a sense of frustration in my voice.

There is a pin drop silence on his side.

After another minute of reticence, he replies with some hesitation.

"Ok let me try something. I will ask our CEO to approve these funds and get back to you today."

I sigh in relief.

An annual budgeting exercise has virtually remained unchanged for 20 odd years. The budgets are allocated at the beginning of the year, which in not vey nimble. However, none of the leaders have the courage to challenge and change the annual budgeting process which is so sacrosanct in the company.

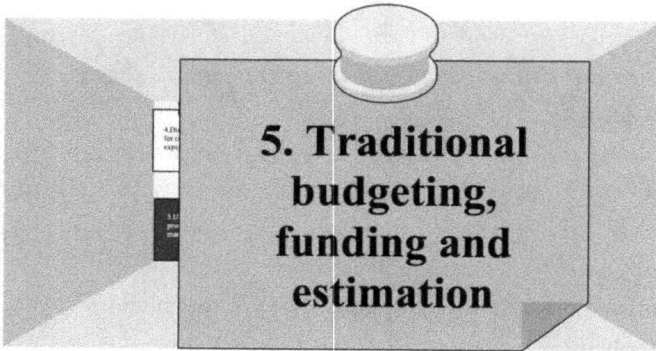

Figure 3.5 WALL No. 5

Table 3.4 *The Writing on the WALL No. 5*

5. Traditional budgeting, funding, and estimation	
What does it mean?	• The budgeting and funding require excessive administrative overheads in releasing, reporting, tracking, and reallocating finances • Funding project generates constant admin effort as projects are temporary endeavors as new projects need to be started regularly • The estimation of time, efforts, and cost is tentative and bureaucratic exercise but defines the funding requests
What are its effects?	• Effort intensive and time consuming for senior management • Nonvalue Adding (zero value of budgeted but unused funds from customer standpoint)

Projects are temporary endeavors, but agile funding needs to support value continuously and in a sustained manner. FA@ST focuses on funding projects which may cease to exist. The funding of value streams is better as these are continuous constructs unlike projects which have an expiry date. The funding for the internal or external projects is largely bureaucratic and of a longer term.

Instead of annual budgeting, the quarterly funding adjustment is much more agile and takes into account the dynamic of the market conditions, consumer behavior, and competitive strategy.

Sid wants to meet but I am busy in formatting a presentation for Richie for the next hour.

"Does Richie really care what format, font, color, and what pictures are added to the presentation?"

"Perhaps, actually I don't know," I shrug.

"I think he could care less as long as it's valuable, and not weird or unreadable. The amount of time you are spending in formatting this presentation is eating the time you could ideally spend on solving a customer problem. Right?

There is a good amount of waste of *over processing* inside companies. This includes making slides decks, documents which consumes lots of efforts and not about the contents."

I reflect on his argument for next few minutes.

I am starving but decide to inform Paris. I knock on her office door and she invites me to join her. She is eating her keto snack. I happily accept the invitation.

"Paris, I have decided to officially communicate that my wife Cindy is recently diagnosed with triple negative breast cancer."

She gets up and walks to pat my hand. "I am so sorry Neil, I don't even know what to say."

"My apologies too for some delay in communicating this. I need some flexibility in my work schedule." I try to pull a brave face.

"Absolutely. You see family comes first. I will take care at HR's end. We have your back. Anything I could help with?"

I am relieved with her support but I am overwhelmed with another reminder for PMO reporting.

Reminder: Status Reporting

The next morning as I walk to from the parking lot, I realize I had snoozed the reporting day reminder yesterday, I check my phone and its Richie's e-mail reminder.

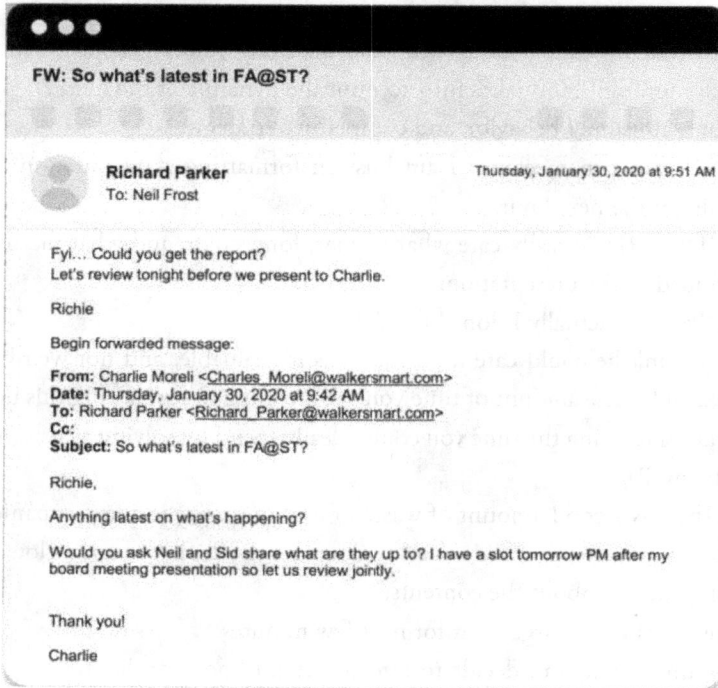

> ● ● ●
>
> **FW: So what's latest in FA@ST?**
>
> **Richard Parker**   Thursday, January 30, 2020 at 9:51 AM
> To: Neil Frost
>
> Fyi... Could you get the report?
> Let's review tonight before we present to Charlie.
>
> Richie
>
> Begin forwarded message:
>
> **From:** Charlie Moreli <Charles_Moreli@walkersmart.com>
> **Date:** Thursday, January 30, 2020 at 9:42 AM
> **To:** Richard Parker <Richard_Parker@walkersmart.com>
> **Cc:**
> **Subject:** So what's latest in FA@ST?
>
> Richie,
>
> Anything latest on what's happening?
>
> Would you ask Neil and Sid share what are they up to? I have a slot tomorrow PM after my board meeting presentation so let us review jointly.
>
> Thank you!
>
> Charlie

Figure 3.6 E-mail—report on FA@ST

He is asking for a status report to be presented to Charlie for our progress, and he is pushing for tomorrow. I am almost visualizing my long and tiring night in office writing this bloody report.

As I meet Sid standing right next to the WALL to show him the e-mail, and he asks me

"So, what about the report, are you really creating one. Is this a common practice?"

"I would like my team to help make the report if that's what you're asking. My team helps draft the status of how things are, our statuses are traffic lights, R, Y, G status, team's problems, and so on. We try to avoid the *red* status as you know, or else someone is explaining to someone else until midnight why it is *red*?"

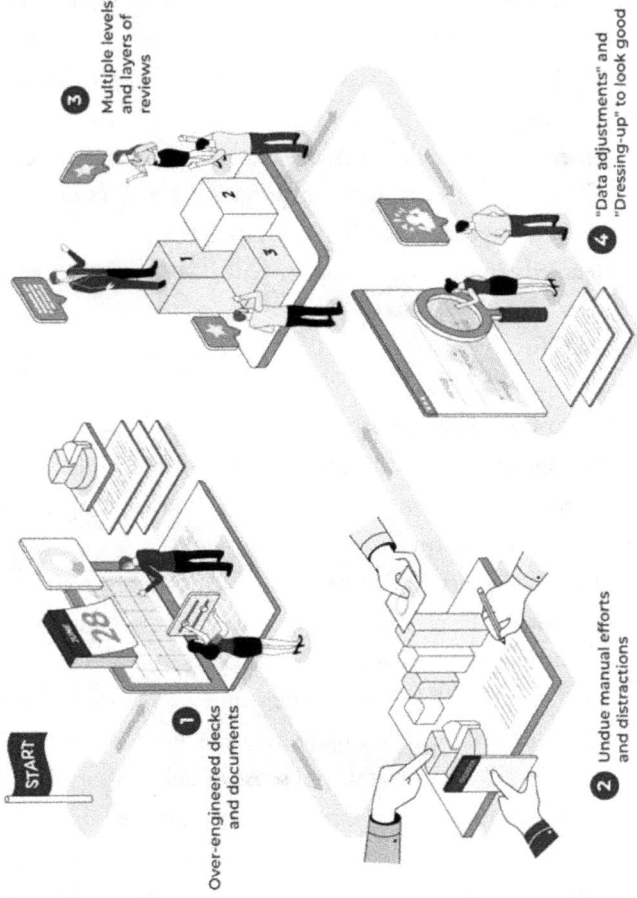

Figure 3.7 *Reporting*

"I am thunderstruck. Could you further elaborate on the process?" Sid demands.

"This process was defined almost over eight years ago when there was a lack of visibility of projects. The PMO wanted a totally standard approach. They have been running multiple project review boards and were still stuck in an old-fashioned PMO-driven style of project management. They mercilessly insist everyone to provide weekly status reports and biweekly full-blown status review meetings lasting hours.

PMO sends at least four to five reminders a week to get those reports from the respective project managers or scrum masters. Each project is presented by the project manager, or in some cases a scrum master. Richie, Tim, and Gus ask questions to grill the project managers. It's not a popular meeting, and this often leads to new additional documents and more detailed reports in some cases. Our PMO is a pure representation of intellect waste."

I reach for a marker and carefully sketch out our typical reporting process.

"We do create paperwork as mandated by PMO, essentially Tim's team. We spend almost 40-person hours on reporting for every team. Seems like one person in the team is full-time working on reports and other internal documents.

If there's a project, PMO needs a report to assess the process adherence and performance. I don't think Tim is ready to give up his process and I'm not willing to continue having our scrum masters and product owners spend 20 to 30 percent of their time on reporting and documentation. Tim has not been willing to concede, even when we all know we are under *deep sh***." I admit with a sense of helplessness.

Sid is rolling his eyes and remarks with a strange look on his face.

"That's not good. It's not value-adding time for the projects to provide the report and never-ending review meetings every week. Additionally, being oversensitive to what is reported to management is a cultural inheritance and does not add real value to customers. Reporting is acceptable when it is an effortless and automated byproduct and not the primary product of what we do. Too much reporting and random movement of status information with an intent to create fear and insecurity is one of the other easiest ways to erase agility in the system."

I show him playbooks on almost everything on reporting and status review meetings, which was built with a team of PMAG consulting folks and multiple review sessions.

Sid argues "A rigid and overprocessed playbook and other documentation alone can make practices rigid and shallow, and adversely affects the broader agility in the organization. We are actually departing from the values from agile manifesto. Instead of working solutions and products, we are focusing on comprehensive documentation and reports."

"We are not going to continue this freaking process. We will not provide status report." Sid sounds forceful and decisive.

"Excessive reporting seems like a waste of time, but I am not ready to give it up immediately. I need to cover my back and other folks need to cover their asses too you know." I am undecided.

"The sprint review is the right forum to showcase the value to all. The sprint reviews and demos are really effectual means to show progress and collect feedbacks than any report! They help establish the feedback loops in the system.

Sprint reviews indeed are the most powerful ways to visualize the progress and how our product which is 'Transforming the transformation' is evolving."

"Could we invite the CEO to the sprint review?" he suggests.

"Tim and even Richie will not be happy with us not doing the reports." I explicitly mention.

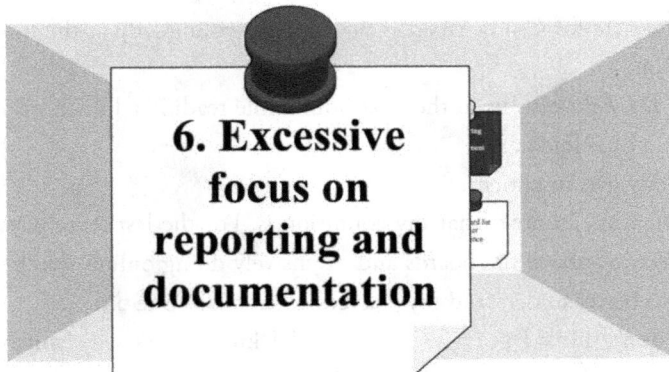

Figure 3.8 WALL No. 6

Table 3.5 The Writing on the WALL No. 6

6. Excessive reporting and documentation	
What does it mean?	• Agile is about transparency, showcasing working product, and tangible business value to elicit early feedbacks not heavy reporting • Devoting excessive efforts and time to generate long reports, forms, templates, and documents mitigates the focus of agile teams
What are its effects?	• Nonvalue Adds and wastes to create, update, and complete many rounds of reviews • Frequently inaccurate, dressed-up, and misleading view of progress

I pick the phone: "Becky, could you check if Charlie could be available to join our sprint review?"

"That's short notice but let me see." She is prompt but looks frustrated with multiple requests.

After hearing that Charlie is being invited, Richie and Tim cancel most of their meetings to attend the sprint review which they had declined just earlier in the day.

Richie wants to review what is being presented if the CEO attends. Tim wants to join too in all preparations. We would need to curtail our working sessions and spend the next two days bringing them up to speed on what we have found.

After a deliberation, I forward the meeting invite to the acting CFO, Bart. It will help me get attention to release funds from Finance.

Hospital Appointment for Cindy

"We are here for Cindy Frost." I say to lively young lady at the hospital reception.

As Dr. Anu calls us in the next hour while reading a bunch of printouts in a blue folder.

Cindy gets impatient.

"Dr. Anu, I know what my condition is. For the last three days I've been reading about the boards and extensively doing online searches for hours to better understand my chances of survival." She blurts.

"I don't think I got one answer and I know that's why you better understand what the current diagnosis is.

Your age and your willingness from what I can see to fight the disease will make a big difference." Dr. Anu assures

Dr. Anu tells me that Cindy will need to be taken inside for next two hours to undergo more tests.

I need to spend that time extremely wisely given what's happening at work.

I recall meeting this hospital's Operations Director at a recent agile conference some weeks back. He had presented a compelling case about how hospitals he is working with have launched a lean and agile transformation.

I check the hospital directory and try reaching him.

He picks up and is gracious enough to invite me to their transformation room which he calls Obeya. I have heard of this term before, and now I am getting too curious to miss this.

He explains to me wastes in the hospital. I see their own version of Tim Woods in the hospital.

Transportation

- Unnecessarily moving patients, specimens, or materials throughout a system is wasteful.
- The poor layout, as the emergency room (ER) department is located too far from the blood bank, pathology, diagnostics testing, and clinical laboratory.

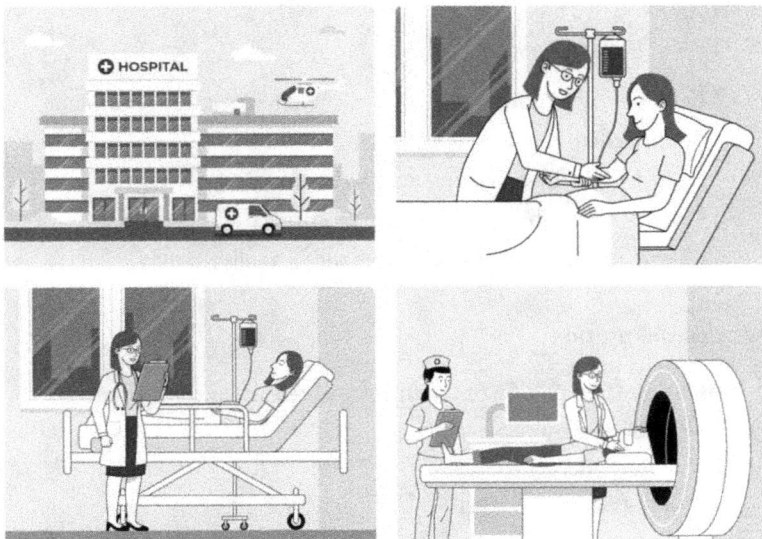

Figure 3.9 Hospital

Inventory

- Hospitals create waste when they store excess inventory costs, storage and movement costs, spoilage, and waste.
- Overstocking leading to expiry of supplies and disposing out-of-date medicines.

Motion

- Lab staff may walk miles every day due to a poor hospital layout, for example, office or hospital layout is not consistent with operations and day-to-day workflow.
- Staff and patients need to frequently move across hospital facilities or buildings like from one department to another department or from one room to another room.

Waiting

- Waiting for the next event to occur eats up time and resources.
- Patients waiting for an appointment.
- Some hospital staff waiting as their workloads are uneven.
- Patients spending hours in waiting rooms or exam rooms.

Overprocessing

- Excess bedside equipment with more devices and instruments than needed.
- Supplies require searching across shelves.
- Doctors prescribing more complex surgical intervention despite having relatively effective medical alternatives.

Overdocumentation

- Unnecessary paperwork, admin, and redundant information collection at multiple steps.

Defects

- Errors in medical billing due to wrong claim codes in insurance Explanation of Benefits.

Skills and Intellect

- Health care professionals working below their level of licensure.
- Trained nurses are focusing much of their in administrative tasks ad hoc activities, follow-ups with doctors, and filing paperwork.

Table 3.6 Kanban board

To-do	In progress	Done
	• Invite CEO to the sprint review	• Lean wastes *TIM WOODS* at Walkers and in context of hospital • Insights into the meaning of agility • Focus on sprint reviews and reduce efforts for status reporting
		The latest Writings on the WALL: 5. Traditional budgeting, funding, and estimation 6. Excessive reporting and documentation

CHAPTER 4

Gemba WALK and Candid Talk

A Value Stream-Based Diagnostics

Thursday, February 6, 2020

I wake up in the morning with a banging headache after having two grueling days of work. I quickly freshen up and get dressed before 7 a.m. Sid has added a number of items to the Kanban board.

Table 4.1 Kanban board

To-do	In progress	Done
• Introduction to Gemba Walk • Gemba Walks in action • Survey for wastes and team pulse • Neil–Daisy 1:1 on preparedness for coronavirus-related disruptions • Sprint review: value stream mapping • Sprint retrospective	• Invite CEO for sprint review	

Meanwhile downstairs, there is chaos going on between the girls and I can hear it from upstairs. I frown, looking at the clock. This is too early for them to be arguing.

"Stop it, that's mine!" Ami roars, trying to get her brand-new jewelry box from Tina.

"Well, I want it!" Tina yells, aggressively fighting her big sister.

Cindy interrupts their fighting and yelling. Cindy hugs the girls with cuddles and kisses, letting them know that she loves them so much.

Lately, the girls have been getting into arguments and fights over little things, and I have noticed their change in behavior since Cindy's diagnosis, especially when it comes to Ami.

I make a mental note to book us in for family counseling in Green Bay.

I sigh, feeling my stomach growling. I am starving but don't have much time for breakfast as I am late for the Gemba Walks.

I quickly grab a croissant and a flask full of coffee and start driving.

Introduction to Gemba Walk

I walk into the meeting a few minutes late. I see Sid with Seth, Saira, and Keisha.

Keisha is talking "I had heard Gemba Walk before in the context of our lean program and also from one of our suppliers who adopted it as part of their lean manufacturing."

"Gemba is a Japanese word which means the place where things happen. Like for a health care worker, the Gemba is where the patient is, and for a crime reporter, it's the crime scene." Sid explains.

"So why do we need Gemba Walk?" asks Saira. She does not completely understand how it can help.

We decide to list down objectives and benefits to have a common understanding.

"Prudently spending time at Gemba brings awareness of fundamental but still not so obvious improvement opportunities by keeping an inquisitive mind coupled with a fresh set of eyes for focused observations. For example:

- It stimulates us to challenge the current state and helps recalibrate the purpose of teams.
- It could help identify opportunities for cross-pollination, reuse, creativity, and innovation within teams but more importantly across teams.
- It defines pragmatic improvements to deliver and sustain business outcomes.
- It inspires team members, leaders, and stakeholders with call to action."

Essentially, Gemba Walks are conducted to help us answer the following questions:

1. What is the purpose of the Gemba and its linkage to organization's purpose?
2. Are the activities and underlying steps adding value for customer?
3. Are people excited, engaged, and creative in their work?

The Gemba Walks in Action

Go see, ask why, show respect.

Everyone now wants to see Gemba Walk in action. We all agree to start soon.

Normally, we would have waited for two to three approvals and aligned for everyone to agree at least a couple of weeks before actually implementing such kind of diagnosis.

We walk with Seth, Saira, and Keisha to three teams. The Ship-to-Store and supply chain optimization teams are in our building. The third is virtual walk at Innovation Hub. We organize remote Gemba Walks using video calls with our international teams in Bangalore, with some team members spread in Manilla, Kraków.

Gemba Walk 1: We walk into the Ship-to-Store team for which Keisha is the product owner.

As we walk toward the teams, we see nine people working in a closed room. It is darkened with dim lights set by the team, who clearly want some privacy and didn't want too much light. *Something seemed fishy.*

We analyze the last six projects to understand the timelines. It is revealing and insightful to see how many months gets lost in waiting, thinking, and complying to guidelines which are purely internal.

They had way too many changes in their mission and roadmap for the team changed every week, and even after 30 odd revisions in last six months, it still is somewhat confusing.

As we try to understand what's wrong, Keisha reminds me that this team been there for over 15 months. They have been set up as an agile team, and it took almost four months to build a solid backlog so they could start. We learn the team has been focusing on primarily building a pile of playbooks and bug fixing for last three sprints. The team members are frustrated, and there is a clear lack of motivation.

It seems like the team is in the silo and folks are staring at their monitors. Everyone looks busy on their phone screens doing their own stuff without much collaboration.

The confusion, boredom and frustration are obvious, but there seems to be a visible reluctance in vocalizing the challenges to us.

Gemba Walk 2: We meet supply chain optimization team with Saira, who is the project manager in this team. And interestingly, she also acts as scrum master for ceremonies.

The team does not have a clearly defined roadmap and conflicting timeline to deploy the solution they will be building. The product owner has received conflicting priorities from business and IT managers. There is a visible lack of clear direction on the next set of sprints. It seems the planning exercise is essential to keep all team members busy without much deliberation of the value they are delivering.

We attend the sprint planning of this team. There is a visible lack of effort to articulate, inspire, or build agreement within the team of the sprint objectives. Most backlog items are left unrefined for the team members to figure out. Most user stories are randomly estimated by team members without proper consensus.

The planning concludes with a number of team members unclear about their work items.

Table 4.2 The Writing on the WALL No. 7

7. Doing but not being agile	
What does it mean?	• These are scrum ceremonies that are rigid, perfunctory and prescriptive, creating burnout charts that are virtually fake, stand-ups that turn to status reporting, and estimations that are mistaken • Building detailed project plans which needs to be changed frequently and frontloading work for agile teams which is not sustainable
What are its effects?	• Demotivation and indifference to agile ways of working • Create a pretense of progress without real outcomes

Gemba Walk 3: Finally, we have an upcoming conduct Gemba Walk virtually in our Innovation Hub primarily based out of Bangalore, India. Seth organizes the sessions with his peer scrum masters.

"Hey everyone," The scrum master joins with the team from the Innovation Hub.

" … Tim Woods and Hana Saito, from Governance, launched this integration project with a six-month duration but it got extended three times and became an 18-month-long project. It had been a blessing and executive sponsorship of Richie."

I recall it had started to die down almost after the initial three to four months of excitement. Very few people entered values, systems became complex, data was inaccurate or did not make sense, and teams made up estimates for logging in their time. It was a misstep of PMO to manage agile teams. Now, Tim is even asking to restart the program and upgrade the system which very few people use.

Our first set of questions do not produce much clarity on what the team is tasked to accomplish.

Sid asks them politely: "I am new to Walkers and it will be tremendously helpful for me if you could share the purpose and objectives for this team?"

The scrum master explains for next few minutes:

"We have an enterprise technology program to integrate all our people management, timesheet management, PTO, agile backlog, and project management tools. It was called agile enterprise operations and networks or AEON for short.

Timesheets and estimated values by agile teams as well as that of traditional projects teams were directly managed by PMO. This system had a too ambitious and unrealistic vision to integrate the time management system (TMS), with the portfolio management, reporting tools and with PTO/leave management systems (LMSs), and agile tools like backlog management.

AEON integrated with our backlog management tool really generates colorful charts. Charts are used by PMO to compare whether one team is doing as good or as bad as other teams. For instance, we generally compare the productivity between my two teams and the other team. Most of the time they are not accurate, and teams are not happy with this micromanagement."

Sid is looking intrigued. "I am afraid I find it strange too. You don't compare teams as each team is unique in terms of skills, background, and technological capabilities of the team members."

We find the Innovation Hub, despite of its fancy name, represents a hidden factory.

This team includes talented, smart and bright data architects, engineers, and data scientists. But Richie, his PMO, and Gus are not using them well. They kept the folks busy giving ad hoc tasks and allocating them to multiple partial projects that had fractional allocations to team members. The team is regularly given odd work like random testing, debugging, tool setups, presentation making, and even data entry tasks.

This is also an unequivocal case of *Skills and Intellect waste.*

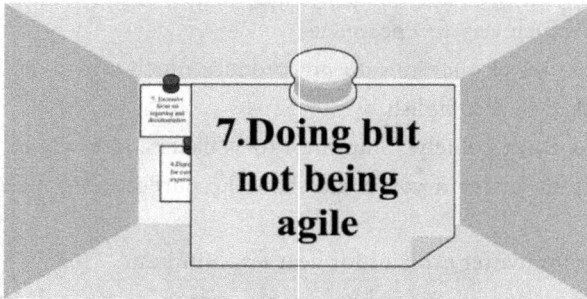

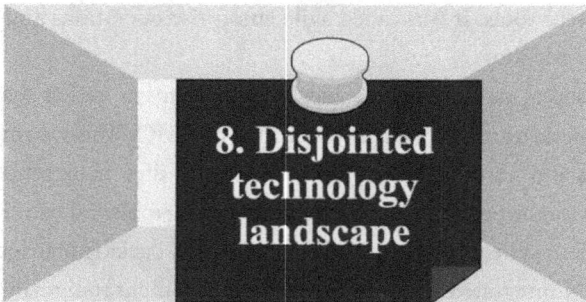

Figure 4.1 WALL No. 7 and 8

Table 4.3 The Writing on the WALL No. 8

8. Disjointed technology landscape	
What does it mean?	• The isolated systems, and tools for each functional silos cause slow and sluggish delivery of value to customers • This leads to deployment of unstable applications to the production environment causing technical glitches
What are its effects?	• Lots of rework, wastes, and manual intervention across the value chain • Longer Time-to-Market to develop and release solutions • Lack of stability and uneven performance post go-live

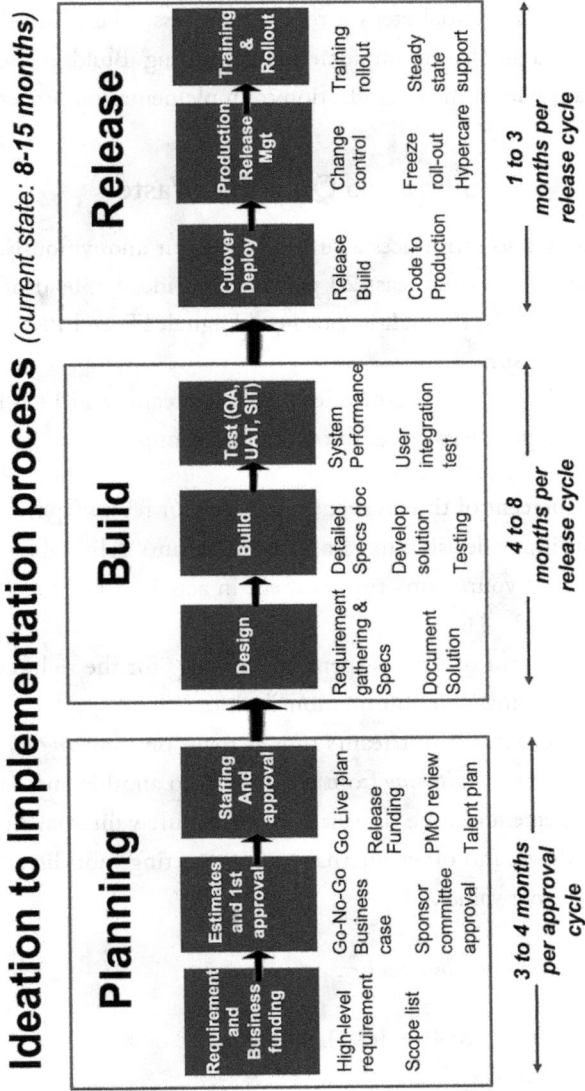

Figure 4.2 Ideation to implementation (Time-to-Market)

We analyze the last six projects in the teams to understand the timelines. It is extremely revealing and insightful to see how many months get lost in waiting, thinking, and complying to guidelines which are purely internally defined but not in the best interests of customers. There is waterfall like sequential steps across the process. The relatively smaller portions of agile-driven implementation during Build phase become insignificant within the long ideation to implementation process.

Survey to Quantify Wastes

Sid parallelly also introduces a survey to be sent anonymously. He suggests a sample size of at least 20 percent (and ideally 30%) of the total population, that is, the staff in Business, Digital, IT, and PMO teams to respond to the survey.

Seth and Saira self-organize to encourage teams and help bring the number of respondents closer to the suggested number.

1. What percent of time is spent in *waiting* for review/approval/clarification/input/decision to complete your/team's deliverables?
2. Percent of your/team's time is spent in activities *not* directly related to backlog?
3. What percent of time is spent on *searching* for the right contact or process of any issue/information/decision?
4. What percent of your/team's time is spent on *searching for information or context switching* from one project to another and back?
5. What percent of time is spent in creating purely internal reports, status reviews, and other internal project meetings not directly related to customer value?

Each question has four choices.

(a) <10%, (b) 11 to 30%, (c) 31 to 60%, (d) >60%

Enter the type of wastes with examples.

Team pulse check: Paris and the HR have conducted an *anonymous* team pulse check survey to measure team dynamics and people satisfaction (pSAT).

How do you describe your job and workplace?
Some of the key themes that came up:

How do you describe your workplace?

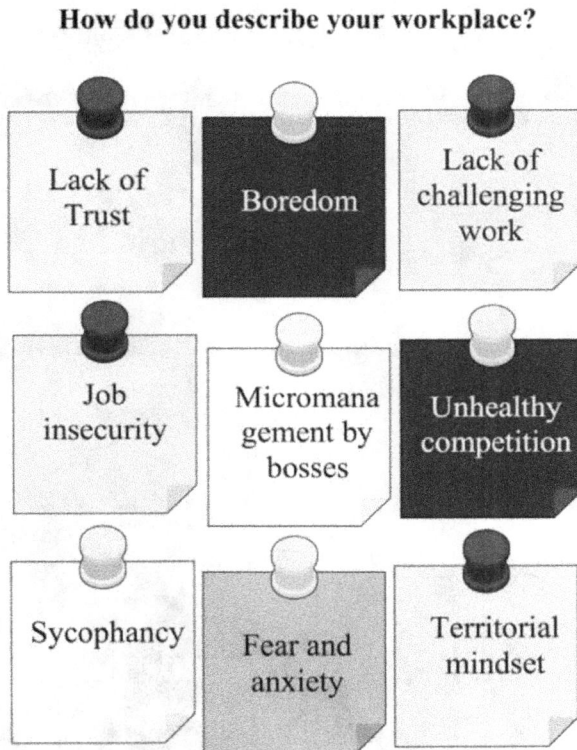

Lack of Trust	Boredom	Lack of challenging work
Job insecurity	Micromana gement by bosses	Unhealthy competition
Sycophancy	Fear and anxiety	Territorial mindset

Figure 4.3 The workplace

The workplace is dysfunctional and fraught with insecurity, frustration, command and control, and sycophancy.

Later in the day, we focus our attention to the Purchasing Operations PMO and spend two hours with the team. It is a PMO within a purchasing department which essentially is a subset of the enterprise-wide PMO which Tim headed. The lack of focus and politics of the group further startles us.

We find most of the group is not really motivated and not so serious about the work. None of the folks in the team show any semblance of craftsmanship and passion.

WILO (Week in life of) – How Purchasing Ops PMO staff spent their time?

| Lengthy and crowded meetings | Sycophancy and 'alignment' with managers | Back-stabbing & Territorial mentality |

| Navigating emails and messages | Excessive paperwork and rework | Administrative work & duplication |

Figure 4.4 Disengaged workforce

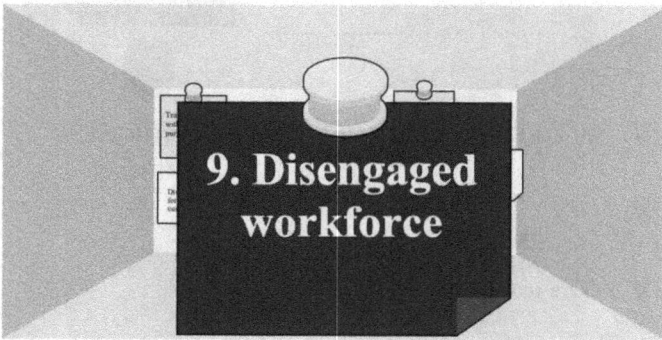

Figure 4.5 WALL No. 9

Table 4.4 The Writing on the WALL No. 9

9. Disengaged workforce	
What does it mean?	About a third of the company's workforce are generally not sufficiently engaged or underutilized due to: • Unyielding cultural, lack of psychological safety, and micromanagement • Lack of clarity, collection ownership, and shared purpose • Teams are advised to embrace teamwork and collaboration, but they are measured on their individual performance which creates conflicts
What are its effects?	• Inadequate sense of urgency, boredom, and complacency • Failure to contribute enthusiastically and whole-heartedly • Suppresses creativity and innovation due to underperformance

We have completed physical walks, surveys, and interviews, and we all add the takeaways.

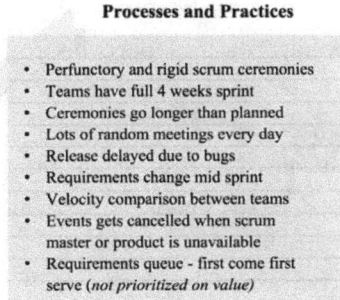

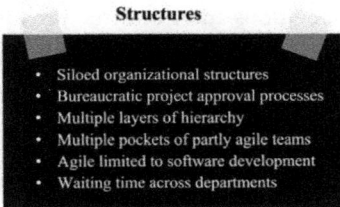

Processes and Practices

- Perfunctory and rigid scrum ceremonies
- Teams have full 4 weeks sprint
- Ceremonies go longer than planned
- Lots of random meetings every day
- Release delayed due to bugs
- Requirements change mid sprint
- Velocity comparison between teams
- Events gets cancelled when scrum master or product is unavailable
- Requirements queue - first come first serve (*not prioritized on value*)

Tools and Technologies

- Confusion in key terms (for example microservices and microapps)
- Competed code sits for weeks to be tested
- Tech debt and risk slow down prod. releases
- Enterprise architecture not clearly understood
- Physical signatures needed for software test
- Technology drives all backlog refinement and sprint planning decisions, NOT business value
- Releases getting delayed by GRC reviews

Structures

- Siloed organizational structures
- Bureaucratic project approval processes
- Multiple layers of hierarchy
- Multiple pockets of partly agile teams
- Agile limited to software development
- Waiting time across departments

People and Roles

People on their phones constantly
Scrum master acting limited to scheduling
PO not empowered on backlog prioritization
Same person is PO and scrum master
Large size 18-20 person scrum teams
Handful of aspiring agile individuals
Handovers and excessive context switching

Figure 4.6 Gemba Walk observations 1

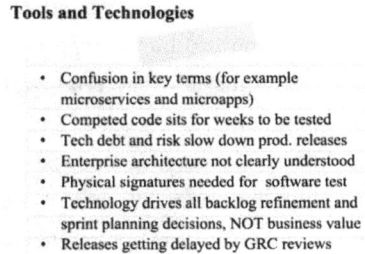

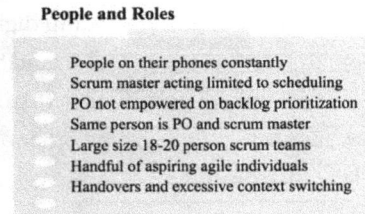

Figure 4.7 Gemba Walk observations 2

I have no time to take a break, and I soon notice that I have an upcoming weekly touch point on a burning topic.

We meet in her office shortly after.

Neil–Daisy 1:1 on Preparedness for Coronavirus-Related Disruptions

I look at Daisy who is engrossed and prepping on her laptop. She stops her work and looks straight to my eyes.

"You know Neil things are so volatile right now and very dynamic. Our international supply chain is drastically impacted, you are copied on those e-mails. Nothing seems to be coming on time anymore from China and Asia-Pacific. There's something new and something changing almost every day due to this virus, potentially threatening fast and exponential variations in the industry in matter of days."

"There's so much ambiguity, the international and domestic supply chains are both under immense pressure. It's a mess due to this drastic impact." She adds.

"It has been more expensive to maintain higher levels of inventory in some product categories, especially groceries like toilet paper, paper napkins, antibacterial, bottled water, gloves, and masks." She further adds.

"There are tangible and exponential shifts in customer buying patterns and behaviors. We need to be adaptable. The Board and COO have asked Richie and I to accelerate e-commerce in coming weeks.

And now, we need to be ready to serve over 80 to 90 percent of our customers online. As you know currently that it's less than 28 percent? This means we need to revamp digital operations and infrastructure for a potential global health and financial crisis! What's your take?"

"Perhaps, it's no different than earlier infections. There is news for a few months and then some other news. I'm really not sure." I admit.

Daisy continues.

"So, I am still working to get time in Richie's calendar, but we can't wait to start for his time. Our supplier and local teams in China are working totally remote now. So, my three questions."

- Are we ready for at least 90 percent customers switching online?
- Are we ready for at least 90 percent of teams working remotely?
- How are we planning to adapt IT infrastructure and operations to support the above two goals?

I confront her, "But isn't the last one Gus's responsibility?"
She folds her arms in a frustrated manner.

"Yes, but can you figure that out within your IT shop?" She reminds she is from Business.

"We could absolutely stay afloat if we have a killer end-to-end digital system or perhaps a digital platform to track. Our shopping apps continue to suck. We need to up the ante on our digital side."

We both agree there is need for both functional and nonfunctional upgrade. The need of the hour is to reimage digital strategy. As I start to get up, thinking my meeting is over, she drops a follow-up question.

"So, when is your production release for new platform upgrade in site-to-store and new digital apps for curbside pickup?"

I begin to explain and push back simultaneously "Sorry Daisy, we don't have a release date. I got funds released just yesterday after huge efforts and back and forth with our acting CFO, Bart. We still need to mobilize our best people and form one or two new digital teams.

We need the data team to provide their project plan, APIs need to be built by Gus's team, and we need an integration team for testing and enterprise architecture to commit to such an aggressive release plan. You see our company is extremely careful in releasing to productions. Hana's GRC needs three to four weeks of review. We take six to nine months generally."

She raises her eyebrows.

"We need to pull our shutters down if we don't get digital apps in order. We are staring at bankruptcy if we don't drive up digital business revenues. We can't imagine such long timelines. You guys are digital and IT experts, so figure out the damn thing."

Fearing she is about to explode; I assure her of some solution.

She is not unreasonable to warn me. I convince myself not to overreact on her harsh tone.

I am starving after a long meeting, so I hurriedly grab a coffee and a protein bar on my way.

Sid joins me to chat over informal sync-ups which he likes to call *Lean Coffee.*

"This isn't an acceptable situation!" I raise my voice in frustration.

We talk about my earlier conversations with Daisy, and we both concur with her sense of urgency. Sid suggests we connect with his old MIT professor, Prof. Nussbaum, over a video call. We will need to check if professor could meet in the next couple of days to get his insights on digital strategy.

Shortly after, I once again knock at Richie's door for budgets.

Richie is busy in reviewing some documents. "I have two minutes before my next meeting. Anything urgent?"

I leave his office with a firm reminder,

"Richie, please help in getting funding before we boil the ocean for the new digital strategy. You see this could be a thin line separating our company's success from failure."

Richie seems noncommittal. I feel helpless too, but still contented that I sounded assertive. I have done what I could, as I walk to the parking to wrap up my workday.

Tomorrow is the first sprint review. Sid pushes us to be totally transparent. I decide to take calculated risk recognizing the very survival of the company is at stake.

The next morning

Sprint Review

Gents welcome to our sprint review. Our agenda includes latest list of problems on the WALL, survey responses with hidden factory analysis, and value stream mapping of *ideation to implementation* process.

Seth says "We have conducted multiple Gemba Walks, physical and virtual walks, and also administered a survey. We have compiled and synthesized the responses."

The Survey Places the Waste as 36 Percent

We are all speechless!

We conduct detailed analysis and group the antipatterns observed across the three teams within four categories. Each category relates to destruction to at least one of the four values outlined in agile manifesto.

The Ratio of Value-Add Time to Total Lead Time Is 18 Percent

The value stream with value-adding activities, waiting time, delays, rework, and inventory which we have observed across the major releases. The VSM illustrates from ideation to implementation. This helps us to substantiate our hypothesis of wastes.

It's becoming clearer why we have defined over 30 percent of the things we do to be classified as waste.

"What does these really mean? This is shocking and awfully revealing" notes our CEO.

The Hidden Factory

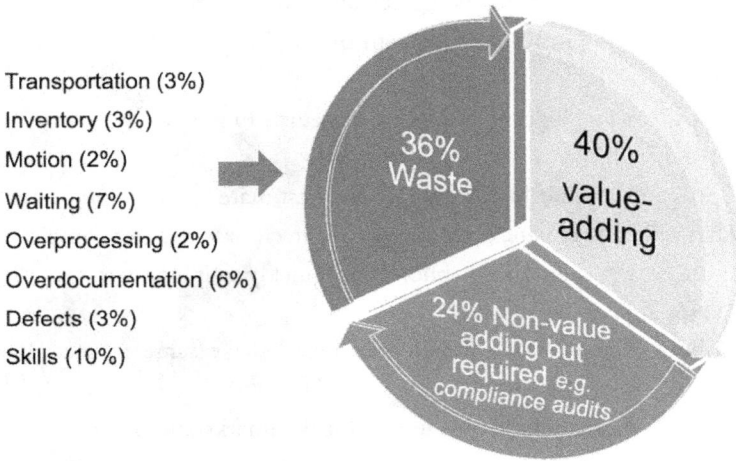

Transportation (3%)

Inventory (3%)

Motion (2%)

Waiting (7%)

Overprocessing (2%)

Overdocumentation (6%)

Defects (3%)

Skills (10%)

36% Waste

40% value-adding

24% Non-value adding but required e.g. compliance audits

Figure 4.8 The hidden factory

Table 4.5 Destruction of agility

Agile Manifesto: four core values	Activities causing destruction of value
Individuals and interactions over processes and tools	• Redundancies and imbalances in skillsets • Lack of creativity and innovation • Bureaucratic process to get access to tools and new licenses • Frustration and insecurity among team members due to status reporting
Working software over comprehensive documentation	• Eight playbooks totaling 655 pages sporadically used in the company • Lengthy 50-page documentation of business case to approve new projects • Software code and test cases are built, but product is not released timely • Gantt charts with multiple versions • Multiple department level "disjoint subset" of project plans
Customer collaboration over contract negotiation	• Lack of customer focus in sprint objectives • Customer feedbacks are prioritized ineffectively and infrequently • Commonplace design of products
Responding to change over following a plan	• Deadlines from top management • Roadmap gets changed multiple times in a week interrupting timelines • Changes in project plans creating widespread instability

I think of what this means in terms of dollars, a typical CEO question that would inevitably crop up, but I am clueless.

Sid does not hesitate in being upfront and provocative.

"You see, about 30 to 35 percent of the things we do at Walkers is a waste!"

"Gosh are you kidding me?" Charlie retorts immediately.

"No. Not really." I respond with speed.

"So, gents, even if I take a conservative estimate, say um.. 30 percent, so what will be the financial impact of 30 percent waste in our company?"

I see Bart pulling out his phone and quickly swiping, perhaps to his calculator app.

"About 30 percent. But this does NOT make sense to me." Bart responds categorically.

"It's my estimate based on industry benchmarks and obviously putting current observations in context of baselines I have seen in other similar organizations, but we will do a very methodical value stream mapping and time motion study." Sid explains.

Bart almost instantaneously presents his calculations on a whiteboard. He adds his own conservative guesstimate, wearing his CFO hat.

Blended average company cost per employee U.S. $

This is company's total employee compensation costs including wages, salaries, and the benefits like health insurance, retirement funds, and so on.

Total number of employees in corporate and regional offices

These include white-collar employees who work in offices and exclude store clerks, drivers, crane operators, helpers, cleaners, contractors, and so on.

"The total Cost of Waste is in the range of $125 to $250 million?" Bart sums up.

"The board will go absolutely crazy with this analysis … .

… So, are we spending up to a quarter of a billion dollars for wastes and other internal non-value-adding things?" Charlie wants reaffirmation.

There is silence in the room for next few seconds.

He continues, thinking of the politically correct words on a sensitive observation.

"Very interesting and for sure equally disturbing!"

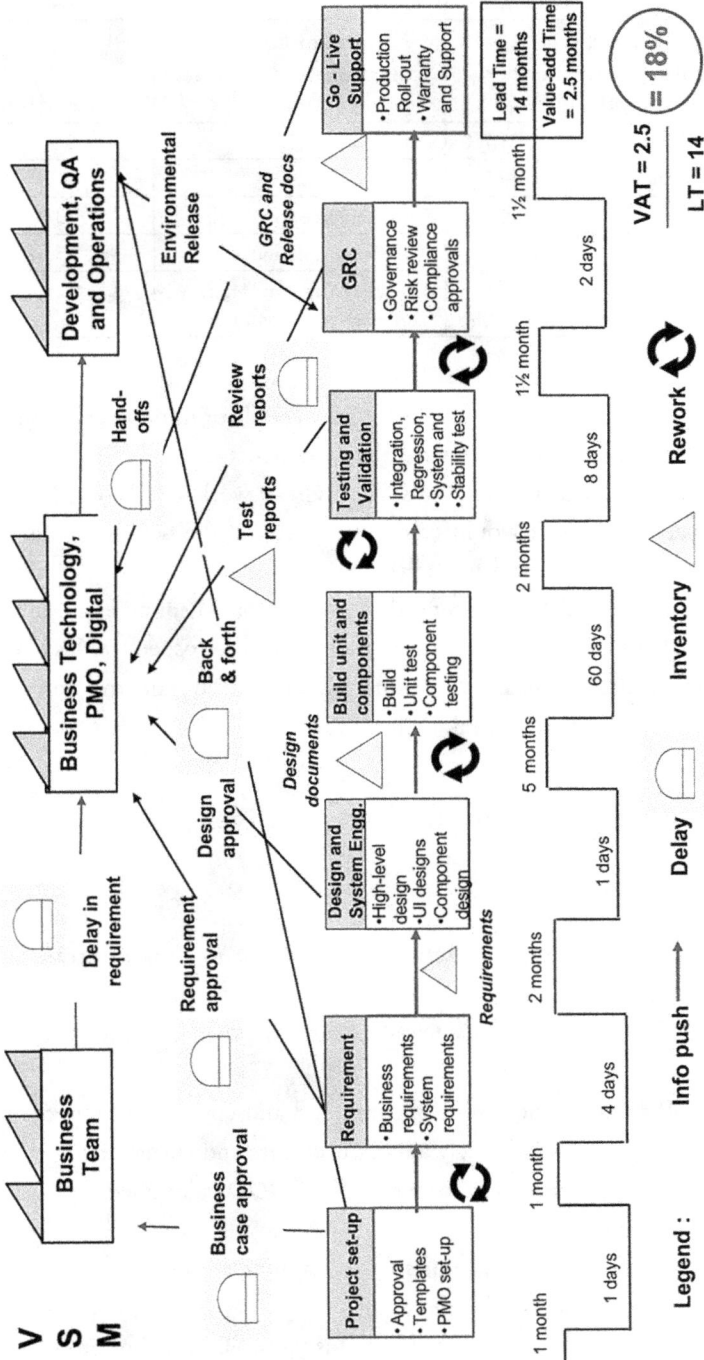

Figure 4.9 Value stream mapping (VSM)

Table 4.6 The Cost of Wastes

Blended average total cost to company per employee (U.S. $)		No. of employees in corporate and regional offices	U.S. $ Million
The United States	88,700	8,950	794
Rest of the world	19,550	2,290	45
		Total employee costs	839
		30% wasted time and effort	250
		20% wasted time and effort (conservative estimate)	125

Then, our CEO is speechless for next couple of minutes as it sinks in. There is an unsettling silence for a few moments.

He concludes the conversation. "Great work all. I support your approach. Though I would really like to see all the details in the value stream mapping. Can you send this to me?"

"Sure Charlie. We will send that to you soon." I sound extra polite.

Sid, Seth, Saira, and Keisha join me for our retrospective. It's a deliberately smaller audience to nurture psychologically safe and controlled environment for all to speak their minds.

Sprint Retrospective

What is working well?

- An inclusive enterprise-wide retrospective to visualize problems in the company
- NPS revealing deficiencies in customer experience and product management
- The management style of command-and-control and micromanagement adversely affect the culture and engagement
- Eight lean wastes in form of *TIM WOODS* identified at Walkers
- Gemba Walks and value stream mapping with ideation to implementation sketch
- Estimated *Cost of Wastes* (CoW) is up to $0.25 billion in the company

- The problems, the Writings on the WALL, identified during the Sprint 1:
  1. Transformation without a clear purpose
  2. Command and control management style
  3. Disregard for customer experience
  4. Uninspiring product management
  5. Traditional budgeting, funding, and estimation
  6. Excessive reporting and documentation
  7. Doing but not being agile
  8. Disjointed technology landscape
  9. Disengaged workforce

What could improve?

- Articulate the purpose of the transformation with objective and tangible outcomes.
- Reinvent digital strategy and agility to respond to disruptions due to coronavirus.
- Transparency and promptness to reallocate budgets and secure funding.

SPRINT 2

Reflection and Reimagination

Sprint Goal

- Develop a comprehensive method to define solutions to the problems.
- Device a superior approach for redesigning digital products and solutions.
- Adopt a fresh perspective to look at problems and embrace a new mindset.

CHAPTER 5

Organization as a LIVING Organism

Systems Thinking to Rebuild an Enterprise

Monday, February 10, 2020

Table 5.1 Kanban board

To-do	In progress	Done
• Approach to generate solutions to identified problems • Rethink the purpose of transformation • OKRs (Objective and Key Results)	• Plan a session with Prof. Nussbaum to reimagine digital • Follow-up with Richie for allocating budgets	

As I reach home at almost 8:00 p.m., I hear the TV is blaring out loud and both my girls are glued to it. Cindy is upstairs in our bedroom.

I hurry to grab the remote control to tune into the news.

On the local TV Channel WI6, a doctor explains "Coronavirus hijacks our cells. The virus makes copies of itself and multiplies throughout the body."

Tina comes running toward me.

"Dad you see that it's about cells." She points out.

"You said last time that when cells grow and grow, they cause cancer, right dad?" She asks.

"Yeah, that's true, sweetheart." I pick her up in my arms.

A three-dimensional model is on the news, illustrating how the virus enters our cells.

"Are cancer cells and the virus cells the same?" She inquires.

I am startled by how much our little one has heard about cells lately. I swiftly decide to put down the TV and focus all of my attention to her.

"There are enormous lessons that we can learn from our bodies. There are 11 interconnected systems in the human body."

Ami is quick to add "... like digestive system, nervous system, immune system."

I quickly nod.

"You know cells are very small." I clasp Tina's pinky finger and tell her that it is made up of millions of cells.

"The Building Blocks for our bodies are our cells, see?" I hold her pinky up.

Tina is curious and asks, "So what is a Building Block?"

Ami comes to support, "Tina, they are like the block pieces in your toys, which we both build and solve like we do with puzzles, right?"

"Exactly, very similar! Ami, this is a great analogy." I smile ruffling up her curly hair.

By now Tina is mesmerized and absorbed in the conversation.

"They are called the Building Blocks of life because they are the smallest functional units making all the living organisms." I continue.

I search the Internet to show them a picture of a cell.

"Any infection like a virus attacks our cells. The virus forcibly makes it to a cell to start making thousands up to millions of copies of itself. The virus uses our basic Building Blocks to multiply and reproduce within our bodies ... "

"... while the cancer spreads due to the uncontrolled growth of our cells. The strength of our inner Building Blocks, our cells to fight infections, virus invasions fundamentally define our ability to stay safe, healthy, and alive!" I explain.

"So, our inner Building Blocks define how strong our body is to fight bad guys."

"If mom's Building Blocks become stronger, then we don't need to worry about cancer or viruses, right?" Tina looks at me for an answer.

"That's absolutely right!" I assent.

I feel relieved having answered their questions.

I soon realize it is equally true for Walkers. If we make our Building Blocks inside the company stronger, then we could fight our competitors too and have a better chance to survive.

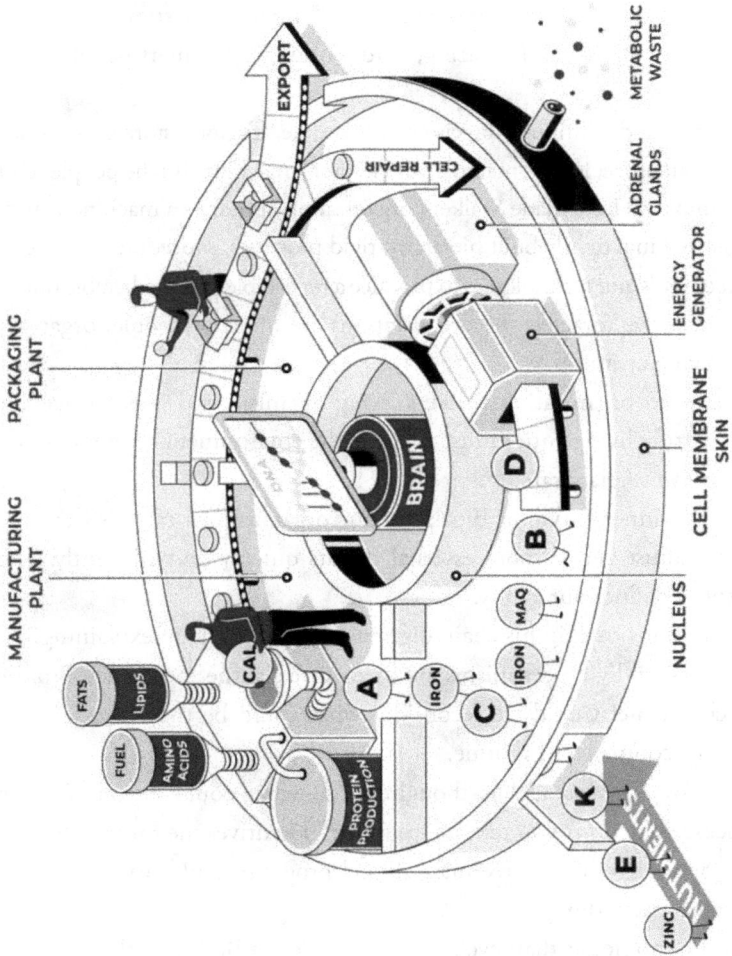

Figure 5.1 The cell

Next morning

Approach to Generate Solutions to Identified Problems

I continue to reflect on the need to bring the similar thinking to Walkers. I see Sid in the office and start the spiel to bounce my ideas:

"How do you define an organization?" I pose a question.

"It's a collection of amazing, hard-working, and smart people." He is quick to respond.

I nod and continue. "Precisely. It is people, it's not a store or a product, it's not an office, it's not material, and it's not a machine. It's the people. Don't you think we have made Walkers' organization appear as a machine which is organized in a tightly built hierarchy, rigid processes, procedures, and collection of tools and technologies to produce a repeatable and predictable output?

What we forget is the organizations are made of people, organisms, and living creatures.

So, our organization is like a living organism and is *not* a machine. And a truly living entity must adapt as the environment changes in order to survive." I elaborate.

"The inner Building Blocks of our organizations establish the ability to adjust and combat external threats quickly and efficiently. Their strength defines our agility."

Sid leans back in his chair, digesting everything I am explaining.

"Like all living organisms are made of cells, the most basic Building Blocks of life! Could we reconsider what could be those blocks which builds a company?" I resume.

"Wow, this parallel is thoughtful, so what could be our Building Blocks? Why don't you take an example?" He drives me for specifics.

"Should we take three main digital programs and start there?" I ask without much thought.

"No, no not at that level. We need to define Building Blocks by considering the entire system of Walkers. You see we have messed up the whole system like I have never seen before and completely missed the compounding effect of interconnectedness.

A system is an interdependent group of parts forming a unified entity. Systems thinking is the ability to see things holistically. It is based on the belief that the different types of relationships and interdependencies exist between the diverse components of a complex system. The constituent parts of a system when viewed in isolation will act different than the system as a whole. Additionally, the components work uniquely over time and within the context of larger systems." He amusingly points to a picture on my desk made by Tina.

"For example, when changing a car tire and expecting the rest of the car to run faster with one new tire. However, the car is a system with interconnected and interdependent automobile components like the engine, transmission, ignition, fuel supply, and battery, which have a significant contribution to performance of the overall automobile."

His analogies really amaze me!

"In the digital space, in order to achieve a true and holistic agility of a software application, it's not enough for the front-end team to just adopt agile, the dependent back-end application, the database platform or ERP need to be agile too, or else the system will not have agility as a whole!

Teams cannot smoothly function as these are vital interdependent components of the system with multiple integration touchpoints impacting the flow of value. Right?" He looks at me, slanting his head.

"Yeah, you are right; we do struggle in visualizing our organization like an interconnected system. Our management and executives are busy in their own territorial ambitions. The consultants we had hired are too busy pleasing the ego of each of their project sponsors. In the process, they are minting money with their exorbitant billing rates, mostly pointing at local optimization opportunities without taking a holistic system view of things."

Figure 5.2 Automobile as a system

"… So how do we change it?" I abruptly interrupt to investigate.

"The Building Blocks will be more effective and robust when we consider the entire system of Walkers. We can no longer optimize locally. We need to be comprehensive. We must recalibrate the strategy, redefine our structures, simplify operations and supply chains, optimize processes, rewire talent and capabilities, and relentlessly ask ourselves how to mesmerize our customers?" He debates passionately.

After nearly 50 minutes, we agree to have at least one Building Block as a solution for each problem in the Writings on the *WALL*.

The Writing on the WALL = Problem
Building Block = Solution

Sid questions me on a tactical plan to execute the idea.

"This space is meant for everyone to add. It's a live WALL and any rearrangement is prone to human error."

"How could you differentiate which solution solves which problems?"

"How do you plan to number the Building Blocks?"

Components of the System

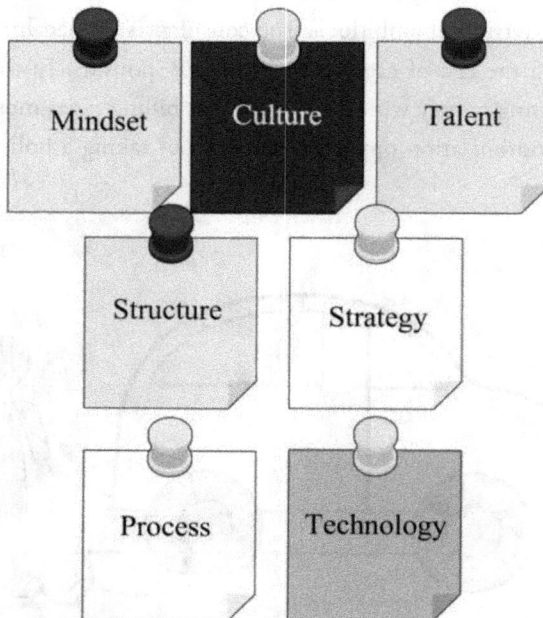

Figure 5.3 Components of the System

We think for the next few minutes. We decide to create an error-proof mechanism.

We define two lightweight rules to establish clear linkage of problems with solutions.

- Continue to tag each problem or "Writing on the WALL" sticky with *numbers 1 to 20.*
- Use an alphabet, *letters from a to z* for the associated solutions "Building Blocks."

Later in the day, I join Cindy at home for a quick lunch and return to the office with blocks from Tina's old wooden puzzle set. She has three almost identical sets anyways.

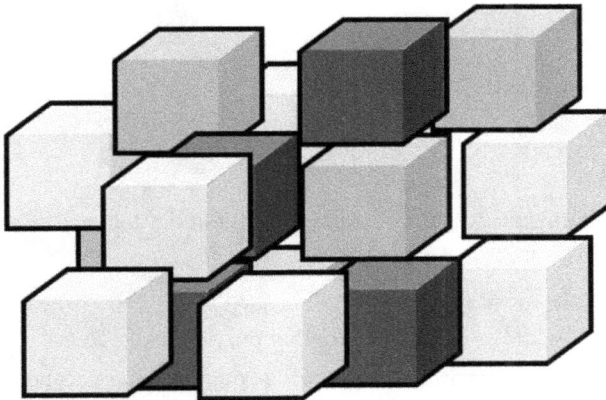

Figure 5.4 Blocks

After I return to office, I walk straight to the supplies room to borrow 10 boxes of sharpies and another 10 sets of post-it stickies.

Next, I send a communication to all of our staff.

It's symbolic and an extremely powerful gesture to be inclusive and rely heavily on our peoples' collective wisdom to solve the biggest challenge in the company's history. We soon start to see it pay off with some thought-provoking responses.

Seth and I meet Sid, who had scrutinized the documents, strategy presentations, and lengthy roadmaps we had shared. In the middle of my discussion, I see an incoming video call from Cindy's phone.

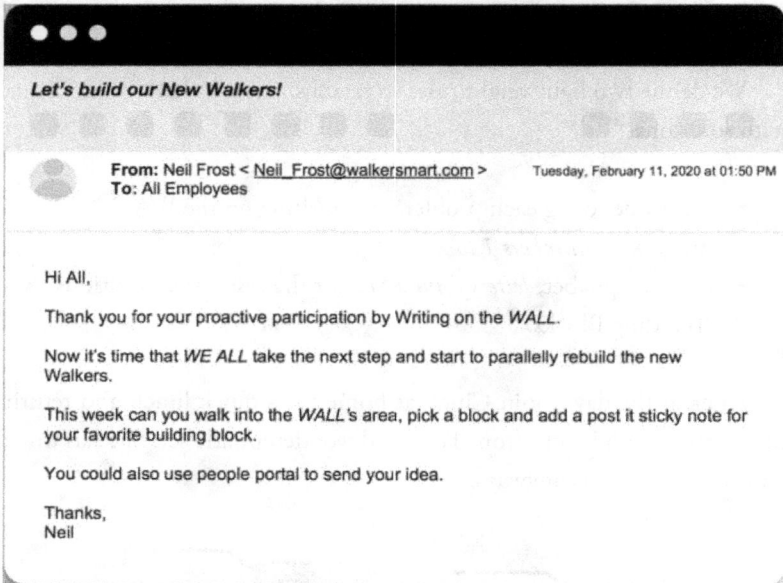

```
● ● ●

Let's build our New Walkers!


    From: Neil Frost < Neil_Frost@walkersmart.com >    Tuesday, February 11, 2020 at 01:50 PM
    To: All Employees


Hi All,

Thank you for your proactive participation by Writing on the WALL.

Now it's time that WE ALL take the next step and start to parallelly rebuild the new
Walkers.

This week can you walk into the WALL's area, pick a block and add a post it sticky note for
your favorite building block.

You could also use people portal to send your idea.

Thanks,
Neil
```

Figure 5.5 E-mail—New Walkers

I pick it up quickly fearing if something is not right. I see Ami and Tina. Tina is not looking happy.

"Hey girls. What's up. Is mom ok?"

"Dad, why did you take my wooden puzzle blocks?"

I try to bribe her with a trip to beach when weather gets better in the spring. She looks willing to negotiate and wants to settle for a date. She swiftly reminds of a long weekend in two weeks.

"Dad, look at the weather today, it's so sunny and warm. We need to go to the beach in two weeks because the weather is so nice now."

Ami immediately interrupts her, with a frown on her face. "Tina, just because the weather is so nice and warm today doesn't mean it's going to be so warm after two weeks. It might be, but there's a high chance it will change."

"But how do you know that?" Tina folds her arms, rolling her eyes.

"Do you know what we are doing today?" She asks,

"Obviously, we are making the yummy ice cream at home!" Tina replies with confidence.

"Do you know what we will be doing after two weeks?" Ami smiles posing a question.

"Aaahhh no we don't," Tina says a little confused after thinking for a while.

"Well, it's just like that. The weather people only predict what the weather could possibly be, but things change. There is a higher chance that the weather predicted for tomorrow is going to be more accurate than what is predicted for two weeks from now. They are mostly very confident about today and tomorrow but they are not confident for two weeks later." Ami makes her point.

"Oh, no … !" Tina exclaims.

I gently remind them about my upcoming session and end the call.

Rethink the Purpose of Transformation

After I hang up, I realize this is precisely what we do at Walkers. We spend humongous efforts in planning programs for three to five years assuming things inside and outside the company will not change. We frequently fail to realize that the next quarters and the immediate year is so volatile and unpredictable. We conveniently ignore the dynamics of the outside world.

"I see Walkers' management usually spends more time planning for two or three years down the line, and much lesser time focusing on what can be accomplished in the next month or quarter.

What makes us think that the System and its underlying components remain constant with time?" I say aloud.

Seth highlights his own challenges "Some commonly asked questions that always come from our senior management team tend to be:

- *How many resources are needed for the next two to three years for our agile projects?*
- *What is the team going to work on two years from now? or even*
- *What is the product roadmap for next three to five years?*"

Sid poses a rhetorical question:

"Could boiling the ocean to plan rigorously for three to five years down the line be considered agile?

Longer-term plans invariably need modification. In fact, they must evolve to stay relevant! There are too many dynamics involved internally as well as externally due to potential changes in customer requirements and dynamics in marketplace. Longer-term plans could become inventory, a lean waste. It's a waste of both time and resources." He continues.

"We define five-year transformation roadmaps without accounting for changes needed to stay relevant in disruptive business environments. Certain changes are much more immediate, and the impacts require swift responses that a multiyear transformation could not respond to. We tend to focus on just rigidly completing goals and disregard how the boarder system gets impacted." Sid is clearly hinting to our situation.

I admit candidly "It's true for us as well. Walkers' transformation was planned for five years, which is actually long and made us lose track of the big picture. The excessively longer timeframes without intermediate milestones and increments essentially meant that the company lost its sense of urgency … .

… We have built plans based on our own internal view without recognition of the tacit digital revolution of the marketplace and a rapid change in customer buying preferences, which is now being so rapidly accelerated with the health crisis around us."

Seth, Keisha, Sid, and I meet for 20 minutes for our stand-up to identify common patterns of our System to consolidate and synthesize the solutions.

A dozen thoughtful and practical ideas start following from the next day. We decide to start with ideas around clarifying the purpose of Walkers.

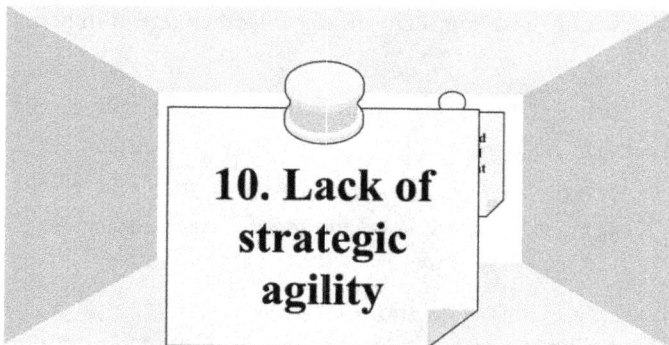

Figure 5.6 WALL No. 10

Table 5.2 The Writing on the WALL No. 10

10. Lack of strategic agility	
What does it mean?	A combination of top-down, document-driven, and overly long-term planning reduces adaptability and flexibility in strategic interventions. • Strategic planning becomes an entitlement for top management to satisfy highest paying person's opinion (HiPPO) in the conference rooms, without meaningful involvement of frontline staff who have first-hand knowledge of customer needs • The business strategy exercise revolves round lengthy business plans, data-heavy charts, spreadsheets, theoretical assumptions, hypothesis, and undue documentation • A disproportionately longer-term planning of three to five years without adaptability to repurpose for incremental outcomes in near-term (like next quarter) diminishes the ability to respond to changes
What are its effects?	• Planning processes are less agile and nimble to align with customer's needs • Lack of clear alignment between business strategy and customer needs • Reduces competitive edge and ability to pivot to respond to a digital disruption

- We need to provide them with clear purpose, articulate objectives, and create opportunities to experiment for a meaningful transformation.
- Start agile transformation with a defined business case and target "end-state" view. For example, visualize a state of agility after 12 and 24 months from the inception.

Objectives and Key Results

We decide to announce the approach in the next town hall and then invite anyone wanting to join in the coming weeks for redefining our purpose and OKR. Keisha and Seth join us, and we begin to draft one of our suggestions on what it could look like.

We all start to build our first Building Block with OKRs.

a) Customer-centric OKRs

Purpose: We will be relentless to deliver the most compelling shopping experience for our customers. We will invest in our people and deal fairly with our suppliers to build longer-term value for our shareholders.

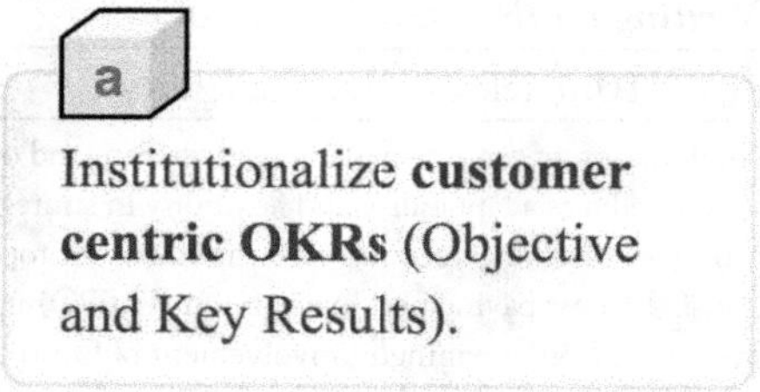

Institutionalize **customer centric OKRs** (Objective and Key Results).

Figure 5.7 BB a

- OKRs comprises of an objective and key results. Objectives are clearly defined goals, and underlying key results are a set of three to five measurable outcomes. The key results are ideally achievable up to about 80 percent. When teams frequently achieve 100 percent of their key results, it indicates that these are not aspirational.
- The purpose behind OKRs is to provide structure for teams to focus on specific, concrete, and tangible results for the company. Objectives are measured with results and need to be translated to value using epics and stories.

Measuring what is important to customers makes the most sense. The three parameters which are most important to measure the outcomes from the customer standpoint are:

Measurement

Cost, Time, and Growth

Cost: Cost of delivering value to the customer
- % Cost saving with supply chain agility
- % Reduction in rework, defects, and waste in processes
- % Reduction in customer complaints and trouble tickets

Time: Time to deliver value to the customer
- Time-to-Market (ideation to release to customer)
- Team happiness (people satisfaction [pSAT] and Net Promoter Score [pNPS])
- Progressive velocity of agile teams (use it meaningfully)
- % Automation of processes

Growth: *Experiences and feelings of customers directly impacting growth in repeat and new business*
- NPS
  - % Growth in revenues from new customers
  - % Growth in revenues from repeat business

Objective 1: Transform our organization relentlessly to deliver a compelling shopping experience for our customers.

Key results for the quarter:

- NPS of 90+ percent promoters
- 95+ percent customers satisfied with "value for money" measure
- 90+ percent of customers satisfied with delivery timelines
- Strive toward 85+ percent repeat customers

Promoters are loyal and enthusiastic customers and respond with a score of 9 or 10. They will be repeat customers and help to power business growth by referring others.

Scoring: 0 (not at all likely) and 10 (extremely likely to promote).

Table 5.3 Kanban board

To-do	In progress	Done	
		• System Thinking provides the approach to generate solutions • Organizations need to have a clear purpose for transformation	
		The latest Writing on the WALL: 10. Lack of strategic agility	The latest Building Blocks: a) Customer-centric OKRs

CHAPTER 6

"You Are on Mute!" A New Definition to Reimagine DIGITAL

Wednesday, February 12, 2020

Table 6.1 Kanban board

To-do	In progress	Done
• Session with Prof. Nussbaum to reimagine digital strategy • Translate new digital strategy into actions (Neil out of office 5 to 7 p.m.) • Lemonade stands with Ami and Tina		

I check my e-mail to view our daily customer traffic report and our stores are almost empty with less than one-tenth of customers. This clearly means more push for digital and e-commerce to stay afloat.

I am sipping my lukewarm coffee at 7:30 a.m. We all are in the virtual town hall on the company's coronavirus preparedness. This is the global event—a first of this kind to tackle the scale and magnitude of the fast-evolving situation.

You are on mute!
Can you see my screen?
We cannot hear you!

We have colleagues, consultants, and suppliers from across 32 locations and 15 time zones. Most of the participants are struggling to establish connectivity. No one seems to be intuitive in using digital technologies.

"It indicates our mediocre digital quotient." I say loud while rechecking if I am on mute.

Twenty-five percent of the time is wasted in resolving technical glitches and handholding participants to use the Zoom features correctly.

How could we possibly fast-track our digital transformation with such hopeless state?

I see a notification and soon we have a call with Prof. Nussbaum.

Session With Prof. Nussbaum to Reimagine Digital Strategy

"Thank you for getting in touch, how can I help?" Prof. Nussbaum looks so gracious.

"The Walkers Mart has isolated systems for each department or function, for example, product management, search, fulfillment, shipping, and returns. We need to rethink and recalibrate current disjointed systems, applications, and technologies in our companies to build an integrated digital landscape of the future. We are calling it *Reimagine Digital!*"

Seth chips in.

"We could absolutely use your behavioral science expertise and your invaluable experience to stand up digital start-ups."

"Of course, let's go back to the drawing board.

So, what does digital mean to you?" Prof. examines.

"Great question, let me share my thought." I try to think fast for the least silly answer.

"There are a set of digital projects and programs in our portfolio." I continue.

The professor interrupts me. "Are you sure that you are thinking about digital correctly?"

"What do you mean?" I answer with another question.

"Ok, let's put this into context. We think about digital in many different ways, right? There are four levels in which digital could be understood. Look at the slides which I'm sharing."

We look at his shared screen on Zoom.

1. For some companies, digital is still about the technology.
2. For others, it's about digitizing some processes and operations.

3. For some, it's a one of the ways of engaging with customers.
4. For new generation companies, it embodies a totally unique way of looking at everything and reimagining digital disruption for everything around us!

Prof. Nussbaum uses digital whiteboard with stickies, *quite technically savvy*!

"Walkers is surely not there in point 4, not even in 3, perhaps between 2 and 3?" Bobby speaks up.

"We would like to be at point 3 in the short term and hopefully point 4 in the medium term" I add, nodding to concur.

"So now then, let me rephrase, what does being digital mean to you?"

- Inclusive (for everyone, by everyone, and from everywhere)
- Efficient
- Cost-effective
- Scalable
- Environment friendly
- Adaptable to our behaviors (and not the other way around!)

We discuss in more detail, as we look at the latter slides.

b) Reimagine DIGITAL strategy

"Wow, this is excellent Prof. Nussbaum, well-articulated, intuitive, and so easy to remember too. So apt given the looming health crisis!" I exclaim and could we continue to get your insights.

Prof. Nussbaum: "Let me open one of my articles so I could explain each one of these."

Democratization of Technology

"What is common theme in *electricity, Internet, social media, and smartphones?*"

"These are technologies of the people, created by the people, and for the people. That's why they are ubiquitous and widespread." Prof. rationalizes.

The new meaning of *Digital*!

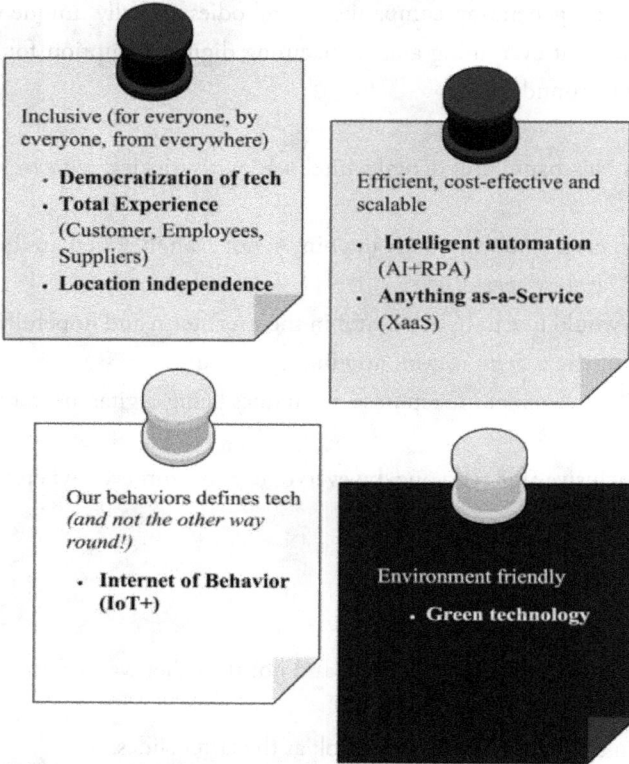

Inclusive (for everyone, by everyone, from everywhere)

- **Democratization of tech**
- **Total Experience**
  (Customer, Employees, Suppliers)
- **Location independence**

Efficient, cost-effective and scalable

- **Intelligent automation** (AI+RPA)
- **Anything as-a-Service** (XaaS)

Our behaviors defines tech *(and not the other way round!)*

- **Internet of Behavior (IoT+)**

Environment friendly

- **Green technology**

Figure 6.1 Meaning of digital

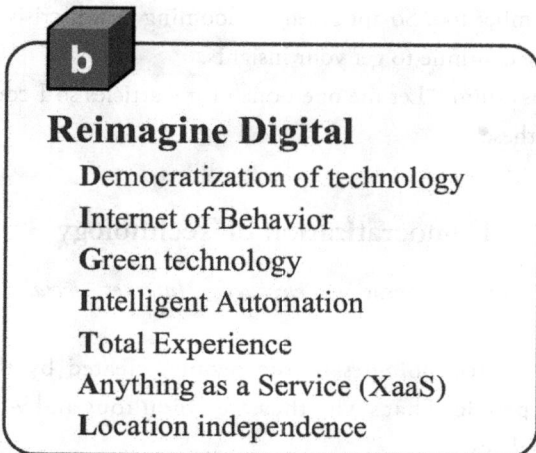

b

Reimagine Digital

Democratization of technology

Internet of Behavior

Green technology

Intelligent Automation

Total Experience

Anything as a Service (XaaS)

Location independence

Figure 6.2 BB b

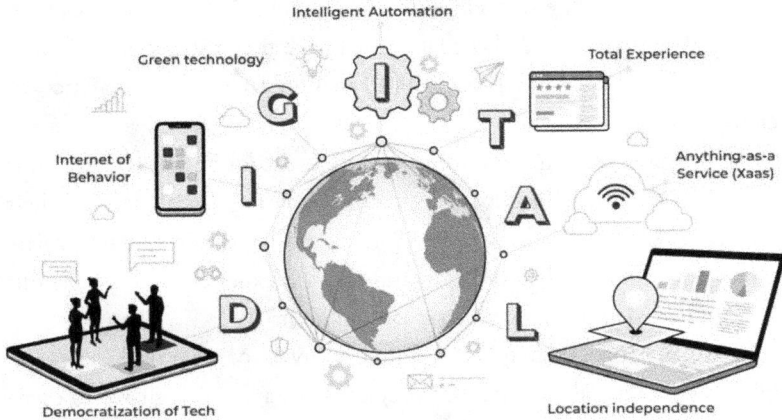

Reimagine domain of DIGITAL

Figure 6.3 Reimagining digital

When technology is created by the people and for the people, there is a purpose and better accessibility, availability, and widespread innovation. The opportunity for everyone to use, apply, and build increases speed, reach, and the spread of digital technology.

For the People and of the People

The people-centric digital technology means keeping common people at the core of the vision during the development. When technology is made for the public, it becomes a noble endeavor with a profound purpose and meaning. It has a far-reaching effort in lifting people up in their social and economic status. It improves connectivity to a global community, faster access to resources, and equitable distribution of knowledge leading to increased collaboration.

This explains why the social media platforms have become an integral part of lives of most people. It means providing easy access to those people who are or do not have the right expertise, proper education, or technical training. This has the potential to change people's lives.

By the People

There is a considerable shortage of skilled digital talent, and most organizations hire talent due to their educational qualifications and specialized professional experiences. Those who don't have these academic or professional credentials are not hired in information technology, analytics, or related fields.

Signaling theory in education infers that the labor market functions by academically qualified persons communicating "or signaling" their skills to their potential employers. When companies hire digital professionals only due to their education and relevant experience, they miss out on large skilled workforce which also has potential.

Generally, people may have different levels of technical expertise, skills, and analytical abilities, but they do not have mechanisms to communicate to the potential employers.

But what if people who do *not have advanced engineering or technical degrees* are given easier access, basic training, and ways to build newer digital technologies? What if companies do not differentiate based on academic qualifications and prior technical experiences?

When appropriate tools, enablement, and mechanisms are provided to people with above average aptitude, then it could become feasible. Democratization supports nontechnology professionals like business analysts and customer service reps to write code or generate data models. Every employee becomes an innovator. Those who are not skilled in a specific technology or have no or low coding skills can start to code software.

Internet of Behaviors

The Internet of Behaviors (IoB) decisively expands the scope and applications of the Internet of Things (IoT), as the IoB focuses on customer behaviors like tastes, preferences, interests, and buying patterns.

The IoT is a network system of interconnected devices that connect to the Internet to collect and transfer data. Over 90 percent of the data which exist today all over the world were collected in the past two or three years.

The IoB is the collection of behavioral data collected by IoT devices. It combines big data analytics, networking technology, and behavioral science with a focus to convert the information into knowledge. Along with buying decisions, IoB could also expose the customer's intimate information—emotions, relationships, and lifestyles.

As people use devices connected as part of the IoT, the companies tend to collect data which illuminate the behavioral patterns of the people.

The IoB outlines a compelling case of gathering usable insights from customers, which companies can immensely benefit from to better understand their customers.

There are clearly manifold implications for cybersecurity. The legal protection and regulations need to be clearly defined and strengthened over time as IoT and IoB become a reality to continuously address cybersecurity challenges.

Three main solutions to cybersecurity challenges:

- Reduce apprehension that data collection is without the explicit permission of the customers.
- Address negligence by both governments and corporates in identifying how the data are gathered, stored, and used.
- Prevent underlying risks to individual privacy and information security.

Green Technology

Conscious selection of IT and communication technologies offers potential to move toward carbon neutrality. The information and communications technology could account for up to 15 percent of the global carbon footprint within the next two decades.

Software has started driving all aspects of our lifestyles right from the time we wake up with digital alarm clocks on our smart phones until we retire to bed after watching our favorite series on streaming services or reading e-books on our tablets.

Migration to the Cloud

The public cloud shared across organizations could help the world reduce millions of tons every year of CO_2 emissions. Factors like improved server utilization rates and energy-efficient infrastructure make public clouds

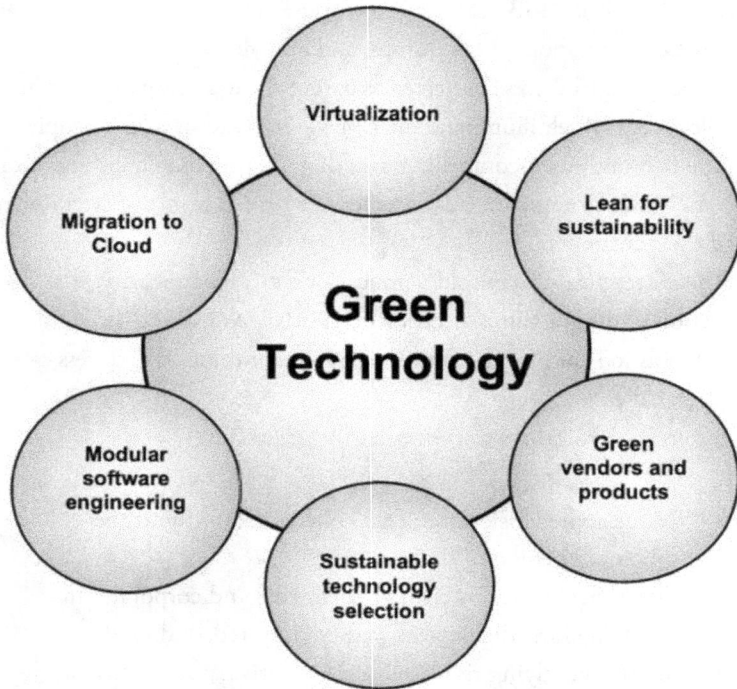

Figure 6.4 Green technology

more cost efficient than individual company-owned data centers. Optimizing and configuring applications for the cloud give an added edge.

The servers used in the cloud data center have fairly high-energy consumption that almost doubles every four years. Relocating and collocating servers will minimize cooling and underlying energy costs. Reduced cooling and harnessed outside air cooling, using separate aisles based on hot and cold temperatures, all helps reduce energy consumption. IT must continuously try to reduce the number and size of servers in a collective effort to reduce unnecessary storage and reduce the number and size of traffic requests.

Virtualization (and Containerization)

The concept of virtual servers is useful in going green. It enables companies to scale up the servers on demand and reduce overall energy consumption. Virtualization helps the creation of manifold simulated environments from a single or unified hardware system. Virtualization could be multiple levels like server, application, network, storage, and desktop.

Functions as a Service (FaaS) defines the concept of serverless computing. The serverless computing considers applications as a workflow of event-triggered functions and helps pivot toward a greener tech. This energy advantage comes from usage of shared infrastructure and related computing resources by executing functions only on demand.

Containerization (which is lightweight virtualization) is for operating system (OS) virtualization. Containerization aids in running applications in an isolated user space termed as containers using the same shared OS. It involves bundling an application together with configuration files, libraries, and dependencies across different computing environments. A container runs an isolated process as a fully packaged and portable computing environment; a group of multiple containers share a common OS.

The serverless computing separates applications at the hardware level, while containerization divides them at the operating-system level.

Modular Software Engineering

The machine learning and other algorithms, programming languages, APIs, and libraries could all ultimately contribute to the carbon emissions. The programming languages are the backbone of developing software. All programming languages are not exactly the same. They differ substantially by a number of factors like the logic, syntax, and compilation methods. The scripts in languages such as JavaScript and Python in most user scenarios consume higher computing resources and energy than the compiled programs built in languages such as C++ and Rust.

The efficient software codes, modularity, and refactoring mean considerably reduced costs due to the simplicity and option of continuous scaling on demand to leverage pay-as-you-use cost sharing models.

Therefore, selecting the most suitable programming language for a business function becomes vital.

Sustainable Technology Selection

The selection of technologies is vital for a greener tomorrow. In terms of systems of engagement, systems closer to customer, the edge computing is environment friendly. On the other end of the spectrum, in systems of records, systems which store data mostly at backend, blockchain is a promising technology but is not so green!

- *Edge Computing* manages workloads at the edge of devices. The applications are run at the "edge of user," and the data are stored and processed near the users and devices. Edge computing helps data to be analyzed locally and notably reduces the resources and time required for data to be relayed back. This fundamentally challenges the notion of having data centers located hundreds or thousands of miles away. It essentially supports optimization of energy by cutting-down the total amount of data traversing the networks. It lessens the latency for the end users and preserves energy.
- *Blockchain* revolves around public ledger, a fixed record of data groups called "blocks." Each block holds information, and the data can signify a wide variety of transactions. Blocks get added to the chain through a process known as crypto mining and use high-powered computers to power the processing. Blockchain is getting popular but consumes a remarkable amount of energy to power computers to sustain and grow the chains. As crypto currencies like Bitcoin get pervasive, the energy required to create and maintain "duplicated" records goes up too. The enormous electricity used by the Bitcoin creators and miners gets generated from a variety of sources including polluting ones like fossil fuels and coal.

Green Vendors and Products

Parameters like net carbon footprint are worthwhile to select providers and product vendors. The companies must have a set of attributes in their selection criteria like green supply chain management and environmental competencies (e.g., carbon emissions, recycling rate, waste management, inventory of hazardous substances, and green research and development).

Prioritize vendors who have R&D greener products and possibilities like:

- Milk products based on natural and smooth textile fabric alternatives
- Plant-based plastic which is 100 percent recyclable and degradable
- A biological substitute for animal leather: Develop yeast cultures to produce collagen (a biological material that skin is formed from)

Lean for Sustainability

Makes an organization more efficient and nimbler in going green by:

- Identification and elimination of redundant and duplicate copies of data, compression of data into smaller pieces helps to conserve energy consumption.
- Continuously auto running background videos on a web page increases energy and resources. This is the best way to prevent it to turn-off automatic video playing on websites.
- Modernize Walkers' stores and warehouses with 100 percent natural energy sources like:
  - Recycled battery power: LEDs equipped with recycled electric car batteries.
  - Solar roof: Shiny, sleek, and discrete type of solar roof using solar panels.
  - Bacteria-based solar cells: Cyborg bacteria to produce acetic acid (a chemical that can be converted into a potential fuel source from sunlight, carbon dioxide, and water).
  - Chemical fuel cells: Electrical current by exploiting a chemical reaction between hydrogen and oxygen.

Intelligent Automation

It combines and amplifies a combination of the robotic process automation (RPA), artificial intelligence (AI), chatbots, and Machine Learning to reduce the toil, process-related wastes, and manual labor needed to perform multiple steps.

- Automate and monitor everything across the critical end-to-end value streams.
- Adopt an optimum mix of agile backlog and collaboration tools with well-defined interfaces for seamless integrations and eliminating manual efforts at all steps.
- In the longer term embark on an IT organizational redesign journey to consolidate agile teams for enabling planning, development, production release, and support operations of key products.
- Using machine learning, data analytics, and AI, it is easier to correlate individual customer patterns of the product returns and exchange.

Total Experience

The experience of every stakeholder across the value chain of the ecosystem is interdependent. Happy suppliers deliver better services, products, and experiences. Happy employees translate to happy customers.

The total experience is important not just from the customer viewpoint but from people, contractors, shareholders, and vendor partners perspective as well. It is a complete and compelling digital experience for virtual distributed customers, mobile users, and workforce.

- Total experience has to be at the intersections of everyone relevant—the customer experience, people experience, user experience, and even the supplier experience.
- Improve perceptions, quality of service, and commitment we need the strategy of total experience. This strategy also helps us to constantly look at improving efficiencies, reducing

redundancies, and relentlessly improving our processes, products, and services.

- Maximize the wow feelings and amplify positive emotions
whenever stakeholders interact with our company's multifarious touchpoints.

Anything as a Service (XaaS)

It is on-demand scaling cloud computing, pay-as-you-go, or subscrip-
tion-based consumption. This comprises of a diverse set of products,
tools, services, and technologies that product vendors could deliver to the
customers over the network with monthly subscriptions.

- Recalibrate tools used across key value streams for the
DevSecOps to migrate toward XaaS model.
- It is about exploring scalable IaaS, PaaS, and SaaS for intranet,
source control, configuration management, testing, release
management, continuous integration, and deployment tools.
- Embrace alternatives to shift toward modular technology
architecture (service-oriented architecture and microservices).

Anything as a Service (XaaS) could be manifested in multiple ways.

Table 6.2 Anything as a Service

• Infrastructure as a Service (IaaS)	• Functions as a Service (FaaS)
• Platform as a Service (PaaS)	• Desktop as a Service (DaaS)
• Software as a Service (SaaS)	• AI as a Service (AIaaS)

Location independence is the single-most critical component for business continuity. It accentuates technology ecosystems to support remote
operations from anywhere for customers, workforce, and suppliers. It
becomes quintessential element like oxygen for companies and economies to survive in a crisis like a global pandemic or a natural disaster. This
includes 100 percent remote operations. It's a make-or-break period.

We decide to discuss next steps with Richie on location independence, which is now led directly by him due to latest mandate from the
CEO and business leadership.

Translate New Digital Strategy Into Actions

"This all sounds great but I am still wondering how do we translate this new strategy to execution. What does this really mean tactically."

Prof. Nussbaum smiles and departs with a few astute questions. "Can you think about these?

> *How do you be digital to build digital?*
> *How do you collaborate with your customers in building solutions*
>   *for them?*
> *How could you ensure a constant flow of feedbacks?*

The girls and I have an afternoon planned at the Pink Bows United Foundation's fundraiser event at a local farm field, where we will be raising money to advance the early detection and treatment of breast cancer.

Today is a bit warmer than usual as the sun is out.

We walk to our setup lemonade stands and get ourselves ready as the fundraiser begins. The field is well decorated with pink balloons, food stands, and tents where various sales and auctions are going on.

Although the virus has not reached our Wisconsin towns, I still insist that the girls to wear the face masks. They are perturbed with my push, but for me it is better safe than sorry.

"Someone's coming!" Ami puts her best smile on, as an elderly woman approaches our stands where we are selling lemonade.

Ami has her own stand selling sugar-free lemonade, while Tina and I are sharing a stand selling the traditional lemonade.

We are competing with each other to see who can raise the most amount of money for Pink Bow United. Ami had just served her first customer, and she welcomes the elderly woman to her stand with her contagious and joyful energy.

"Hi, would you like some lemonade ma'am?" Ami says to the old woman scanning her baby face.

"Hi sweetheart, yes. But I have diabetes, so can I have a medium sized cup of the sugar-free lemonade." She says, noticing all the ingredients on the table.

As Ami mixes and seals the cup with a plastic lid and fitted straw, the woman gladly pays her. I laugh as Ami winks at Tina and I, fully knowing that our stand is not doing so good.

As we prepare more glasses with more customers coming, the elderly woman returns after a few minutes.

She stands by Ami's stand and happily exclaims, "This is the best lemonade I have ever tasted with the right amount of everything!"

"Well, I am very glad you like it! Thank you," Ami smiles at her.

"You know what, I like this so much, I'll take three more large sized cups! Keep the change." She pulls out a 20-dollar bill from her brown leather purse.

"Oh wow! It will be ready in just a minute with the same condiments!"

"That would be wonderful, thank you."

"Here you go." Ami hands over the three cups.

"Thank you, sweetheart." The old lady smiles and walks away.

Soon after sunset, we are packing up.

"Well, I got about 28 dollars! How much money did you guys make?"

"We made seven dollars." Tina answers, and starts to throw a dramatic tantrum in the field.

"Ami always wins all the competitions! It's not fair!" She yells,

"Come on get up Tina. I can tell you why I won and how you can win next time."

Ami encourages her. "Yeah. Okay so, you know how you already had three jars of lemonade premade?"

Ami begins to explain, we both listen.

"Well, I only had one jar premade and bought all the condiments on the table so I could make special orders. For example, old woman had diabetes. She could get sugar-free options. She liked it so much that she got three more cups!"

"Good job Ami, you really learned a lesson and taught us one too today." I appreciate her.

As I drive back, I am ruminating over Prof. Nussbaum's questions. I feel I have a response.

I think about why Walkers doesn't engage in as much customer collaboration, in a manner that I had witnessed earlier today between my daughter and her customers. Despite this being so obvious, we don't focus on customer feedbacks as regularly and relentlessly.

"Our new digital strategy could translate to execution with an enhanced digital system for customer, product vendors, and people to collaborate by establishing feedback loops."

Is this an epiphany, the eureka moment for me?

I set up meeting with Bobby the next morning, who pushes me to define the problem and solution statements.

Business problem: We don't have a best-in-class digital process to regularly collaborate with customers, people, and third-party vendors (whose products are sold by Walkers).

Solution approach: Feedback loops with customers both internal and external. The defect or change later in lifecycles are more effort intensive and costly than doing it timely based on robust feedback loops.

He is receptive but needs specifics. "What does this look like and what do we include in business case?"

We use the remaining time to define a clear problem statement, purpose, business value proposition, projected benefits, and approach of Feedback Loop Orchestration Workflow (FLOW).

The FLOW ultimately would lead to improved responsiveness, quick resolution of customer request, sophisticated predictive analytics, and faster delivery of digital features.

The key benefits of *FLOW*.

- *Increase in customer retention:* The personalized product search and recommendations leveraging machine learning help us to get a competitive edge by integrating product demand, supply chain, and inventory management in their warehouses and retail store. The analytics provides smart recommendations and tips on size, color, model, and so on. It improves repeat business and retention. It could vastly improve its ability to deliver tailored search results and targeted marketing promotions based on page views, signups, clicks, past purchases, and other patterns using predictive analytics.
- *Supply chain optimization:* It helps to predict consumption patterns of customers in a geographical region and during specific times of the year (Independence Day, Christmas). This in turn helps to predict demand in advance and improves efficiency of inventory management at warehouses and stores.

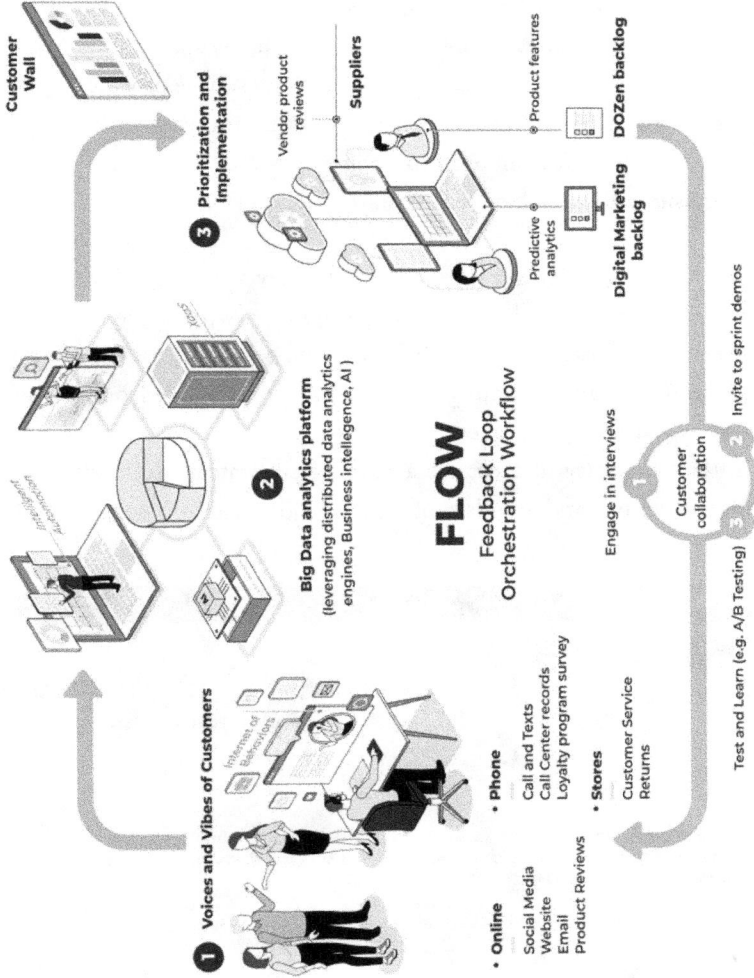

Customer Wall

3 Prioritization and Implementation

Vendor product reviews

Suppliers

Product features

Predictive analytics

DOZen backlog

Digital Marketing backlog

2

Big Data analytics platform
(leveraging distributed data analytics engines, Business Intellegence, AI)

FLOW

Feedback Loop
Orchestration Workflow

Engage in interviews

Invite to sprint demos

1 Customer collaboration

3

Test and Learn (e.g. A/B Testing)

1 Voices and Vibes of Customers

Internet of Behaviors

• **Online**

Social Media
Website
Email
Product Reviews

• **Phone**

Call and Texts
Call Center records
Loyalty program survey

• **Stores**

Customer Service
Returns

Figure 6.5 The FLOW

- *Consultative selling*: The customers would get important recommendations in selection of products and identifying corresponding local installers based on customer reviews, which could be digitally available chat/call/text on The Walkers website and Mobile app. This makes the entire selling process more consultative and collaborative.
- *Attractiveness of local business services*: This helps drastically reduce marketing and selling efforts of local service providers, handyman, plumbers, electrician, and installation suppliers—who could shift from push (of their services) to pull from consumers when they become part of the FLOW.

Sid and I meet over lean coffee later in the day as I see the e-mail.

"I wonder how do they estimate the budget without considering future state and roadmap. Nevertheless, for now we have a direction to reimagine digital and assuming you also have the required budget, so what stops you now?" Sid takes a sip of his latte.

"It's not that easy to executive a new digital strategy given with our traditional culture and mindset of risk aversion, internal politics, and

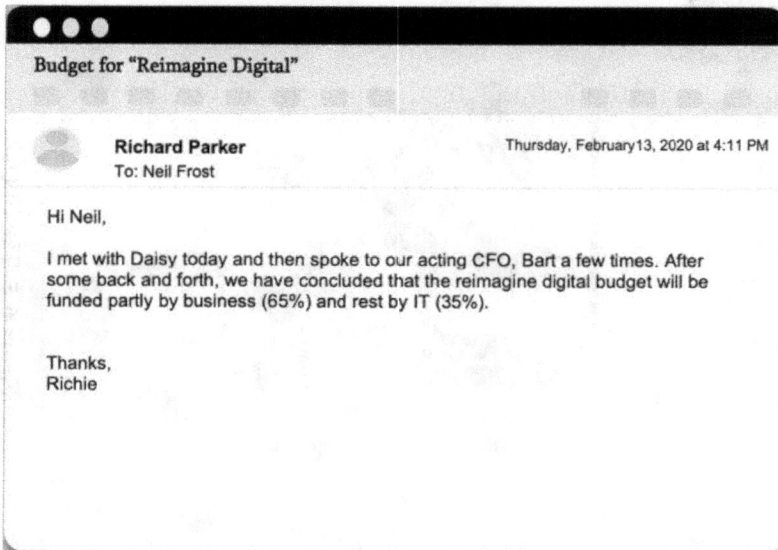

Budget for "Reimagine Digital"

Richard Parker
To: Neil Frost
Thursday, February 13, 2020 at 4:11 PM

Hi Neil,

I met with Daisy today and then spoke to our acting CFO, Bart a few times. After some back and forth, we have concluded that the reimagine digital budget will be funded partly by business (65%) and rest by IT (35%).

Thanks,
Richie

Figure 6.6 E-mail—budget

red tape. People want the status quo to continue" I retort without much hesitation.

"I agree, this is a clear Building Block. Changing the culture, mindsets, and behaviors seems like a no brainer, though it will not happen overnight ... but needs to start right away ... .

Table 6.3 Kanban board

To-do	In progress	Done
	• Techniques for Inner Agility	A holistic digital strategy entails reinventing everything! the processes, practices, and experiences, and this is not limited to just technology
		The latest Building Block: b) Reimagined digital for Walkers include the following seven levers: 1. Democratization of technology, 2. Internet of behavior, 3. green technology, 4. intelligent automation, 5. total experience, 6. Anything as a Service (XaaS), and 7. location independence

... However, what is the plan to actually change these things on ground?" Sid asks pensively.

"We need Inner Agility." I attempt to ramble for a few minutes.

"But how?" Perhaps, Sid is noticing ambivalence in my thoughts.

We both realize we don't have a crisp answer or a concrete plan of action.

"Let's spend quality time with other leaders. Why don't you reflect on what you and others could start to do differently as leaders?" he insinuates.

CHAPTER 7

The INNER Agility

The Power of Pause and Mindfulness

Friday, February 14, 2020

Table 7.1 Kanban board

To-do	In progress	Done
• The first chemotherapy (*Neil out of office 7 to 9 a.m.*) • What is Inner Agility? • Ways to embrace Inner Agility • Define Inner Agility Manifesto		

"Happy Valentine's day hun!" We hug for the next few minutes. Shortly after the doorbell rings, it's our delivery order of heart-shaped pink- and red-colored donuts. The girls come running downstairs to open the box.
"Frosts like our donuts frosted ... right?" Cindy tries to cheer us all.

The First Chemotherapy

A few hours later, I find myself walking up and down the hallway of the hospital to help time pass by. The nurses are helping Cindy prepare for the first chemotherapy session in a private room.

The hospital is less busy, and most of the junior doctors and nurses are having their break as I notice them socializing near the vending machines.

I see Dr. Anu in the passage across the chemotherapy room. Perhaps, by know she knows I am edgy.

"So, Dr. Anu I have been reflecting a lot in the last few days and I am really curious about why and how Cindy got the cancer. And how do we avoid it in future."

"Mr. Frost, I don't think that we can pinpoint to any one source. It's a combination of factors, including family and medical history. But with my research, there is generally one common pattern in the patients. That is, the mental well-being of a patient plays a pivotal role in their fight." She explains.

She wants to know if there was anything unusual in Cindy's life.

I pause to recollect some images.

"The two images include my mother-in-law in tears in her death bed and losses Cindy experienced in her real estate business."

Cindy was a successful realtor when we married. Cindy owned her own real estate company. She was known for her witty nature and treating her staff with respect. During the same time, her mother was sick for many months. "Cindy could not spend much time with her mother due to her frantic work and professional commitments."

I pause for a sip of water "And soon after the death of her mother, a couple of her deals did not go as planned either. She had to let go all many of her employees. She blamed herself for months for not being next to her mother in her last days and then laying off her colleagues. It made her depressed for months."

Dr. Anu takes a deep breath: "You see, we are always in the quest for more and more! More money, more influence, the latest smartphone, the best social media presence with desires to drive the most luxurious car, or live in a mansion. In our quest, we may grab the best gizmos, tools, and latest technologies. But in this never-ending desire to do more things, we tend to ignore the most basic and fundamental of all the tools and technology, *our body, mind, and soul.*"

"The physical, mental, and spiritual well-being are connected at a fundamental level. During and after treatment, it is well known that the mental well-being, will power, and resilience are quite important for the effectiveness of treatment and longer-term survival."

"We need our inner strength and resilience to face unpredictable circumstances." She adds.

Dr. Anu suggests Cindy to start a mindfulness course to nurture her mental health, to which we both agree. I volunteer to join her in most sessions to provide emotional support and camaraderie to Cindy.

We both decided to join the hospital's mindfulness course run by the city's renowned Zen Center. Fortunately, it starts next door in next hour.

We carefully and quietly take off our shoes. We put them sideways fitting it in dark brown shoe rack tightly packed with shoes, chappals, and slippers of various hues and sorts.

People are sitting on the dark red and blue mats. Most are sitting in a cross-legged position, and some are in a full lotus position. We feel intense energy and positive vibes. I take a deep breath and feel a sense of calmness taking over. The smell of incense fills my nostrils.

I whisper in Cindy's ears, "I love the scent. It's very clean and refreshing."

We look at the writing on a poster in the room.

- Zen is about having a peaceful mind, calmness, and the simplicity which brings us concentration, simplicity, and focus.
- Zen comes from a Japanese word which itself is derived from the ancient Indian language. In essence, it really means meditation ("Dhayan" in Sanskrit, Ch'an in Chinese, and Zen in Japanese).
- A Zen mind is like a beginner's mind, which is an open mind just like the child's mind—children have a lot of questions which may seem silly.

Sensei assures me that he will help answer this question after a breathing exercise. We all start to sit in lotus position.

"Start by closing your eyes. Take in a deep breath for about four seconds and pause for another four seconds. Breathe out for the next four seconds through the nostrils and not your mouth."

My attention comes back, as I look at Sensei. I raise my hand and ask a question.

"As adults, we all tend to think children are impulsive and they need to learn a lot, so why do we as adults need a child's mind?"

"The naturalness and spontaneity are vital characteristics that should not be confused with recklessness or impulsiveness. A beginner's mind is open and receptive to say *why not, or let's give it a shot.*" Sensei enlightens.

What Is Inner Agility?

I still feel somewhat vague about the idea, and so I run it through Sid, perhaps looking for some sort of affirmation before I invite others.

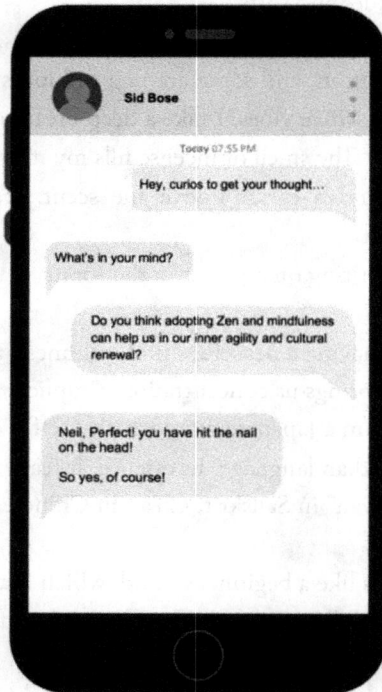

Figure 7.1 Text—Sid and Neil

My invite starts getting accepted ensuring an active participation in the session. I already feel excited and start to create a brief presentation to crystalize my thoughts.

Zen in a nutshell itself means meditation and mindfulness—or more accurately, a way of life. It could have different meanings to different people. It is about a peaceful mind, calmness, and a simplicity which brings us concentration, simplicity, focus, and awareness of who we are more. It is the motivation to make a real difference in our work, lives, and ultimately bring about happiness.

"It is what we need in this company, a new way of thinking and way of living and doing things. It focuses on plainness and intuition rather than traditional thinking focused only on self, limited to certain tasks, or excessive preoccupation on just rigidly completing goals.

Could we embrace inner agility?

From: Neil Frost < Neil_Frost@walkersmart.com >   Friday, February 14, 2020 at 08:15 PM
To: Richard Parker; Sid Bose; Tim Woods; Gustavo
Perez; Daisy Love; Hana Saito; Seth M; Saira
Ahmed; Keisha Thomas

Good evening!

It is no secret that our company is going through a really rough patch. There is a possibility of pandemic, when our company is already struggling. The environment around us could likely become more uncertain, ambiguous and volatile.

A range of emotions have crossed me lately. Then I read somewhere *it's better to light a lamp than to blame darkness.*

As I have started mindfulness sessions *"Zen ways of thinking and living"*, I have come to realize the power of pause.

To run faster, we need to slow down at first, and reenergize!

Zen is simply the state of mind which is about emptiness of a beginner's mind – a highly open mind and one which is full of compassion, humility, ethics and wisdom. It could help us to embrace our inner agility and enable us in our cultural renewal.

When we embrace an open mind, we can empathize meaningfully with our customers because we are not restricted by possibilities. We could approach our rather hopeless situation with an abundance of possibilities, creative solutions and innovations in our lives and work.

Could I invite you to thoughtfully consider how do we start this journey with ourselves?

Neil

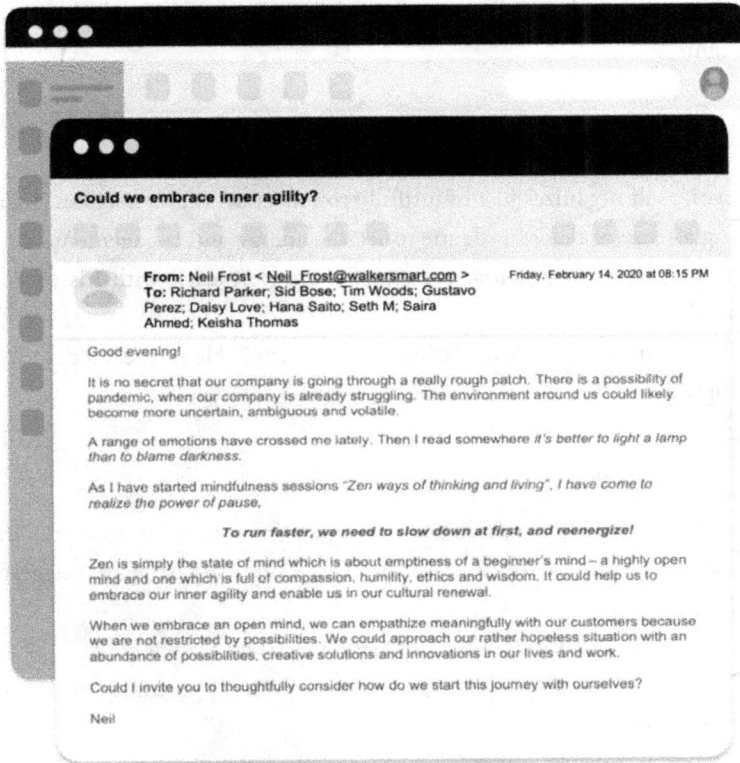

Figure 7.2 Could we embrace Inner Agility?

With what is happening in my personal and professional life, I have come to realize that there is a very real and profound connection of our minds with the way we think and behave in our work environment."

"Do you guys agree?" I look around and see the room is silent.

"Zen is simply the state of centeredness with an open mind and includes compassion, values, and wisdom to make a real difference around us!" Saira adds.

"And it's correlated to respect for the individual, and acting with patience, situational awareness, right?" Seth nods.

"I think it could help in embracing change as an ally?" Daisy concurs.

"Yes, yes, and yes!" I almost yell.

I look at Tim, who looks a bit hesitant.

Keisha inquires "Could we make it real, tangible, actionable, or else it could remain an abstract concept buried in our minds."

We resolve individually or in pairs that each one of us will share our thoughts.

Ways to Embrace Inner Agility

Everyone self organizes just beautifully to reflect on the Zen values. I am feeling a sense of relief inside me to see the energy and engagement.

Sid whispers "a *Shibumi moment!*" I am perplexed with his choice of words.

"It's an instance of flow, clarity, and harmony!" He assures to describe at length later.

Beginner's Mind

"The fear of making a mistake or risking an error or being told you are wrong is constantly with us. And that's a shame. Isn't it?" Paris suggests rhetorically.

To support the argument, Saira reads an extract from a book.

We should observe the problem as an opportunity without preconceptions.

A child is one who approaches life with the beginner's mind, bringing a diversity of thought, freshness, and enthusiasm. In contrast, an expert or an experienced individual is generally conditioned to think in a pre-defined way.

Our expert minds are generally bound by past experiences and are not receptive to newer untried possibilities. Adults tend to think that they are experts, and more often than not, they could be biased to think that this cannot be done.

But if you are not willing to make mistakes, then it is impossible to be truly creative. The best solutions come from an environment that fosters fresh and new perspectives that are not driven by fear and risk avoidance.

We need to have a child's mind to challenge the status quo and question the laws of the universe by thinking, doing, and testing the various possibilities. This is a mind that is open to exploration, discovery, and experimentation, and this is not constrained by old habits or obsessed about the way things are done around here.

The beginners' minds are open minds full of possibilities without limitations. They have an abundance of possibilities and potential solution. They are being intuitive, intrinsic, and innate and manifest in spontaneity. It creates environment conducive for intrinsic motivation.

Children are not biased by what can and cannot be done. They are curious and inquisitive and have a number of ways to look at things, they are unbiased, and they have multiple ideas which may sound strange and outlandish. It is possible that some could turn out to be really creative and even feasible.

A beginner's or child's mind is not worried about how things were done, older ways, previous habits, or how things have been until now. If we approach an activity or task from our open beginner's mind, we are not afraid of being wrong.

Here and Now

Tim and Keisha have two flipchart sheets.

You see, our minds are constantly disrupted because of all kinds of interferences, external factors, and abnormalities, for example, when the right tools are not in place or due to unreasonable requests from bosses like when we are asked to prepare a document that very few will have read. This makes it difficult to concentrate on the real task of bringing optimal quality, rigor, and creativity.

Generally, we all have preconceived feelings and judgments about events, challenges, and even biases about people around us. We usually tend to become judgmental and start with some conscious and unconscious biases in our minds.

In order to yield the most optimal outcomes, we must pay attention to the present moment without biases. The way we think without preconceived notions could make all the difference!

Here and now refers to a state of mind in which the person is totally immersed and exists in the present moment, entirely at peace with it. They are prepared to boldly face any situation with a steadiness, calmness, and composure. It means less distraction by least non-value-adding tasks, in the absence of unnecessary stress, office politics, and frustrations.

In a nutshell, this allows us to be fully present in our work. So, the goal of a well-performing workplace is to free up the minds of its most important asset, that is, people from unnecessary burdens, follow-ups, and office politics!

Thinking and living in the moment is about freeing ourselves from the delusions that keep us restricted in insecurity, self-centeredness, pretense, and narcissism. It helps us to stay open, focused, patient, and curious.

Imagine how our sense of quality and balance would improve if we could simply drop the old habits and predispositions, looking freshly at every moment with open minds. It's about accepting the challenge of each moment, to maximize our impact in simple ways. We must provide the right working environment for people to perform their jobs effectively and to ensure that they are not performing tasks on "autopilot" but with full concentration and focus.

Everyone is impressed by Tim and Keisha's clear explanation and applaud them.

We all pause for the yoga pose, the *Standing Forward Bend.*

"Standing straight with the feet together, bend forward at the waist, try to touch the ground placing palms down firm and flat, and keep your back and knees straight. Hold for up to one minute and go back up to mountain pose."

Experiential Learning

Richie and Seth have visual cards to explain the concept of experimental learning.

The formal education is rigid, rules-driven, and test-based. The education cannot just be limited to the reading and writing of words and letters or transferring of information.

The informal learning of "practice" is free from a set of rules. This informal learning is that which flows with one's life experiences and is practical in nature. The learning needs to be contextual, adaptable, and vibrant. We must practice what we learn to actually learn and confidently teach others. We should not just remember instructions or memorize theory but explore opportunities for empiricism and experimentation.

The best method of learning is learning by doing and experiential learning, which focuses on learning from past and present experiences. Those experiences then stay in our minds and help us to actively apply what we learn in multifarious environments and settings. We learn by the observations and experiences of the teacher, the Sensei, but at the same time, everyone is encouraged to observe, reflect, and verify teachings by themselves as well.

It is pragmatic to learn through direct experience and empirical insights. It includes learning by example, through observation and inspiration, by reflection, and by application of skills.

Leaders could serve their teams well by creating dynamic environments where their teams can learn and have experiences at the same time.

Continuous Flow

Hana and Daisy have an article to share.

Our lives are a great illustration of change. Life is a chain of natural, spontaneous, and incessant changes. We should let things play out and flow naturally.

Things have to be in an even flux, a smooth flow, moving on or passing by, as of a stream, or like a river where there is a constant *flow of water*. We need a continuous and unbroken flow in processes, practices, structures, and technologies. Just like the time which endlessly *flows*, we need to build uninterrupted *flow in our value streams* to delight customers.

In the same way that machines need periodic maintenance to optimally function and reduce the chances of overheating, wearing out, and ultimately breaking down, people need quiet time open mind and space for creativity to sustain their natural flow of talent. When teams are in the state of flow, we are all completely focused on the task at hand, feel happy, and become creative and productive.

Inner Agility starts with compassion. And if you're compassionate, you are imagining an abundance of possibilities. We could empathize meaningfully and practically with others because we are not restricted by possibilities to solve their problems.

Table 7.2 Zen values and adoption

Zen values	Ways and means of adoption
Beginner's mind	• Embrace a mindset of abundance • Pledge commitments "Inner Agility Manifesto (I AM)" • Design (re)thinking for effortless customer experience and excellence
Here and now	• Self-organized, truly independent and empowered teams, i.e., a unified *development and operations team to reduce* interdependencies and distractions. • A visual management space to foster collaboration and concentration, the Obeya
Experiential learning	• Define a place for immersive learning by doing and experience • Use A3 Thinking for succinct and comprehensive visual manifestation • Integrate "*Kaizen*" for unsolved problems from team retrospectives
Continuous flow	• Adopt "obligation to WAR" (waste avoidance and removal) in all sprint retrospectives • Flatten the organization to promote uniform flow of value • Establish a continuous flow of talent and capabilities

Just like a child, we should be thinking about a problem, a situation, or a challenge in a fresh and independent manner. New insights and fresh perspectives to solving a particular problem are essential for an *abundance of possibilities.*

Saira quickly draws a visual illustration of abundance mindset.

"But I still don't know how we could use it in our work" asks Saira.

"So how do you create an abundance map?" I probe.

Sid draws a small table and we all get up and start writing some of our thoughts on the abundance map.

Sid, Tim, and I have a call with Richie and Charlie after our session to brief him.

I am provocative "This sounds great on paper, but how could we avoid half-hearted adoption like previous initiatives?"

"We must invite the company's leadership to collectively define, commit, and embrace the 'Inner Agility Manifesto (I AM)' for collaboration, self-organization, and servant leadership." Charlie affirms.

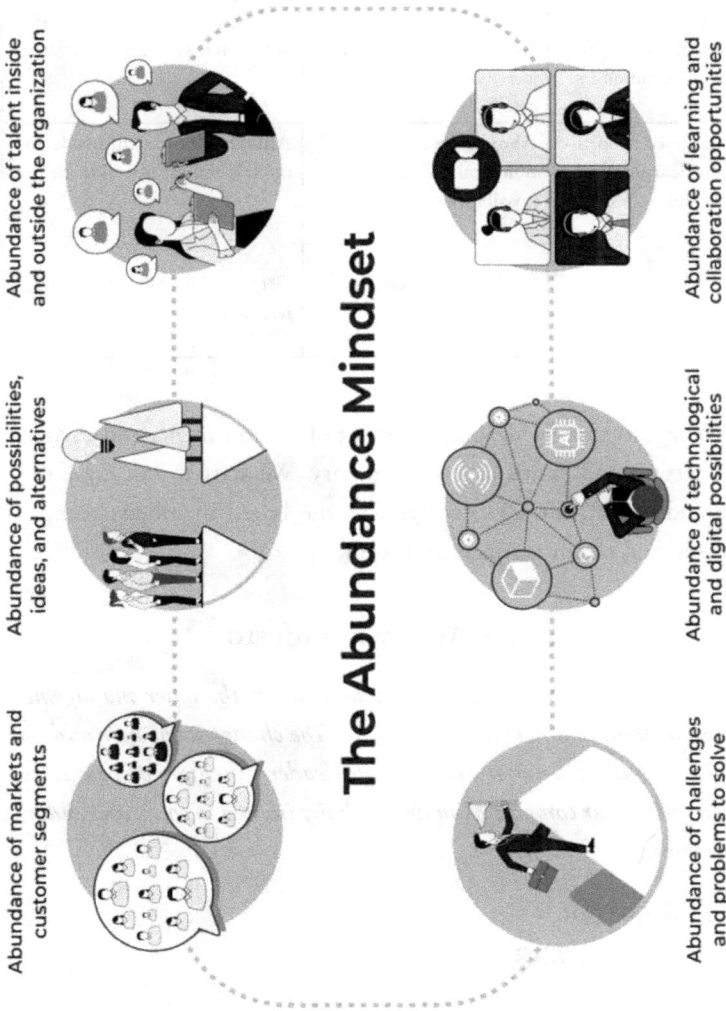

The Abundance Mindset

Abundance of talent inside and outside the organization

Abundance of learning and collaboration opportunities

Abundance of possibilities, ideas, and alternatives

Abundance of technological and digital possibilities

Abundance of markets and customer segments

Abundance of challenges and problems to solve

Figure 7.3 Mindset of abundance

Table 7.3 Abundance map

Abundance map		
Abundance of markets and customer segments	Abundance of challenges and problems to solve	Abundance of possibilities, ideas, and alternatives to explore
We need to define user personas representing 80 percent of our customers	*Let's look at Customer Wall and journey map to identify why deliveries get delayed?*	*UV for sanitization of packages needed in today's environment*
Abundance of opportunities for learning and collaboration	Abundance of technological and digital possibilities	Abundance of talent inside and outside the organization
Revisit our vertical organization structure to improve collaboration	*Explore drones, Green packaging Expand digital fluency*	*Get new digital talent faster and regularly*

He suggests that we draft a statement of commitments and invite all the leadership and teams to be a signatory. We start to outline a draft memorandum for our CEO to send to the board members, company executives, and senior management team.

Inner Agility Manifesto

As the Executives of Walkers, we need to unlearn the older management practices to embrace a new leadership style. The change starts here and now and with us all, as tenured professionals, leaders, mentors of new talent, and stewards of our company. You are cordially invited to co-create, endorse, and promote.

(c) **Customer Wall**
(d) **Obligation to WAR**
(e) **Abundance map**
(f) **Inner Agility Manifesto (I AM)**
(g) **A3 Thinking and Kaizen**

If we have a *Customer Wall*, we could respond quicker and successfully to our customers' needs and their changing behaviors. We decide to set up a *Customer Wall* to regularly consolidate and continuously update the

Table 7.4 Inner Agility Manifesto

DRAFT
Customer
• We shall inculcate empathy and ingenuity for customers and respectfully challenge all colleagues in best interests of customers and *not* focus on self-centered agenda.
People
• We shall exemplify the servant leadership style to help unlock intent, instill a sense of shared purpose, decentralize decision making, and *not* permit micromanagement.
Culture
• We shall promote a culture of respect for enabling trust, psychological safety, liberty to dissent and self-organization of the teams, and *not* allow command and control.
Shareholders
• We shall be accountable for our shareholders, company's performance, customers, talents, suppliers in a balanced manner, and *not* have bias toward anyone.
......
I AM committed to this manifesto
Signatories
Charles Moreli | Daisy Love | Richard Parker | Tim Woods | Paris Fey | Neil Frost | Hana Saito| Bobby Hanks ....

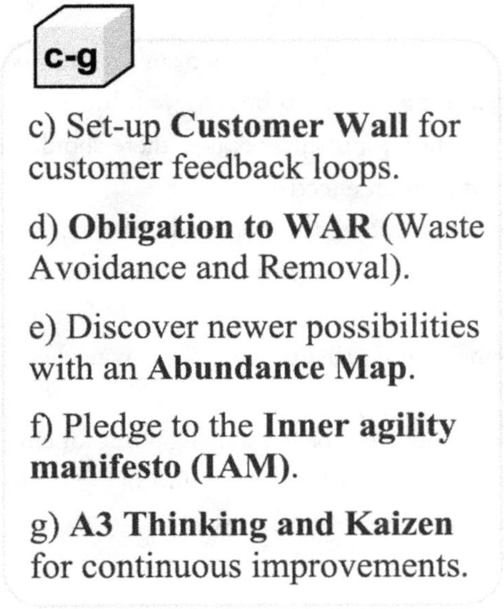

c-g

c) Set-up **Customer Wall** for customer feedback loops.

d) **Obligation to WAR** (Waste Avoidance and Removal).

e) Discover newer possibilities with an **Abundance Map**.

f) Pledge to the **Inner agility manifesto (IAM)**.

g) **A3 Thinking and Kaizen** for continuous improvements.

Figure 7.4 BB c–g

relevant customer voices, vibes, compliments, quotes, ideas, and verbatim feedbacks. A physical wall is a setup at the side corridor with set of three giant whiteboards.

A3 is the crisp and concise visual manifestation for impactful communication, planning, innovation, and problem solving, all in one all-inclusive view of A3 size paper.

The word Kaizen is a positive word. For example, the word Kai means change, and the word Zen means good, and together that word means a *good change.*

Kaizen should be viewed as those improvements which are identified in a team's retrospectives but require engagement and alignment with other groups in the organization.

Retrospectives are when you are reflecting back to what went well and what didn't. The team must plan improvements as soon as possible if it's within the team's control, but if there are improvements which are outside the gamut of the team or are enterprise-wide improvements, then Kaizen is most helpful.

Kaizen epitomizes the philosophy that small improvements at regular periods can lead to sustainable improvements and outcomes overtime. Engaging teams in small improvements almost every day (and at least once every spirit) helps lead to a bigger change. Kaizen is for *everyone, in every sprint, and everywhere.*

Kaizen as a viewpoint recognizes that a continual pursuit of excellence should be treated not as a goal to be achieved, but rather as an intrinsic belief and a never-ending pursuit, because there should be no boundary or an end to getting faster, effective, and better.

It's about taking small, incremental, and steady steps, rather than large and rapid leaps, and it's the key to confidently and constantly moving forward, and thus achieving long-term success. In fact, we could interpret Kaizen philosophy as the principle that there is no best practice, only a better one.

A Kaizen event could also be the starting point for enterprise improvements. We plan 10 percent of our time improving what is not working and set up continuous improvement cycles.

Structure and Steps for Kaizen

We adopt a *PICASO* format to make it easy to remember for A3 Thinking and problem solving. In order to keep it succinct and focused, we formalize A3 Thinking for Kaizens.

- **Problem**: What *problem* we are trying to solve?
- **Importance**: Why is it *important*?
- **Current state**: What is *current* state?
- **Alternatives**: What are *solution alternatives*?
- **Success metric**: How do we *measure* which solution is best?
- **Ownership**: Who *owns* actions and by when?

Later on, in the day at the office, Paris and the team conduct a revealing assessment of our managerial culture and needs for talent transformation.

Keisha concludes, "Really worthy solutions and valuable options could be imagined if we are open to explore, discover, and *test and learn*. It can bring us a plenty of possibilities and opportunities."

Table 7.5 A3 problem solving

A3 problem solving	
Problem *What problem we are trying to solve?*	**Importance** *Why is it important?*
Current state *What is current state?*	**Alternatives** *What are solution alternatives?*
Success metric *How do we measure which solution is best?*	**Ownership** *Who owns actions and by when?*

Sid and I meet over our lean coffee.

"Much needed food for your thought and actions." Sid mentions.

"But at the same time, you see we need to boost our business performance. The digital products of Walkers still are quite mediocre. I didn't have a good experience ordering on the Walkers app the other day. It just takes long; the app has technical glitches and requires lots of effort to search the damn stuff." He emphasizes.

"Yeah. We need to make the shopping easy and intuitive. I like a term I heard called Design *Re*thinking, seems like a fair next step? But how do we go about it?" I probe.

"Let me connect us to a design guru in the next day or so. He is known to have designed one of the early smartphones in Silicon Valley way back in 2007. Let's bring some fresh design ideas and kick-ass viewpoints. He takes Zen one step further to Design Thinking."

"Did you know even Steve Jobs was inspired with Zen of design" he guzzles his double shot espresso at once.

Table 7.6 Kanban board

To-do	In progress	Done
	• Plan a session with *Guru of Design, the* GOD.	Zen values for Inner Agility: *Here and now; Beginners' minds; Experiential learning;* and *Continuous flow*
		The latest Building Blocks: c) Customer Wall, for aggregate feedbacks d) Obligation to WAR e) Abundance map, for newer possibilities. f) Inner Agility Manifesto (I AM), to embrace change g) A3 Thinking and Kaizen, for continuous improvements

CHAPTER 8

The Shibumi Sprint

The Zen DESIGN (Re)Thinking Cadence

Wednesday, February 19, 2020

I wake up before everyone, keep aside some morning coffee, and breakfast for Cindy before hitting the road at 7:45 a.m. after adding the items to

Table 8.1 Kanban board

To-do	In progress	Done
• Meaning and relevance of Shibumi • Zen of Design: The seven principles • The case for Shibumi sprint (what, why, and how) • Sprint review • Sprint retrospective	• Plan a session with *Guru of Design, the GOD*	

Kanban board.

As I walk to the office building from the parking lot, I see Cindy's text.

I smile to myself as I read Cindy's encouraging words for the day. I feel good of her strength and resilience, despite everything that is happening.

As I enter, I am imagining the appearance of GOD, Sid's Guru of Design. I recall Daisy had forwarded my invite to our Head of Marketing to join us for this session.

I reach the office at 8:34 a.m. and I see Richie surrounded by Saira, Daisy, Keisha, Hana, and Paris waiting in the conference room.

"Good morning, everyone!" I greet everyone.

"Look around Neil, you have taught us pretty well to be *Here and Now*." Daisy jokes.

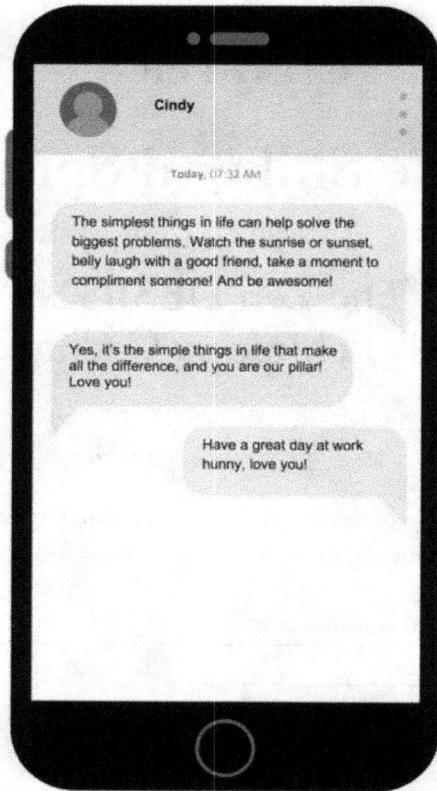

Figure 8.1 Text—Cindy and Neil

Everyone smiles and it appears they are all are cheerful and good-humored. I am still bewildered and mystified with the entire notion of Zen of design.

The GOD is now online.

Sid introduces us to his Design Thinking mentor, whose first name happens to be Guru. But he is often affectionately called *the GOD, the Guru of Design!*

A tanned man with a peculiar smile, perhaps in his late 50s with round thick glasses holding a large, light green, and white colored mug of coffee with brown stains, appears on the screen.

He has a uncanny geeky look, which is not unusual among artists, and a clearly stubbly chin and cheeks. Evidently, he is in the thick of some unique creations and has not shaved for the last few days.

His gray hair in tight curls covers most of his forehead.

His curls bounce up and down as he waves at us, greeting us all. We all wave and smile, but most of us are distracted by the matrix of gizmos and screens behind him covered in green codes and a live feed of simultaneously changing formulas and data points.

"Friends, based on my experience as a shopper, a number of your digital products or features are just not cool enough." The GOD adds.

Daisy wants to know details, "What do you mean GOD? Can you share an example?"

"A segment of your consumers are millennials, teenagers, and young shoppers, but the product mix and customer experience have not been able to keep up with the faster evolving tastes and preferences of this target audience." The GOD continues.

Close your eyes and think of the most wonderful product, service, or experience.

"When we started using a smartphone for my mother's continuous glucose monitoring," Hana gets sentimental.

"When I look down at lush green fields from my light-sport aircraft," Daisy shares her passion.

He asks us to open Walker's shopping app "Are you happy with what you see and what you could do?" He asks.

Daisy does not hesitate to speak her mind.

"No way, I am not happy! Our apps are mediocre in ease of use and user experience."

The GOD: "Right! You need to provide a *Shibumi feeling* to your customers …"

Meaning and Relevance of Shibumi

"Shibumi is a Japanese word and has no direct translation in English. It denotes instants when we feel harmony, connection, and a sense of equilibrium, grace, and elegance. When something has been designed really well and it really works, there is a clear understating and effortless beauty. That's Shibumi!

Shibumi is a moment, an experience, or an image when we have elegant, effortless, and authentic feelings.

The quality of Shibumi evolves out of a process of complexity, though none of this complexity is manifested in final product. You see sometimes it's somewhat difficult to put in words, but you can feel it from the bottom of your heart."

It can be described in multiple ways:

- Understated beauty
- Articulate brevity
- Genuine gracefulness
- Elegant simplicity
- Profound naturalness
- Pristine splendor
- Effortless experience
- Perfect imperfection
- Unobtrusive attraction
- Pure excellence

Saira types the words on her computer and does a quick word cloud.

Keisha gets up to express "So, we need this feeling ... something that is cool but not flamboyant, yet still minimalist! A state of refined but yet natural, poise but still common appearance, the balance, and harmony."

There are many ways to understand and express Shibumi.

Figure 8.2 Shibumi

Zen of Design: The Seven Principles

"Overall, Zen aesthetics are all about intentionally imperfect beauty." The GOD explains.

He continues with a pause, opening his arms wide.

"It's a state of being pretty, precisely what it needs to be and it's not over-engineered."

The GOD continues in more detail, as he leans back in his office chair with a calm smile.

"It employs a direct and simple way of doing things, without being too extravagant and flashy ... using products, technology, or services which are pleasant and cool without too much pretense. It's something as pleasant as ripples in the water, the nature of a fresh breeze or tepid intensity of the sun, drops of rain on skin, or the smell of mud when it starts to rain. In a nutshell, it's a feeling of awesomeness."

"I am still somewhat overwhelmed. Where do we start? How does it help us in solving our immediate problem? You know what I mean, don't you?" I ask with my arms folded.

"We need to use our creative and intellectual energy in a constructive sense, to simplify things and not make it more complex. We need to recontextualize mindfulness.

The simplicity in purpose and aesthetics enriches us. It is imperative to be straightforward and genuine. It helps us to improve our empathy for all, especially for customers and how we serve them with our prettified products and services." The God answers.

"Don't you think it could make the design of any process, framework, practice, product, or technology simpler by its usefulness, rather than execute by a formula? We need to design like ARTISTS."

The GOD shows us a page from his presentation.

1. Austere *(Koko)* is focus and clarity by eliminating what is nonessential.
2. Refreshing *(Datsuzoku)* is breaking routine and not bounded by convention.
3. True to life *(Shizen)* is the natural flow without pretense.
4. Imperfection *(Fukinsei)* is the asymmetry and irregularity.
5. Simplicity *(Kanso)* is the plainness.
6. Tranquility *(Seijaku)* is the silence within flow.
7. Subtle *(Yugen)* triggers curiosity and interest about what is not obvious.

"Generally speaking, Zen cherishes simplicity and straightforwardness in staying grounded to reality and staying present, *Here and Now.*"

I see most of us are curious but it's still not clear. We ask the GOD to explain each one of them in more detail.

"We need to use the Zen atheistic to design like ARTISTS."

"You leverage the minimalist concepts as ways to explore, relate, and design, instead of being driven by prescriptive formulas to repeat or copy. You can design everything *with a mind of an artist, spirit of an artist, and a creative bend of an artist.*"

Saira has an imaginative illustration.

Zen of Design visualized by ARTISTS

(The 7 Zen Aesthetic Principles)

Austere	Refreshing	True to life	Imperfect	Simple	Tranquil	Subtle
(Koko)	not routine (Datsuzoku)	(Shizen)	(Fukinsei)	(Kanso)	(Seijaku)	(Yugen)

Figure 8.3 ARTISTS

In Zen, there are a total of seven aesthetic principles for effortless and appealing, yet simple and prettifying designs:

1. *Austere (Koko)* signifies minimalism.

It means to eliminate clutter or noncore by keeping designs basic, bare essential, and weathered. Or in other words, it's the very subtraction of the nonessential by accentuating restraint and omission for designers.

- Austere sublimity embraces the idea of keeping things simple with a sense of clarity, wisdom, and maturity.
- Design could be aesthetically reduced and simplified.

Zen design principle 1: rigorously avoid adding anything that is not really needed at the first place.

2. *Refreshing (Datsuzoku)* is the welcome break from routine.

This represents an escape from daily routines and introduces an unexpected thought and unfiltered openness like a beginner's mind.

- It embodies being free from conventional and traditional adherence to strict rules, laws, and restrictions.
- It breaks most common habits and fosters freedom.

The ultimate break is our sleep—which really changes our mind's perceptions unconsciously. In fact, we get some of the best ideas in the bathroom or when walking.

Zen design principle 2: An intentional "break" from routine is often critical for discovery.

3. *True to Life (Shizen)* denotes naturally self-organizing.

It means an absence of pretense and superficiality without artifice.

Ironically, there are examples of the spontaneous nature of the Japanese garden which exemplifies it. It does not mean to replicate nature, nor does it mean to let nature have dominance. It means to create a natural state through human intervention.

- The goal is to strike a balance with nature and not against it.
- It also requires a deeper and realistic appreciation of nature.
- It's about creating a fairly natural feeling with purpose.

Zen design principle 3: Embed natural forms, patterns, and rhythms in the designs.

4. *Imperfection (Fukinsei)* is the asymmetry or irregularity.

This principle is extraordinary because it embraces the incompleteness and imperfection of existence. An asymmetrical balance is lively and breathtaking. In nature, trees are asymmetric, heterogenous, and uniquely imperfect, but they are yet so balanced and beautiful.

- Our human nature makes us inclined to seek symmetry.
- Most humans think linearly and look for consistency and uniformity, but there could be things which are uneven or irregular but still delicately balanced.
- The goal is to invoke our natural instinct and desire for symmetry—if things are left asymmetrical or imperfect then as viewers or users, we tend to creatively participate in cocreating and completing it.

Zen design principle 4: Provide collaboration opportunities to co-create and enable platforms for open innovation.

5. *Simplicity (Kanso)* is the plainness.

It manifests in plainness, simplicity, or elimination of clutter or what is not adding value. It reminds us of precision that may be achieved through omission or exclusion of the nonessential.

- It imparts a sense of being neat and uncomplicated—not too lavish or overelaborate.
- Kanso is more than just visual simplicity—it's the thought to exclude what doesn't matter much to deliver space for what is quintessentially required.

Zen design principle 5: Create space for things that matter by omission of what is nonessential.

6. *Tranquility (Seijaku)* means solitude and quietness.

This represents periods of active quietness, energized calmness, brief periods of silence, and internal and external peace and tranquility. It's like a pause, when you breathe in and out in meditation. It is a removal of disturbance and noise from one's mind, body, and surroundings.

- Plan daily time for cleansing the mind of too many thoughts, doubts, and worries, doing nothing in reality and freeing your mind.
- It is often the hardest part, but it could be rewarding to refresh and recharge!

You see we need to realize that being busy all the time is not always better than doing nothing. The same is true for our leaders, we need to let team members have periods of doing nothing.

Zen design principle 6: A momentary silence could lead to bouts of creative energy flows.

"As we know that over 30 percent of costs, effort, time, and resources tend to get wasted in things that do not add value to customers, even when we adopt stringent time management, traditional planning estimations?" Sid adds.

"It's like we do too much of really minute estimation and capacity management, which I now understand is against Seijaku." Tim admits.

7. *Subtlety (Yugen)* is implicitness.

Whenever I try to visualize it, it is partially hidden shadows and part darkness, just like opaqueness but with a vital purpose. Some are partial suggestions rather than a full revelation.

In our designs, something is left to our imagination. It's a puzzle with a purpose. This provokes us to uncover and discover.

- Yugen is a beautiful but easily misunderstood principle.
- It's not about lack of transparency, which is critical for any transformation, but it's in the context of designing marketing campaigns, songs, novels, suspense and thriller movies, and other creative works.

Zen design principle 7: Be subtle by stimulating human curiosity and imagination.

By the time we end, Saira has created a masterpiece with Zen design principles. It epitomizes our conversation with visuals of Zen design and aesthetics.

This is getting confusing and too conceptual. How do we tactfully adopt it? I challenge the audience to get biased for action and think about implementation.

Seth jumps in.

We could leverage *seven Zen aesthetic or design* principles for improving the design of everything—processes, products, and experiences! Could we organize the task within a *Shibumi sprint* to keep Zen of design approach timeboxed within a week to establish a predictable structure and cadence?

(h) **Shibumi sprint and seven Zen design principles**

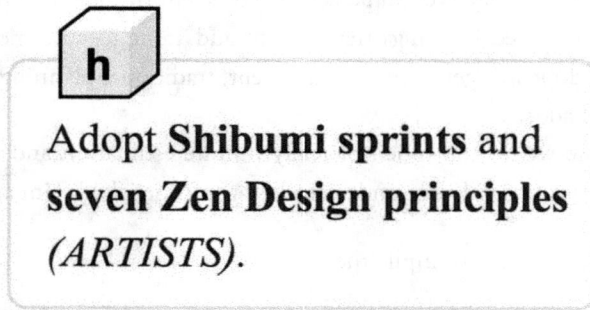

Adopt **Shibumi sprints** and **seven Zen Design principles** *(ARTISTS).*

Figure 8.4 BB h

The Case for Shibumi Sprint

What?

Shibumi sprint is to gather customer voices and vibes, create personas, map journeys, (re)design, and conceptualize with basic principles of Zen of design.

Shibumi sprint is a one-week (or sometimes two weeks) Design *Re*Thinking sprint organized at least once in a quarter to profoundly empathize with customer desires, needs, and aspirations for creating exceptional, powerful, and unforgettable experiences.

Why?

Shibumi sprint helps in the following:

- Awareness of simple but not so obvious possibilities.
- Demonstrate technological feasibility and functional utility.

- Inspires and animates all! a test drive, prototype within a timebox!
- Convince a potential investor, sponsor, or a stakeholder to invest!

Shibumi is a moment, image or an experience. Its process may be complex, but these *seven Zen principles* can help you approach Shibumi in your own designs.

Customers make their own views of the products and services based on how they feel in multiple touchpoints and channels. We need to think of customers as humans who want to be heard, cared for, and need solutions for their problems. They need to feel like they are in control of the decisions they make and are informed, engaged, empowered, and valued.

How?

The Shibumi sprint centers around better understanding customers, extensively leveraging.

   i. Go-n-See: Vibes and Voices of customers
  ii. *User Personas*
 iii. *Journey Maps, Empathy Maps*
 iv. *Seven Zen aesthetics principles,* to experiment with design alternatives

Voices and Vibes of customers: Voices are explicitly what is told by customers, and Vibes are implicit observations considering their emotional state and feelings in different steps of their journey.

We could reimagine Design Thinking with Shibumi sprint and seven Zen design principles for improving design of everything—processes, products, and experiences.

Daisy and Keisha introduce four personas from in e-commerce research presentation.

Each of our self-organized breakout group will meet after two days with new designs for Process Experience and Products. We create a group chat to collaborate for sprint reviews. I offer to move across all breakouts to help orchestrate and everyone agrees.

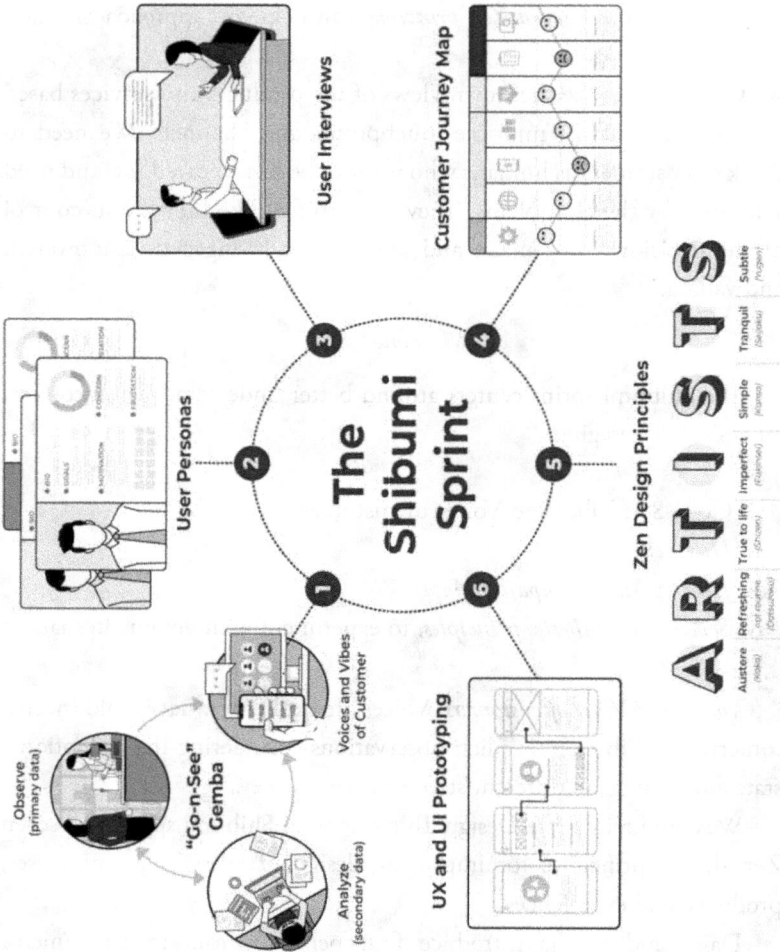

Figure 8.5 Shibumi sprint

Table 8.2 User personas

Persona No.	User personas	Insights from user interviews	User's Shibumi moment
Persona 1	Michael Fast, 28 years old	Mostly late in shopping for essential needs, restocking, or reordering. Laid back and recognizes very late that they are running out of something in their home or office and make shopping decision spontaneously	Home delivery in one hour or less
Persona 2	Monica Green, 42 years old	Lives in a downtown of large city. Zealous about "go-green," saving planet, and environmental friendliness. Is willing to pay a premium for green packaging and shipping options. Passionate about using environment friendly packaging	Zero carbon footprint and eco-friendly packaging
Persona 3	Anita Bucksmall, 23 years old	Works as an executive assistant for large multinational company. Buyer is highly price sensitive. They look for discounts at lowest price. Is highly social, outgoing, and brand conscious. Currently, she defers shopping garments, shoes, fashion apparels, and other accessories so that she could get try different options, sizes, and colors in a brick-and-mortar store	Lowest price and convenient delivery
Persona 4	Ron Staywell, 58 years old	Buyer is not technology savvy and needs help of his teenage daughter to search products online. The shopper is health conscious. Prefers organic options in groceries. They are willing to jump the ship and buy completely from Walkers if they get options for safe, sanitized, and secured delivery of their packages at home	Ability to use digital apps independently and health conscious

Sprint Review

1. *Product (Fulfillment and Delivery)*

Daisy and Sid define the problem statement for Persona 1, Michael Fast.

Business problem

The company continues to struggle and have much longer delivery time-frames to serve certain geographical locations compared to our competitors.

Solution approach

Sid is provocative from the get-go. "So, if pizza can be delivered in 30 minutes and ride sharing apps can send you a ride in 10 to 15 minutes, why does Walkers need three to five days to deliver? Can we deliver online orders in less than an hour for a set of products?"

Reduce delivery time to 92 percent of our geographies by 30 percent with 40 percent delivery now marked as eligible for two-day shipping.

Table 8.3 Product fulfillment and delivery options

Delivery options	Reimagine warehouse hubs	Innovation
• Three options for express shipping on eligible products ⇒ 50-minute shipping ⇒ 3 hours ⇒ 1-day shipping	• Renting six warehouses in Kentucky and Indiana centered around Daviess County, Indiana, the median center of U.S. population. Explore a new delivery hub • Working on an agreement with our delivery service provider to route a number of its air cargo planes through Indianapolis, Cincinnati, and Louisville • Drones to connect warehouses and customers in geographically remote regions	• Tie-up with a ride sharing app • Start with under 50 minutes delivery to about 300 zip codes across the country • Complete testing and request expedited approvals for self-driving trucks • Drive-thru, click-and-collect and curbside pick-up spots as self-serve pick up options.

2. *Product (Packaging)*

Seth, an environmentalist at heart, takes up the challenge and calls up his buddy who works green packaging innovations Inc.

Business problem

Environmentally friendly customers like user Persona 2, Monica Green, don't prefer Walkers because we have traditionally used considerably larger boxes and more amount of packaging than our competitors to fill unused spaces in the cardboard boxes.

Solution approach

Zen design principles:
Austere, True to life, and Simplicity

Walkers uses different sizes and types of packaging materials for shipping the fragile materials such as glass items, tableware, electronics, toys, certain fragile furniture, and even clothes. This is needed to ensure that the shipped items are stable and do no shift, turn, or move a lot during shipping and transportation. We stuff more packaging for risk mitigation.

Saira invites Packaging SMEs at Walkers to define a collaborative approach. The packaging department commits to switching to 100 percent biodegradable peanuts for our packaging needs. With this, we could save costs by recycling, save the planet, and virtually eliminate the polystyrene, a plastic polymer mainly in form of Styrofoam which is environmentally nonfriendly and ends up in landfills.

- Made from natural ingredients: potato starch and corn starch
- Biodegradable and could readily dissolve in water
- Reusable and easily recyclable
- Eco-friendly, dust free, and nontoxic
- Nonsticking due to antistatic (without electrostatic charge)
- Durable, sturdy, and abrasion resistant

A compelling punch line for our TV commercial:

Walkers will reduce estimated 15 million cubic feet land-
fills with biodegradable packaging, eliminating Styrofoam.
Want to join us save our planet?

3. *Product (Clothing and Fashion Apparels Category) Redesign*

Paris and Keisha present their design for users like Persona 3, Anita Bucksmall.

Business problem

There is a sharp decline in revenues in certain segments like clothing and fashion apparels.

Solution approach

A persona analysis, customer journey map, and two design principles are used.

Zen design principles:
Austere, True to life

- Walkers had recently conducted an extensive market study leveraging advanced analytical techniques like machine learning and complex event analysis, with an objective of identifying key levers to improve its sales revenues in retail.
- Analysis has shown that revenues in certain segments (particularly clothing and women apparels) are falling drastically.
- One of the main findings suggests that online customer returns in casual clothing, fashion apparels, and shoes have been constantly increasing for the last two years.
- The primary reason provided by customers is greater preference for online shopping, which means that they are not able to try different sizes. Customers are not buying online due to the unease in selection in wrong size or incorrect fitting.

The company's Clothing and Fashion group jointly design an experiment to crowd source prototypes of an *Etzy-Tailor app* which could be downloaded by customers on their smart phone for accurate size measurements.

Depending on the product being considered by potential customers, the *Etzy-Tailor app* needs measurement of following up to 99 percent accuracy.

On one hand, the Etzy-Tailor app would help to substantially reduce the percentage of returns in these product categories attributed to size mismatch, and on the other hand, this would substantially improve the confidence and comfort level of customers to purchase clothes and shoes without worrying about size mismatch and potential hassles of returning the product.

Machine learning algorithms will accurately determine one of the two scenarios based on specific measurements: (1) where one of standard sizes could work and (2) where tailoring/alteration are required before shipping.

Punch line for TV commercial:
Tap your Walkers app twice for a personal Tailor

4. *Experience Redesign (Digital App)*

Tim joins Richie to define the problem for Persona 4, Ron Staywell.
Business problem
Mediocre to poor customer experience of digital app users reflected in lower Net Promoter Scores of less than 48 percent (promoters).
Solution approach
Customer interviews (primary data) and research (secondary data) analysis:

- Demand for online shopping has drastically increased due to coronavirus. Still some customers are not technology savvy in using online search features.
- There is a striking 450 percent increase in time spent on digital apps. It also meant experience and ease of use becomes critical. In most customer cases, we identified four to six clicks required to complete a transaction. A number of clicks or taps are too many as compared to our competition.
- Customer surveys and feedback found that average visitors spend 15 to 20 minutes more in online search than in-person shopping for similar products (excluding time to commute). This is leading to poor customer experience.

Explore a unique UV light driven sanitized delivery of packages. The purpose will be to deep clean, sanitize with UV which is proven to kill the virus and bacteria.

Zen design principles:
Refreshing, Simplicity, Subtlety

The team decides to define a seamless workflow to search and order online—reduce the time/efforts by 80 percent and clicks by 60 percent for customers with online profiles.

- Create significant opportunities to personalize every touch-point along the user journey based on customer profile and shopping patterns.
- Help customer use images and voice (and not just typing text) to search and purchase products. This makes them efficient, smart, and decisive.
- Provide machine learning-based platform for personalized search utilizing demographics of customers (e.g., factors like age, past order history, gender, and geographic location).
- Make consumption leaner and effortless—reduce the labor to consume the products.

The prototypes are built, and A/B testing will soon start with customers. A/B testing (or split testing) helps to show and test two alternative variants of the apps to different segments of visitors and also helps with the conducting of statistical analysis.

Walk in and out in 2 minutes when you use newly designed Walkers app

As the session comes to an end, we *thank GOD.*

"This is so great." Tim has a wide smile on his face.

"Honestly, I hope we can meet you one day, you're a real asset." Daisy agrees, commending him.

Sprint Retrospective

What is working well?

- Building Blocks approach to organize relevant solutions to the problems on the WALL.
- Recalibration on the purpose of transformation with OKRs (Objective and Key Results).
- Inner Agility is about peaceful mind, calmness, and simplicity for focus and concentration.
- Zen values for Inner Agility: *Here and Now*; *Beginners' minds*; *Experiential learning*; and *Continuous flow*.
- Design *Re*Thinking with seven *Zen design* principles of ARTISTS (Austere, Refreshing, True to life, Imperfection, Simplicity, Tranquility, Subtle).
- A unique way to reimagine digital disruption for everything around us.
- Providing Shibumi moments to customer for *elegant, effortless, and authentic experience.*

What could improve?

- Endless obstacles and controls due to processes mandated by the FA@ST.
- The latest Writing on the WALL: Lack of strategic agility.

Analysis and Improvements

Sprint Goal

- Evaluate the performance and effects of the scaling framework.
- Reinvent the organizational structures for a nimble and leaner enterprise.
- Define the approach for revitalizing culture and rethinking talent strategy.

CHAPTER 9

Fragile FRAMEWORK

Limitations of Emulating Scaling Frameworks

Monday, February 24, 2020

"Ahh, this fatigue, headache, and muscle pain. I cannot breathe well."

Cindy looks completely worn-out walking at the hospital parking. She is under the weather with chemotherapy side effects. I have taken the day off.

I ask Dr. Anu about the possibility to suspend her chemotherapy.

"Normal cells become cancer cell when they continue to grow and divide out of control. It is this unchecked cell growth which keeps spreading when untreated. We need to expedite her chemotherapy before it is too late. We are ensuring that we track down the reasons of any more abnormal side effects." Dr. Anu assures.

"We will need to keep her in the hospital for more tests."

I try to wave our hands from outside the glass door. Cindy has a faint smile on her face and waves back.

I return home in the evening to Ami and Tina after a rather subdued day at the hospital. I finally get the chance to update the Kanban board.

Table 9.1 Kanban board

To-do	In progress	Done
• Identify challenges in FA@ST • Testing the hypothesis: Does scaling framework bring agility? • The TIM WOODS analysis • Explore a simplified alternative for backlog management	Doctor appointment	The latest Building Block: h) Shibumi sprint and seven Zen design principles

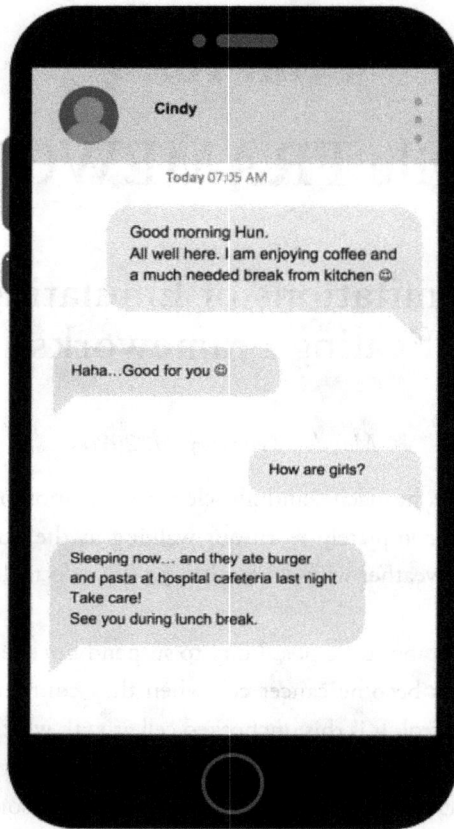

Figure 9.1 Text—Cindy and Neil

Early in the morning, I see a text message from Cindy, letting me know that she is feeling much better after yesterday's scare. All her tests came back normal.

I come out of the shower and quickly make sandwiches while getting Ami and Tina ready for their schools.

Soon after, I hear a ding of missed call and find a voicemail from Seth.

"Hey Neil, Hana is insisting for compliance reviews and risk documentation, which could take about two to three weeks for us to start the project officially, and Tim has asked us to follow FA@ST processes for funding and business case approval processes. We cannot meet Daisy's timelines with all of these."

Did our agile framework make us fragile? I ponder.

I decide to get exception approval to exempt following FA@ST.

I start my day in the office late, at 11:05 a.m. with a list of tasks to action by the end of the day.

As I am walking toward the elevator, I see Paris in the large conference room with employees from store planning. With the subdued look and somber mood of the room, I instinctively realize they are being let go!

In the next room, the repetitious and mandatory three-hour monthly introductory training on the framework is in progress. I see closely that there are 12 folks, most peeping at their laptops or phones. I shake my head, realizing that they are still doing their day job during the trainings.

Too many projects and programs. We have more than needed people in certain roles like project managers, but we have asked them to shift overnight to agile ways of working. Some project managers are partially allocated 8.33 percent to a total of 12 projects. We have a mammoth 400 IT and digital projects in the company.

I always wonder how could a human being work precisely 8.33 percent of his time on a project? How could they turn off at a precise number, even when the work is not done? Are all projects equally important?

I can't help but reminisce on recent conversations with Dr. Anu about the uncontrollable growth causing cancer. I start to think deeply about this, as I realize that there might be another type of uncontrollable processes, tools, and red tape at Walkers.

We have excessive forms, templates, policies, procedures, and too much documentation. And not mention, our many status reports, many siloed departments, too many consultants, excessive processes, practices, multiple types of meetings, systems, and tools—all leading to an ocean of Nonvalue Adding, that we are drowning in.

Is this not creating a kind of unchecked growth?

We have created the huge inventory of methodologies. In the next hour, Sid, Seth, and Saira join me in the WALL area.

"But … why is agile and lean managed by two different groups?" Sid raises a brow.

I openly admit that I am one of the parties in that entire saga, along with another person named Doug Dicky from Lean CoE.

I vent my frustrations for the next few minutes explaining constant bickering between me and Doug. I propose to come back to this problem in the next session, so we don't derail the agenda.

Everyone nods in agreement. It is almost noon, and everyone looks to be hungry.

We make time for a lunch break at a nearby Indian restaurant to continue our conversation. We are at the *Mirchi Chowk* restaurant known to have the buffet style lunch. Our mouthwatering plates served with kebabs, chicken tikka masala, palak paneer, mushroom chana, aloo bhaaji, poppadoms with naan, and lassi arrive at our table.

The only sounds I hear for the next 10 minutes are the sounds of everyone enjoying their meals, *crunch, guzzle, gobble, and gulp.*

Sid breaks the ice and initiates the conversation on our framework.

Identify Challenges in FA@ST

"So, how do you guys feel about FA@ST? The Framework for Agile@ Scale Techniques."

Keisha is the first one to share her thoughts.

"I find this framework to be complex and rather prescriptive." She looks at me and chooses her words carefully, noticing that I was a champion of FA@ST.

"Clearly the framework did create a fair amount of excitement initially but did not deliver the results, we anticipated. There are delays, problems, release-related disruptions, and stability issues in the software." I add to encourage an unbiased conversation.

"But it was positioned to us as the best framework in the industry. Many certifications and trainings were organized locally in our branches, domestically and internationally." Seth adds.

I nod in agreement "Yeah, I know. I still own the annual budget of almost $10 million for its adoption."

"So, improving FA@ST is part of this budget, right?" Sid asks, taking a sip of his mango lassi with a smirk written all over his face.

"Who wants a dessert? Lunch is on Neil, our director!" He jokes as everyone laughs.

I bring them back to the topic "But on a serious note, our company is heavily invested in adopting the framework with almost 600 people getting trained in the last two years with at least 350 plus certified practitioners in the organization. Most of them have started adopting cursorily and some even left the organization, piggybacking on their new credentials."

Tim and Hana need to hear it too. I quickly forward the invite to them, to join us before heading back to office.

"Don't you think most people got trained and certified because they think it will get them a better job?" Keisha implies, reminding there were three resignations recently.

"Yeah, in the course of rising popularity of FA@ST, hundreds have got trained and/or certified in agile from ubiquitous providers. Most of the people have a shallow awareness centered on fancy buzzwords with limited understanding of intent and relevance of lean–agile values and principles. It's a charade of transformation!" I admit with a sense of failure.

As we reach the office, I see both Tim and Hana, looking spellbound and staring at the WALL.

All are looking at me to kick off the meeting with two additional audiences.

"Our hypothesis is that our scaling framework slows us down due to more roles, processes, and formalities than needed, consequently leading to confusion, waste, and reduced innovation. It lowers customer centricity as we are always looking inwards and getting internally focused. The teams need to thoroughly unlearn their older concepts, roles, and then learn newer versions of a framework." I make the opening remark.

Hana speaks up, surprisingly "We have tried somewhat to sloppily align our titles, funding, structure, and tools but there are too many changes, and change was all too fast due to FA@ST."

"The roadmap to make transformation a true success for our customers, our talent, our vendor partners, and our shareholders was actually never there. We suffered a lot in GRC" Hana continues to complain.

"The framework was required by all the teams and it also created a lot of shortcuts and a whole lot of hidden factories of processes, where things were getting done for the sake of it without much value for the teams." Tim acknowledges.

".... And this doesn't sufficiently encourage a philosophy of self-improvement. ... This reminds me of our earlier efforts of ISO and CMMi, where the focus was primarily on getting certification and not always to maximize the value for customers." Sid suggests.

Leads to more questions than solutions

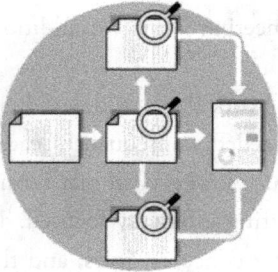

Prescriptive processes

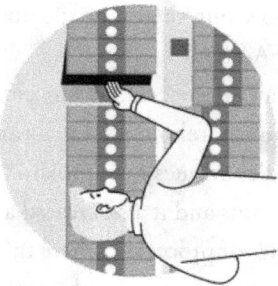

Too much documentation

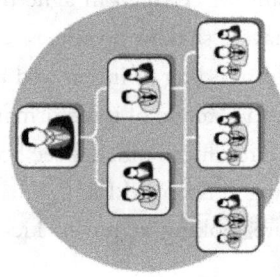

New roles and layers added to hierarchy

Focus shifts on framework adherence

Figure 9.2 Fragile framework

Testing the Hypothesis: Does Scaling Framework Bring Agility?

"Let us talk about how well framework supports agile manifesto." Hana raises a good point.

We all unanimously decide to leverage the agile manifesto and lean thinking to demonstrate a hypothesis of how a scaling framework becomes heavy, prescriptive, ceremonial, and ultimately fragile.

Tim asks, "How many roles have we added?"

"I think seven or eight. But let me call Paris to confirm on this." I insist.

"So actually, the empty and cursory aspects of the framework could make it highly counterproductive to genuine agility and business value." Gus says.

"In hindsight, this provided a false sense of transformation. It is a masquerade, totally perfunctory. Instead of agility, the framework ended up obliterating whatever was agile earlier. It made us fragile." I admit.

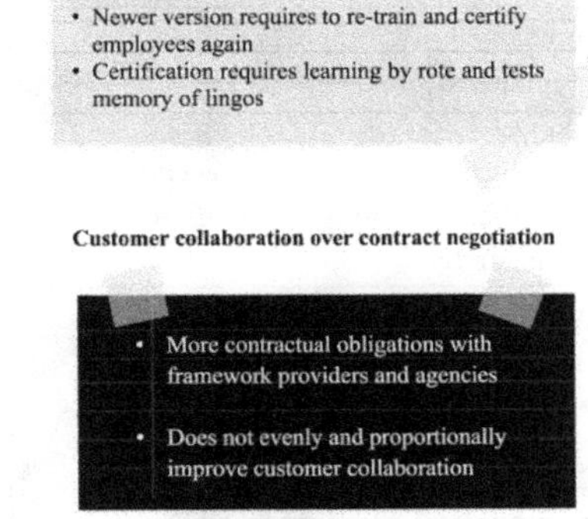

Individuals and interactions over processes and tools

- Focuses on processes (not culture and mindset)
- People get recognized as experts after memorizing terms
- Makes common practices like prioritization too complex
- Team is confounded and confused due to buzzwords
- Newer version requires to re-train and certify employees again
- Certification requires learning by rote and tests memory of lingos

Working software over comprehensive documentation

- The Framework is prescriptive and rigid
- Hundreds of pages of theoretical documentation full of text
- Over 25 new documents and playbook for new concepts

Customer collaboration over contract negotiation

- More contractual obligations with framework providers and agencies
- Does not evenly and proportionally improve customer collaboration

Responding to change over following a plan

- It's a "set" and rigid methodology so requires effort to customize
- Has a "one size" fits all roadmap for implementation
- Diminishes agility because of the prescriptive nature

Figure 9.3 Manifesto view 1 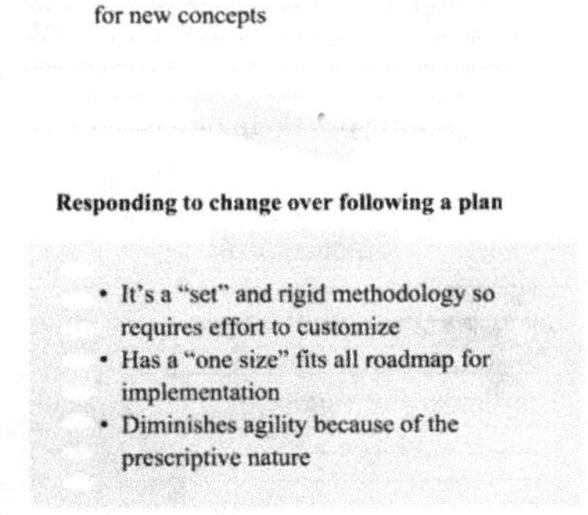   *Figure 9.4 Manifesto view 2*

Table 9.2 Contradictory effects of scaling framework

Agile Manifesto value	The contradictory effects of the scaling framework
Working solutions over comprehensive documentation	• The framework has multiple versions, whatever has been learned needs to be quickly unlearned, and there is a need to learn newer versions in a matter of a few months. A new version every year requires constant retraining and recertification of the people • Frameworks get over engineered because they need to be commercially viable and sell faster. More documentations get created adding to an ocean of content
Customer collaboration over contract negotiation	• The framework led to contractual obligations with three types of companies: framework consultants and coaches; training providers; recruitment agency for staffing new roles • Created a whole new set of training providers, event organizers, and freelance consultants and coaches but reduced customer collaboration
Responding to change over following a plan	• Many aspects of frameworks are "one size fits" all with little or no flexibility to adjust • More money spent on consultants for creating additional models, presentations, and methods and ultimately leading to additional complexities
Individuals and interactions over processes and tools	• A two-year plan was defined by our service provider to adopt the framework covered on practices and processes. The culture and mindset shift were not given enough attention • The framework has added more processes and procedures that have recreated top-down bureaucracy and hierarchy in different names, shapes, and forms

Table 9.3 The TIM WOODS analysis of scaling framework

Transporting something farther than necessary: • Reorganizing people in different levels: portfolio, program, and team	*Inventory* due to supply in excess of immediate and reasonable demand: • Production of new training content • Creates additional practices, roles, and hierarchy
Moving people more than required: • Moving people for large planning gatherings and multiple ceremonies	*Waiting* for the completion of a step to start the next step: • During the set up of new tools, teams, practices, and structures • During the mobilization of new roles
Over processing to an extent that customer may not find valuable: • Lots of theoretical concepts • More buzzwords and jargons • Expensive in terms of time spent	*Over documentation with* more than required content: • Lengthy descriptive playbooks • Large events creating additional documentation

Defects that require rework or redoing: • Half-baked interpretations	Skills (and Intellect) due to underutilization of the talent of people: • Effort for mastering the lingo • Focuses on memory of models and not understanding of concepts

Table 9.4 The Writing on the WALL No. 11

11. Fragile scaling frameworks	
What does it mean?	• A formula centric, purist, and prescriptive execution of agile by blindly following a scaling framework and *going by the book* becomes counterproductive • Cosmetic standardization and consistency efforts without rationale
What are its effects?	• Diminishing return on investment in longer term • More complexity in processes, procedures, and practices • Less focus on the softer aspects of change in culture and mindset

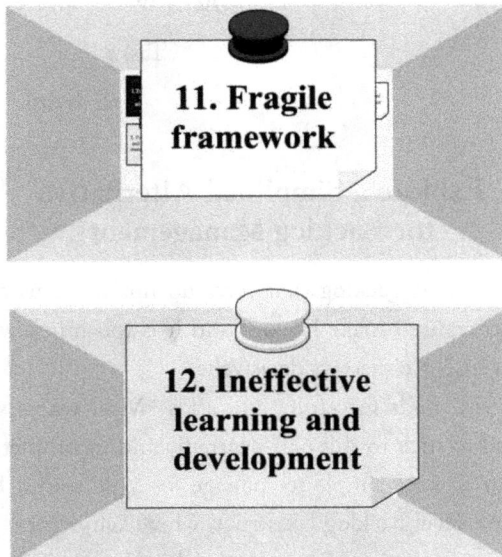

Figure 9.5 WALL No. 11 and 12

We finally see that the framework gave us a highly complex tree structure for our backlog.

We see nine levels of backlog decomposition.

Table 9.5 The Writing on the WALL No. 12

12. Ineffective learning and development	
What does it mean?	• The training emphasizes theoretical and academic aspects which people fail to apply in their work • The unintentional consequence of stressing the certification of frameworks leads to learning by rote
What are its effects?	• Waste of time and effort of all • Does not translate to the intended business results

    Program

        Project

            Functions

                Epic

                    Feature

                        Story

                            Activity

                                Tasks

                                  Sub task

Explore a Simplified Alternative for Backlog Management

"I believe our current backlog structures do not make us agile; on the contrary, we struggle to make it work and it is too much work to align creating overheads." Keisha says decisively.

"I agree." Seth nods forcefully and adds "Most teams were told to follow and tried to stick to this half-heartedly and incompletely."

"It needs to be kept simple to manage for agile teams. In most scenarios, it's a four-level backlog construct, where Objectives, key Results, Epic, and Story are sufficient. The tasks need to be used if the team wants to add more details." Sid adds.

ORES: Objectives, key Results, Epic and Story.

"Just like ores are natural rocks containing valuable minerals, this construct of ORES encapsulates valuable requirements. We need to remove the layers of backlog, to reduce the overhead and complexity. The ORES helps to keep it simple, easy to remember, and intuitive.

Does it make sense?" He looks at all of us.

Most of us are still thinking this through and I insist that we align on the specifics of its implementation.

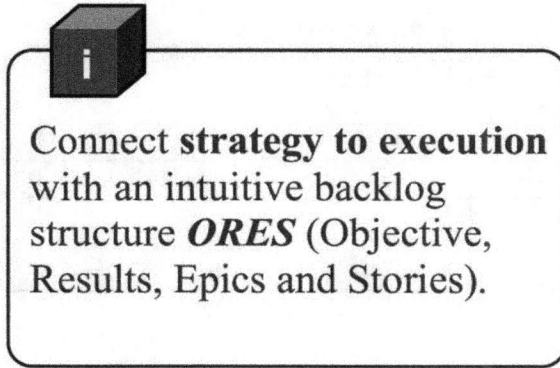

Connect **strategy to execution** with an intuitive backlog structure *ORES* (Objective, Results, Epics and Stories).

Figure 9.6 BB i

(i) ORES: Objectives, (key) Results, Epic, and Story

OKR—Finalize epics or OKRs (Objective and Key Results) based on relevance to customer experience and financial performance:

- *Objective* for one to four quarters.
  - ○ (Key) *Result* is reset for each quarter.
    - *Epic* is at least one quarter.
      - *Story* is for the one sprint.
      - Task is a day or less.

Commonly observed numbers in the ORES construct: For each Objective, there are 3 to 5 key results to measure and 1 to 3 underlying Epics to implement; for each Epic, there could be 10 to 30 stories, and if needed, 3 to 10 tasks for each story which could be created at individual levels.

Do not estimate every *minor* effort—anything which is 30 minutes could be task, but don't create more than three to four tasks in a day; otherwise, it could be overkill and lead to overheads.

Keisha has another tricky question: "How do we know which objective is more important than others and which epic has a higher priority?"

I suggest we use a simple matrix I had learned during six sigma training.

A customizable matrix based on quality function deployment technique of neutral rating and establishing a score-based correlation of objectives with epics. Example:

Table 9.6 Epic to objectives correlation

No.	Objectives	Weightage	Epic 1	Epic 2	Epic 3
1	Objective 1	6	3	9	3
2	Objective 2	3	6	9	3
3	Objective 3	9	9	9	6
4	Total score		117 $(3 \times 6 + 6 \times 3 + 9 \times 9)$	162 $(9 \times 6 + 9 \times 3 + 9 \times 9)$	81 $(3 \times 6 + 3 \times 3 + 6 \times 9)$

- For the "Objective," the weightage is 3, 6, and 9.
- 9 is most critical objective.
- 6 is highly important but not critical.
- 3 is moderately important and not critical.

"Epic" needs to have a correlation or enabling effect to an "Objective."

- The weightage is 1, 3, 6, and 9.
- 9 means the highest correlation.
- 1 means the lowest correlation.

In the example:

⇒ Epic 2 with the highest score of 162 becomes top priority.
⇒ Epic 3 with the lowest score of 81 is the lowest priority.

Key subject matter experts join the C-suite leadership to conduct a team-based voting to decide weightage of the Objective and correlations. Democracy wins, and not the one who is the highest paid individual.

After a quick coffee break as I walk back to the room, I see Paris entering with her laptop. She projects her laptop screen on the large screen.

"I am pleasantly surprised by how quickly our projector got connected this time," Paris smiles.

"We can clearly see that there are more roles than we thought. There is a total of 10 roles as per HR records are directly attributed to this framework for our managers and team leads, and some did exist earlier." I say it loud for all to hear clearly.

Wow that's exactly what I was thinking about.

1. Business owner
2. Epic manager
3. Value stream manager
4. Project manager
5. Program manager
6. Portfolio manager
7. Product manager
8. Agile development manager
9. Business product owner
10. Technical product owner

We see six levels of hierarchy.

- Leadership team
- Segment
- Portfolio
- Program
- Agile team of teams
- Agile team

Tring tring. We hear the classic telephone ringtone. Tim walks out for a few minutes to take a call. I use the chance to sensitize everyone on ground reality.

"Last year, Tim had used his closeness to Richie and pushed HR to ensure each program and project manager has a dotted line reporting to PMO. A common KPI was now added by HR in their performance evaluation 'Adherence to company's project management processes defined by PMO'."

Each of the agile teams is considered a project team as well. Each member of agile team is mapped to a project in the official HR roster. And each project is expected to also follow the PMO processes, many of them overengineered by Tim and his team of PMs. Folks spend 20 to 30 percent of their time for this kind of stupid process adherence work. There is this constant friction between the PMO, agile teams, and the projects.

"The projects which are agile are funded based on what they deliver, while projects are funded for their entire schedule irrespective of its timeline. If you have a project, you need to have it on the PMO sheet; otherwise, it will not be funded. The PMO has already alienated and disengaged most of the project managers and scrum masters, playing with almost interchangeable rules to satisfy the PMO needs." Seth is distraught.

We have bias and inequalities in our funding model. This conversation is another cue for us that we need to resolve funding complications with PMO.

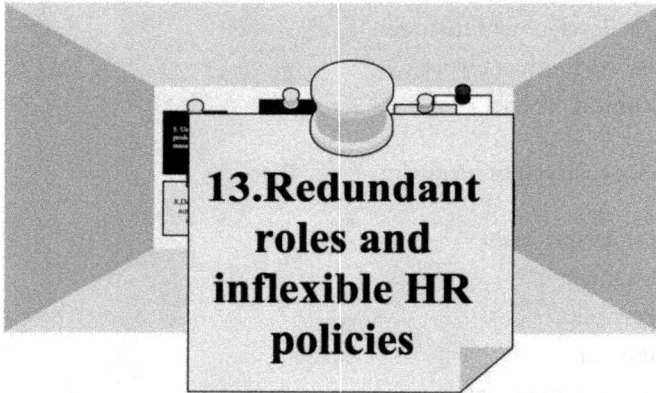

Figure 9.7 WALL No. 13

Table 9.7 The Writing on the WALL No. 13

13. Redundant roles and inflexible HR policies	
What does it mean?	• The numerous departments, manifold team structures, geographies, methodologies, and frameworks have created an inventory of roles, titles, and designations which create confusing identities and redundancies in roles and responsibilities • Certain roles by design are about (micro) managing people and lead to unhealthy dynamic when people have more specialized knowledge, skills, and competencies than their managers
What are its effects?	• Hidden factory of overheads, complexities, and overlaps • Lack of accountability and ownership (*when everyone is responsible then no one really is!*)

Table 9.8 Kanban board

To-do	In progress	Done	
		• Contradictory effects of the scaling frameworks to enterprise agility • Complex frameworks translate to diminishing return on investments in medium to longer term	
		The latest Writings on the WALL: 11. Fragile scaling frameworks 12. Ineffective learning and development 13. Redundant roles and inflexi-ble HR policies	The latest Building Block: i) ORES (Objective, Results, Epics, Stories)

CHAPTER 10

Structural Side Effects

Bureaucracy of a Hierarchical ORGANIZATION

Thursday, February 27, 2020

Table 10.1 Kanban board

To-do	In progress	Done
• Shortcomings in a hierarchical organization • Analyze long Time-to-Market	• Identify common grounds between agile and Doug's Lean CoE • Resolve funding-related complications	

I am on the dental chair for next 55 minutes with manifold dental tools and fluids inside my mouth ... the mirror, sickle probe, suction, syringe, anesthetic, drill, spoon excavator, mold, scaler, and finally polisher cup!

During all this time, the dentist keeps talking to me.

Weird. Does she not realize that I cannot talk with so much metal inside my mouth? It is painful both physically and mentally.

Those 55 minutes are the moments of epiphany. I continue to debate myself. Is this something similar which keeps our employees silent?

How could our people speak their minds when they are stuffed with unyielding HR policies, rigid performance appraisals, conditional bonuses, unbending promotion rules, and risk of getting fired? Their paychecks are directly proportional to overlooking certain things. Our talent cannot freely express themselves and confront their bosses without risking it all.

How can we expect our people to have an obligation to WAR when their survival in the company depends on them not raising problems? They don't have an adequate psychological support system to freely raise their concerns and solve the problems.

Back to the office on Monday morning.

I see a Kanban board to update on my follow-up on Lean CoE. "You see there has always been a Lean CoE in Walkers even before we embarked on agile transformation. The Lean CoE is headed by Doug Dicky. I am meeting Doug today." I mention.

Identify Common Grounds Between Agile and Lean CoE

I discuss the dynamics with Sid "Doug had a dotted reporting relationship to Daisy and a direct reporting to her boss, the chief operating officer of the company. You see the reporting relationship defines what you can and cannot do in this company. It is the political minefield you see!"

I tried to raise it to Richie a few times, but he couldn't do anything as it's outside his territory. I continue. "Doug's team implements lean-driven business process improvements in the supply chain, fulfillment, logistics, and store operations. People in business and operations think lean is theirs and people in digital think agile is ours." I say with a feeling of helplessness.

"I know Doug thinks of me as someone who is coming from the agile camp and competing to land grab his Lean CoE. He thinks I'm his rival. Despite having tried to reach out to him to collaborate on a few projects on a number of occasions, *I've lost count.*"

Sid jumps in, "Unfortunately, this is common for most companies. One of the side effects of traditional organizational structures is spawning distinct cultures, mindsets, and opposing interests. Like children we want to play with our own toys and sometimes we are not so good in sharing each other's toys."

"Why don't you have a heart-to-heart with Daisy to get her support? Tell her how critical it is for timely digital releases to have joint firepower of lean and agile." He sips his smoothie rather brashly.

I write to Doug and copy in Daisy and Richie clearly to up the ante.

Daisy responds with a one liner, affirming my approach.

"Neil, Great effort. Thanks."

Doug and I plan a working session to resolve the long running stalemate.

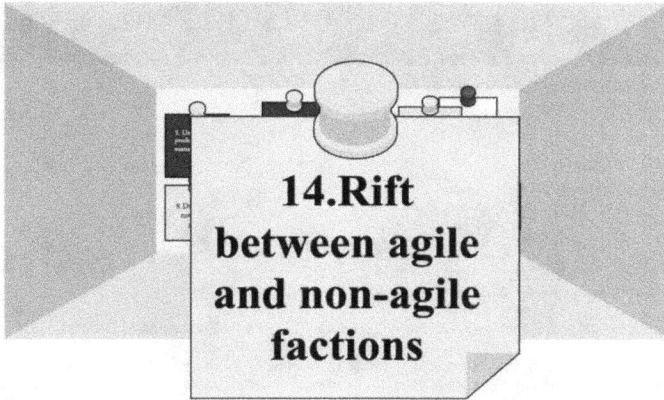

14.Rift between agile and non-agile factions

Figure 10.1 WALL No. 14

Table 10.2 The Writing on the WALL No. 14

14. Rift between agile and nonagile factions	
What does it mean?	• The chasm between two conflicting ways of working (agile and traditional project management) causes discords and rivalry • The role of agile practitioners' conflicts and clashes with traditional roles like project and program managers
What are its effects?	• Creates friction, frustration, and confusion in the workforce • Unproductive conversations and adverse impact on customer centricity

He accepts my invite, and we meet later in the day on his side of building.

Doug starts with a combative tone "Daisy wants me to almost shut down lean CoE. I have half a dozen lean consultants and coaches. We all cannot just become part of agile CoE. And so, whose fault is this?"

"But guys let's be clear what we are trying to do here? And what do you want from me?" Doug removes his spectacles.

"We have a toxic culture of old and new fighting with each other. Our groups constantly lock horns." I sound like a broken record.

Sid quickly interrupts. "Guys, could we first clarify a few things on lean and agile methods?"

We both nod vigorously.

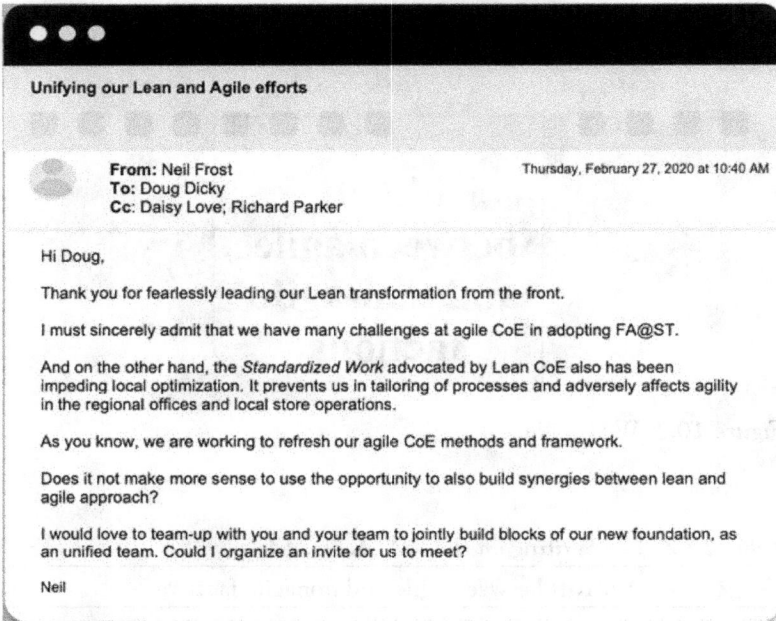

Unifying our Lean and Agile efforts

From: Neil Frost
To: Doug Dicky
Cc: Daisy Love; Richard Parker

Thursday, February 27, 2020 at 10:40 AM

Hi Doug,

Thank you for fearlessly leading our Lean transformation from the front.

I must sincerely admit that we have many challenges at agile CoE in adopting FA@ST.

And on the other hand, the *Standardized Work* advocated by Lean CoE also has been impeding local optimization. It prevents us in tailoring of processes and adversely affects agility in the regional offices and local store operations.

As you know, we are working to refresh our agile CoE methods and framework.

Does it not make more sense to use the opportunity to also build synergies between lean and agile approach?

I would love to team-up with you and your team to jointly build blocks of our new foundation, as an unified team. Could I organize an invite for us to meet?

Neil

Figure 10.2 E-mail—unified lean–agile

"What we know as agile today is built in the last two decades, and I believe agile has some clear roots that we can relate to lean thinking. Agile started in IT/software and is now being imagined enterprise-wide, while lean principles can be applied virtually anywhere, though they could trace their roots in automobile manufacturing context like Toyota production system (TPS).

So, in a way, we could think of lean thinking as a genesis of agile!" Sid suggests.

Doug looks happier and suddenly his eyes brighten up. "I love it. You mean it? Right?"

"I believe they are extremely complimentary and symbiotic, and a meaningful combination is the best way forward!" Sid adds.

"Lately, most of the leading industry frameworks emphasize both lean and agile as two important foundational pillars of agility across the enterprise. Agile is an umbrella term which may refer to scrum, Kanban, XP, and lean software development." I suddenly realize I am back to defending my own terror-tory.

"We do not have to restrict ourselves to one method or standard, but we can borrow other frameworks and methodologies with an eye on business outcomes and customer experience. Zen design for exceptional

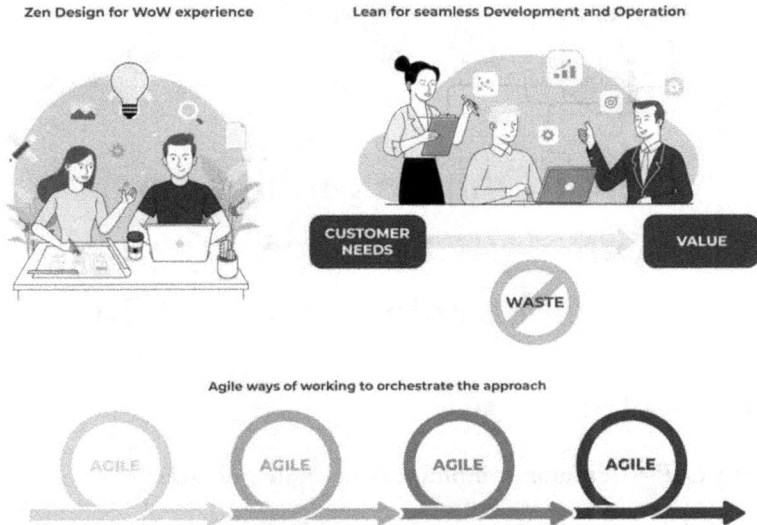

Figure 10.3 Lean, agile, and Zen

experiences lean to cut wastes and agile sprints to orchestrate and integrate methods." Sid proposes.

"So, what's our goal here?" Doug asks.

"It has to be to advance the overall, holistic, and end-to-end agility." I am careful to say agility and not agile.

"The focus needs to be on *No Regret moves*, anyone could do them. These are universally accepted best practices from lean and agile and you can't get it wrong."

Finally, Doug looks to be on board.

"The most basic thing that you could do to applaud and appreciate your teams?" Sid asks, bringing his two hands together.

"You clap?" Doug responds.

"Precisely, that is what we could plan to do to appreciate, endorse, cheer, and energize our teams with this minimum common guidance."

The CLAP is a modest yet a powerful symbol for everyone about the feeling comfortable, excited, and being welcomed—the psychological safety for teams to adopt common-sensical practices. Finally, we all agree on something.

Adopt **Common**-minimum *Lean–Agile Practices (CLAP)* across the entire organization.

Figure 10.4 **BB j**

(j) *CLAP—Common-minimum Lean–Agile Practices*

Adopt elementary lean–agile values, principles, mindset, and common-sensical practices for all teams including those not deliberately practicing agile. Establish mechanisms and forums for regular engagement and collaboration between agile and "nonagile" groups.

Clarity of purpose:
- Any one live lightweight document which is adaptable like OKRs (Objective and Key Results), a product roadmap and mission statement, and a roadmap.
- OKRs include an objective which is a clearly defined goal and set of three to five key results which are measurable.

Timebox with cadence:
- Sprint and release—both are not same.
- Sprint is a timebox of two weeks to complete a sprint backlog. (Sprint backlog is the collection of stories/tasks for a sprint.)

- Release refers to epic or a group of features from product backlog made available for customer. (Product backlog comprises of the epics and stories for a cluster of sprints.)
- Invite nonagile or traditional teams in all key lean and agile events.

Communication flow:

- Fifteen to twenty minutes stand-ups or huddles to collaborate, sync-up, identify blockers/impediments, re-energize, and plan subsequent conversations (This is not a status reporting.).
  - *Accomplishments/outcomes further to the last stand-up*
  - *Blockers, if any, impeding the progress*
  - *Customer-centric story, tasks, or conversations planned*

Visual management with Kanban:

- Three columns of "To-do," "In progress," and "Done" to visualize work.
- Set a work-in-progress (WIP) limit so that there is a maximum of three items "In progress" column per person.

Prioritization: (a) A simple MoSCoW classification

- *Must have: Must have* are critical requirements to the current release and sprints.
- *Should have: Should have* are quite important but not essential for delivery timebox.
- *Could have: Could have* are desirable and "good to have" but not necessary.
- *Won't have (immediately): Won't have* are least critical and are not for immediate considerations but could be reconsidered and refined at a later point in time.

Retrospective: Looking back at events so we identify what went well, what didn't go so well, and what actions we could take to actionize our learnings.

Continuous improvement:

- Relentless obligation toward Waste Avoidance and Removal (WAR).
- Kaizen and A3 Thinking for focused and structured improvements.

- *A3* is the crisp and concise visual manifestation all in one view of A3 or similar size paper.
- *Kaizen* is about small improvements at regular periods which lead to sustainable improvements and outcomes eventually.

Shortcomings in a Hierarchical Organization

We decide to map the organization and see how we could navigate the organization.

During value stream mapping, we had a chance to observe how each of our product departments are run by a VP with a dotted or sometimes solid lines reporting relationship to Daisy.

The organization structure complexities are compounded due to several other permutations and combinations in our reporting structures. Three VPs have direct reporting to Daisy, while two of them also had dotted reporting to Richie for some reason. All of them had direct reporting or in some cases reporting dotted to Charlie our CEO. Two of them have reporting to our head of Fulfillment and one to our head of Merchandising. It was a maze, a perfect tangle, and a constraint!

We are left in this labyrinth to navigate the intricacies of Walkers' cryptic organizational structure. No one moves across teams even when it made a lot of sense without a "go ahead" from their three to four bosses who are too busy fighting their own battles!

Each VP had nine more levels of employees within each of the product category departments (PCDs) like grocery, household, home, furniture and décor, fashion apparels, shoes, and so on.

There are four layers of product management that must approve, before I can approve for release. In cases where the GRC team has raised risk and compliance issues, it requires further approval from the CIO, Richie himself.

Sid shares a few perspectives on redesigning our company.

"Our structure is vertical with reporting managers defining the work. Lean–agile as a philosophy is ideally to imbibe a coach's mindset and not a traditional manager, so *reporting line should not be a primary concern and never the starting point.* The focus should be more on agile broadly

STRUCTURAL SIDE EFFECTS   183

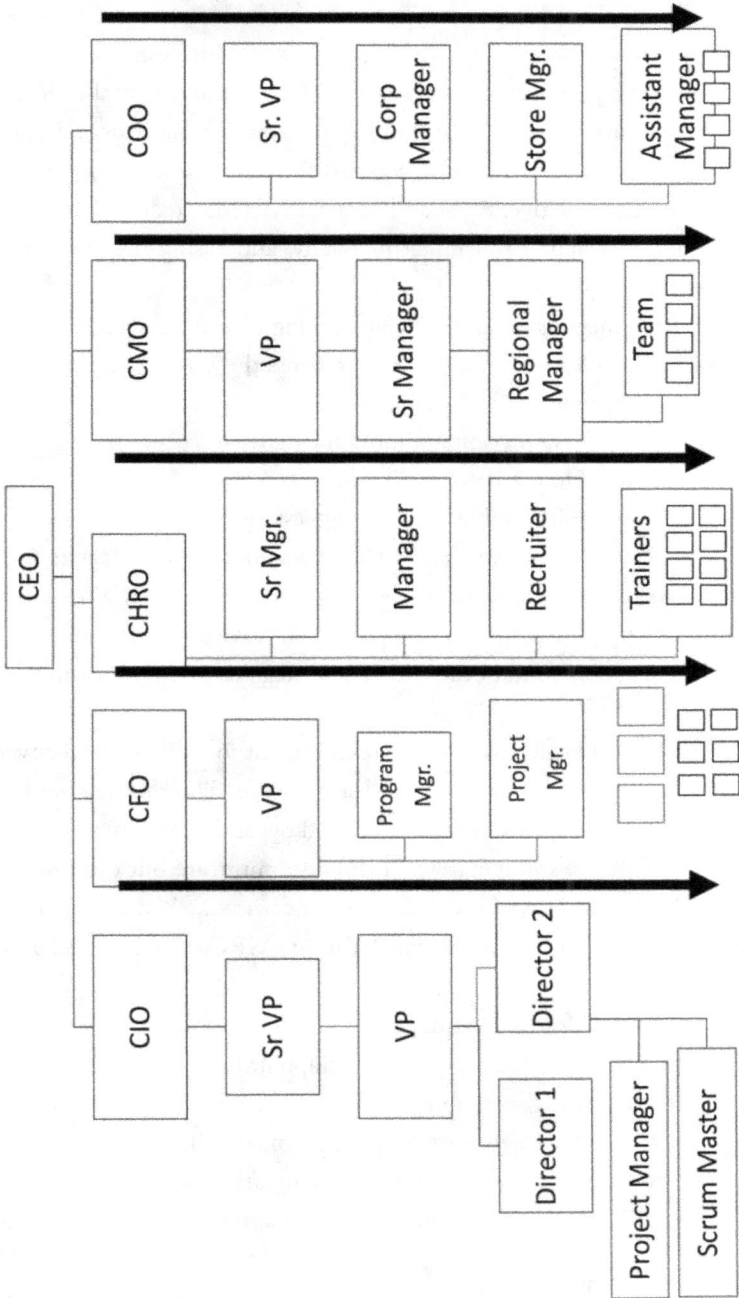

Figure 10.5 Vertical organization

to reduce too much hierarchy, loosening formal reporting structures and easing the command–control style of working."

"Too much emphasis on reporting could also mean teams may have to dilute their independent thought, creativity, and fearlessness to challenge their reporting managers to change status quo. However, most organizations still need to have a line of reporting, and there may be nothing wrong as long as it's constructive. Agile and lean are all about reducing solid line reporting, eliminating too much hierarchy, and easing the command–control style of working."

After my meeting, I can hear Hana calling me from the far end of the corridor as I walk to the colored printer across the WALL area.

Hana Saito, the head of governance, risk, and compliance, is highly risk averse and resists anything nimble and agile!

"Hey Hana. How is it going?" I ask.

"Am I the one in trouble again?" I say jestingly.

This is a joke that we share whenever someone from Hana's GRC team makes a guest appearance. They always ask us to delay a release, fill some form, or ask us to submit long compliance documentations.

Hana is not so fond of the joke. She disregards it with sarcasm and a forced smile.

"Hey Neil, I heard that you are reaching out to all those smaller vendors who are not in our approved list. I do not like the way we have started contacting the external vendors and bypassing my team."

I confront her immediately. "I did communicate but did not sign any SoW. But anyways how does this concern you? You don't control the vendor conversations, do you? You are GRC, Governance, Risk, and Compliance."

She nods and folds her arms.

"Indeed, we are GRC for vendor standpoint too as there is no OSAP at all. We used to advise them on all vendor risks as well. And when you keep us out of the loop, you are triggering a major risk. It's a reputational risk and we have internal control, forms, templates, checklists, and policy documentation you need to comply with, get approval before we approve such vendor meetings."

"You should know that by now." She says with a hint of disappointment.

Are you kidding me? We don't even know if Walkers will still exist in the next few months and this person is reminding me of some archaic rules, checklists, and forms? *God save us!*

I feel the need to scream but I restrain myself.

As she continues with some other internal controls that I have never heard about, I wonder if she is part to blame for some of our rapidly growing issues and delays. She is really getting on my nerves!

"Let's address this situation without getting upset." I calm her down and continue,

"Hana, listen I don't need to lecture you, but we need timely and transparent exchange of information with vendors. We need regular dialog with vendor folks at the frontlines. For us to be truly agile, all communications internal and external need to be unambiguous and timely to encourage participation and timeboxed actions. I need your help on this."

She does not like my discourse, but does not to argue further.

I suggest meeting her later. She agrees with some reluctance.

To prepare for our meeting I explain to Sid the structural problems at Walkers.

Analyze Long Time-to-Market

"The manifold and even redundant departments, PMOs, CoE end up becoming silos, so the value stream construct helps to align the horizontal to the vertical by placing stress on the horizontal flow of value to consumers and reducing the red tape and bureaucracy which cause delays and inefficiencies."

The organizations are organized vertically, while the value flows horizontally.

"Traditionally, top management has always preferred for Walkers to have a structure which has multiple layers of managers and supervisors to manage and most of the time micromanage our teams. Decision making is rarely delegated. There are many vertical mini-hierarchies within the large hierarchy." I complain.

"As we see they don't fit in with each other. We have all these different functions for each department organized vertically with their respective

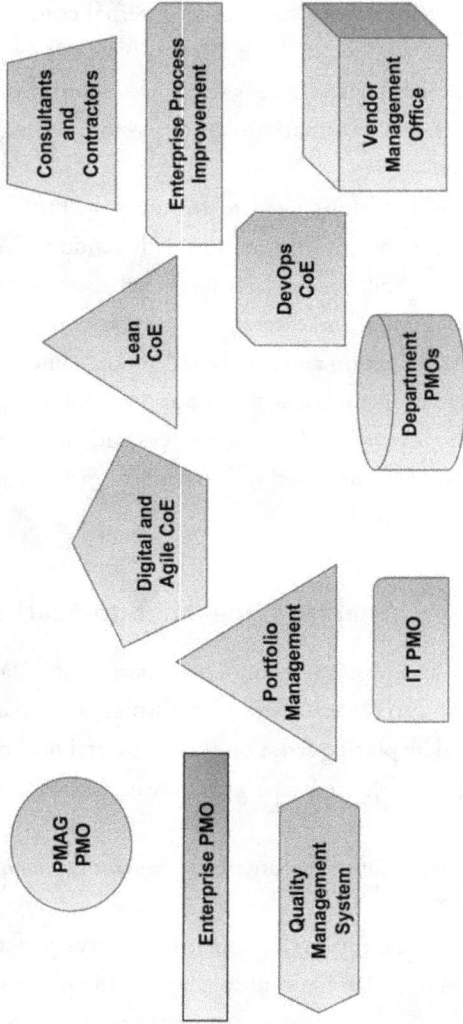

Figure 10.6 Redundant and fragmented groups

measures while the value is flowing horizontally to the customer. Therefore, the organization always believes in multiyear product roadmaps and budgets." Sid extends his understanding.

"The departments slow down and throttle the pace of decision making and implementation of actions due to the vertical focus of each department official reporting to the head of the department, and not across the horizontal value chain where the customer is consuming the value." He explains.

The departments are organized vertically while the flow of value is horizontal which creates communication gaps and friction as teams report to the head of functional department, and not to the customer—who are at the end of the value chain. The different units and teams have a manager or supervisor and the team rolls up to this individual, while the customer is at the end of the value stream. They do not care about the internal organizational setup of the companies. The organization always believes in multiyear product roadmaps and budgets.

Teams are organized by their specialties which in turn creates silos. Organizations become a collection of vertically organized silos each led by different managers. Managers start to fight turf wars and largely focus on their internal territorial battles more than worrying about customer experience and actual customer problems. Although the intentions initially come from a good place, most of their efforts are quickly undone.

I am taking down notes, as Sid sheds some light on our very present issues.

"Let's look at our organization right from the time a customer need arises. So, it's then analyzed, and documentation is provided to the

Table 10.3 The Writing on the WALL No. 15

15. Communication gaps due to silos and layers	
What does it mean?	• The territorial silos and structural complexities in companies create newer barriers and challenges in regular and seamless internal communications • Office politics, lack of psychological safety, and vested interests weaken one of the foundations of agility—transparent and timely communication
What are its effects?	• Hidden factories erode trust and prolong the schedules • Unpleasant surprises lead to unstable products and solutions

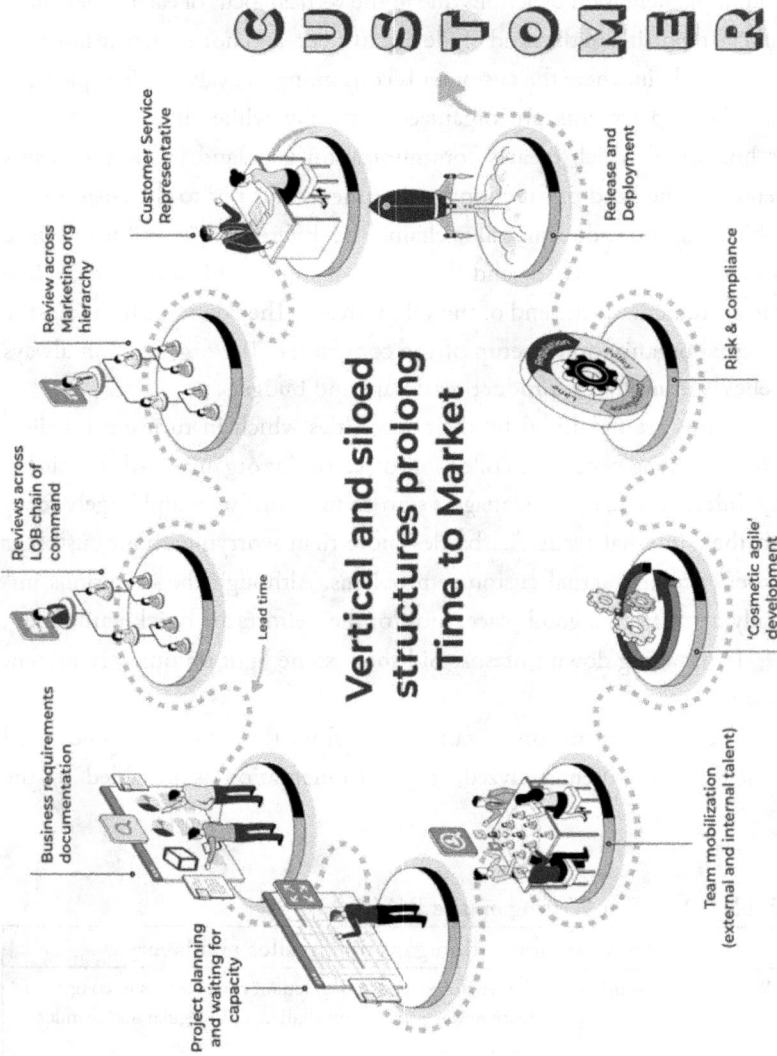

Figure 10.7 Longer Time-to-Market

product team, and then the solution is bland belt testing released back to the customer needs. How many departments or groups do you think are involved here?"

"I see each group creates an additional loop of reviews and decision making which prolongs the entire process. This is unacceptable.

The conception of horizontal organization is far better for a continual enterprise which persistently provides business value to the customer." I concur.

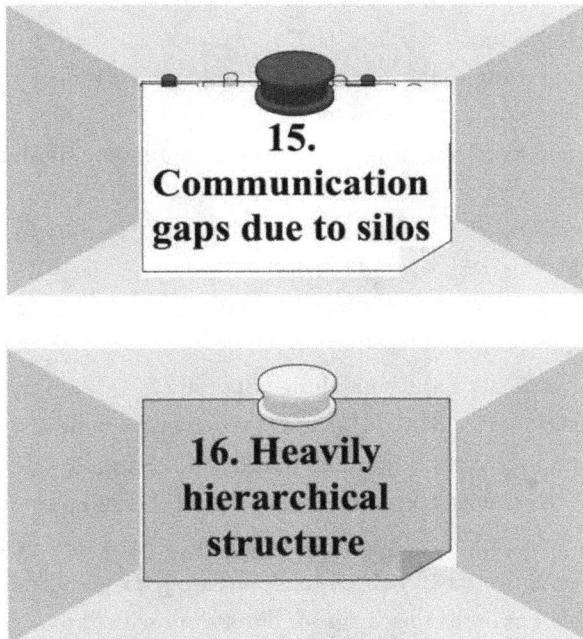

Figure 10.8 WALL No. 15 and 16

Table 10.4 The Writing on the WALL No. 16

16. Heavily hierarchical structure	
What does it mean?	• Disproportionate centralization and multiple layers of bureaucracy slow down communication, lower collaboration, and waste valuable resources • Decisions making becomes very slow due to review and approval required across the manifold echelons of the company
What are its effects?	• Hidden factories diminish trust and increase Time-to-Market • Bureaucracy, red tape, and inefficiencies lower engagement and productivity

Resolve Funding-Related Complications

I slowly approach Tim's office. I have not been in there for a while, as Tim's office always overwhelms me.

He has an old-fashioned office, with wooden and antique pieces. The only modern items, as far as I am aware, are monitors, the printer, and the two projectors. His office is always full of paperwork, whether it is at his desk, by the trash can, or scattered across the table. I don't remember the last time I was in there when there were no files, folders, or pieces of office stationery piling up on his desk. The clutter is a precise reflection of the underlying issues.

"Good morning Neil." Tim sees me walking to his office.

"Hey Tim, how are you this morning?" I smile, lightening the mood.

"Well, you know the drill, Richie wants the funding, project budget reports, and our guys don't do their work properly so as usual I am drafting nasty e-mails!" He sounds condescending, *this is typical of Tim.*

"So, what's up, you wanted to talk?"

Tim continues to look at his laptop, talking to me as if he has more important things to do.

"I wanted to talk about something important."

He is busy in his e-mail. He doesn't look at my eyes, he just nods.

After almost a minute, I give up waiting and continue.

"It's no secret what kind of mess we are in! We all know Walkers is going through a real rough patch, and with this virus, I've been tasked to expedite digital projects. I've been told everything is on the table. One of the ideas that I'm in the final stages of discussions with Paris is new funding model, and it also impacts compensation.

So, we need to align the cadence of people compensations with the business value."

As soon as Tim hears funding, compensation, and costs, he stops typing, thinks for a few seconds, and looks straight at me.

"Neil." He almost raises his voice.

"What does that even mean? Take a pay cut or you don't get paid if you are on a long-term project?" He inquires.

"Everyone who is a part of the teams delivering continuous value continues to get pay checks every other week as per our C&B, the compensation and benefits policy. For those in teams which are not able to show business value their teams are producing, they could see a shift toward a quarterly frequency of pay checks." I try to make something up.

"All those colleagues in product development who are part of teams in IT and digital would be measured based on the frequency of releasing business value to one of the four deployment environments. This needs to be for the customer, and if its an internal project, it needs to be aligned to one of the Walker OKRs." I share an example.

"So, you could be working on anything ranging from an app for a customer, enhanced experience design, a new product enhancement, an upgrade in architecture, customer services, or also something which is internal but has a strategic component associated to our OKRs, you know!" I ramble somewhat.

"So, if a project is supposed to last five months and deliverables are due only at the end of the project, then perhaps release may happen even later, and the folks don't get paid?" He asks in pure disbelief.

"They get paid for sure, but later at the end of quarterly milestone when we can see the value that they have produced." I try to sound believable.

He stresses on "deliverables" and I continue to emphasize the "value".

"Is it even legally allowed? Did you check with Hana? I don't think it will work." He refuses.

I try to make up something in my head fast. I am pulling a bluff, but it is my only way of winning Tim over to my side. I chose my words carefully without mentioning any other name.

"I have deliberations in progress so we could make this decision quickly." I continue to bluff.

"So, if I have a set of projects which are not releasing value for the customer or any internal user I don't get paid?" I nod with a serious look on my face.

"We don't need to deliver value and make releases every other week. I think that we should still get paid, we want to get paid!"

"Hey, Tim." I try to explain him.

"Is this even fair to those who are working in an agile way with faster cycles and those who don't have the luxury of spending time on internal stuff to make long reports?"

He sighs.

"They need to act fast for the needs of our customers. Don't they have to?"

"When we expect to be paid every other week, why can't we build something of real value with the same cadence?" I ask him.

I take his silence as an "I gotcha" moment.

Tim realizes there is no point continuing the argument. "Some of our projects are already in agile mode. For those which are not, I will focus more on faster delivery and at least one of the business values you mentioned?"

As I leave, I make it a point to look him in the eye. He has wasted last year creating all the resistance.

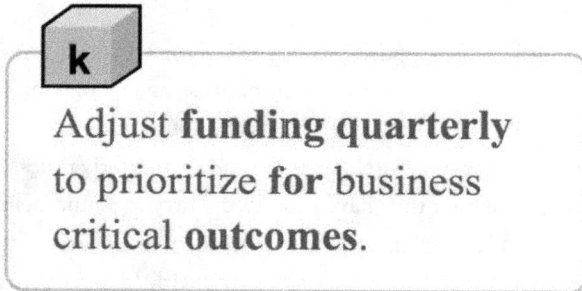

k

Adjust **funding quarterly** to prioritize **for** business critical **outcomes**.

Figure 10.9 BB k

(k) **Funding for quarterly outcomes**

Table 10.5 Outcome-based funding

Guidance for outcome-based funding
• **Tailored and crisp business cases (and not heavily documented):** Focused business cases tailored for the nature of the products and team instead of focusing on very long documents or templates
• **Committee-based funding:** Funding is most effective when decided by a committee and not controlled by a single person or by HiPPO based on hierarchy in the organizations
• **Funding of value (and not projects):** Projects start and end, but agile funding needs to support value delivery continuously. Focus on business value by funding outcomes using OKRs
• **Shorter time horizon (and not too long):** Funding needs to be for shorter increments in quarterly timeframes (and not annual). Shift from annual budgeting to quarterly course corrections and reprioritizations

- **Continuously adjustable funding (and not fixed):** There must be a mechanism to adjust funding (every one or two quarters) based on value delivered and for course correction to respond to changing market conditions. A reprioritization of funding is helpful though overall total funding within product organization may not change
- **Funding for enabling teams too (not just Dev teams):** Funding needs of other related teams like production support; DevSecOps tools or enabling functions should also be considered continuously (and not just core Software dev/Solution delivery/ product teams). Example: Dev team may need agile tool/licenses and CI/CD automation which may likely be owned by another centralized group
- **Funding for test and learn:** Funding needs to be planned to encourage entrepreneurial efforts with Design Thinking, test and learn initiatives, and creative problem solving, and Kaizen continuous improvements should not be underestimated

Later in the day Sid and I go to the corner meeting room. Hana is sitting silently making notes on her writing pad. She has a bunch of papers, neatly arranged in their red, yellow, and blue colored folders.

As I knock, Hana pauses for a few seconds to look at us and goes back to her paperwork.

Hana was in meetings for the entire day given her involvement and in a wide variety of legal and compliance topics. Their team's explicit approval is needed on almost everything. And no one in her team dares to approve requests without a review meeting with her.

"Hana, do you mind helping us understand what your group does? So far, we understand that the GRC group includes risk management, compliance, legal, control audits, and governance, is that right?" I respectfully ask her to define specific responsibilities of GRC to reveal their overreach in interfering in almost every area.

Compliance to Internal Controls, Policies, Procedures, or Guidelines

- Compliance to external or government-defined regulatory framework and policies
- Risks management which preempts and the potential failure modes or deviations from the desired results and expected outcomes
- Legal group which primarily focuses on legal implications, data privacy, data breach, and guidelines on complying with legal framework

Sid says "Invariably, the control functions tend to be overzealous and extra-cautious. This is not a bad thing in itself; however, this could substantially reduce the speed, agility, and efficiency of the solution development and timely movement of value to customers. It's a genuine obstruction to agility, when combined with the one of the following scenarios:

- Lack of clearly defined accountability and responsibility with the control functions
- Overlapping and redundant guidelines provided by control functions
- Only one or two decision makers in upper echelons for work-arounds or exceptions
- Lack of assigned compliance and GRC SMEs to the agile teams"

Hana looks offended and spreads her arms.

"My team focuses on the regulatory requirements to protect our customers. For instance, there are many apps in our phones which could track our locations and communication without us knowing. This is a blatant invasion of our privacy and needs regulatory policies to be constantly reviewed and enforced for preventing this." Hana explains her case.

"There are a multiple interpretations and implications which need to be studied and examined for the implementation. What we receive from the legal and regulatory compliance standpoint is 'what' and not 'how' the practices need to be governed. This means we are always asked to ensure compliance without clearly defining the 'how'!" She expounds.

I jump in,

"Yes, absolutely we all need to help in the privacy protection. But this opens the GRC to a much wider interpretation and micromanagement. Tight command and control by any function suffocates innovation and downgrades agility. GRC needs to be engaged and stay collaborative in the boarder lean–agile transformation. They definitely could bring more focus on oversight but keep it pragmatic.

In a nutshell, the GRC needs to continue setting higher bars for themselves by proactively defining specific, actionable, and easy to understand compliance requirements."

Sid wants to get tactical: "Perhaps, let's have some rules?"

Lightweight Rules of GRC Engagement

- GRC to build A3 size sheet to provide unambiguous guidelines without expecting follow-ups by the agile teams.
- The agile team including the product owner, scrum master, and data architect should provide a clearly defined intent of the solution.
- Assign right GRC SMEs, subject matter experts in part-time capacity to agile.
- The GRC SMEs must be clearly explained the intent and the key components of the solution, the data flow architecture, potential data privacy, and other risks.
- The GRC team members:
    o Spend two half days in a sprint with the team.
    o Join at least two stand ups in a week with teams.
    o Attends the demo/sprint review sessions of the digital teams.
    o The guidance is added to the acceptance criteria and ensure definition of done does not compromise compliance and stability.

I return home late in the evening after a long day at the office. I find myself drowned in worrying headlines and coronavirus updates on the local news, with the rate of virus infections in the town on the rise. There is a Governor's live press conference.

"Dad is watching the news again mom!" Tina reports me to Cindy. Ami and Tina could hear the TV echoing from upstairs.

Lately, the girls have been noticing how anxious and worried I get when I watch the news. The rate of infections and deaths related to

COVID-19 in neighboring states where our extended family live have me worried about Cindy, as the risk of her catching the virus is high during her chemotherapy sessions.

I stop myself from getting lost in my worries and thoughts, and head upstairs, where Cindy and the girls are snuggled up eating pizza and watching a movie. Instead of worrying, I join them and spend the rest of the evening with my family. "What a welcome diversion elevating all our moods!" I exclaim.

Table 10.6 Kanban board

To-do	In progress	Done	
		• The hierarchical organizations are organized top-down vertically, while the value flows horizontally for the customer • Clarity in roles of GRC in internal controls and regulatory compliance • Lightweight rules for systematic GRC engagement	
		The latest Writings on the WALL: 14. Rift between agile and nonagile factions 15. Communication gaps due to silos 16. Heavily hierarchical structure	The latest Building Blocks: j) CLAP—Common-minimum Lean–Agile Practices k) Funding for quarterly outcomes

CHAPTER 11

Flattening the Curve

Shift From Vertical to HORIZONTAL Organization

Wednesday, March 4, 2020

Table 11.1 Kanban board

To-do	In progress	Done
• Principles to establish end-to-end team • Optimal size of an end-to-end team • Define a horizontal organization	• The next chemotherapy rounds (Neil out of office a.m.)	

I wake up to hear Cindy wheezing and coughing. Cindy has been coughing intermittently, and she doesn't sound good. At this point, the girls are awake, and they run downstairs to check on her.

"Are you okay mom?" Ami looks at Cindy with a worried face.

"Could she have the virus? Could I have given it to her?" Tina adds.

I hold the girls close to me, as I feel and hear the anxiousness in their innocent voices. Cindy looks worn out before her next chemotherapy. We surround her and help her to the living room so she can feel more relaxed on the recliner.

"Thank you, it's okay girls. I am fine," Cindy assures them, but coughs a little more.

"I just drank too much water at once, that's all," Cindy comforts them as the girls hug her, wanting to make sure she is okay.

"I love you both. Let me lie down for an hour, I need to rest?" She asks, giving them both kisses on the cheek.

The TV is on. Ami raises the volume of our TV, pointing at the host to grab my attention. The host is asking Dr. Jha, a leading virologist.

"So why is it important to flatten the curve?"

"So, we can properly manage the virus caseload. Already swamped health care system becomes overwhelmed and could potentially and completely crash."

I feel a sense of worry overcome me as I listen.

"All other regular surgeries and medical treatments will need to be put on hold, risking many other lives."

I look at tears rolling down Cindy's eyes, and we both start to wonder how it could affect her treatment. We hug for next few minutes when I hear a door bell.

In that moment, our usual babysitter arrives and gives us enough time to hit the road. As soon as we arrive at the hospital, the nurse does her usual routine checks. Dr. Anu is looking at some papers, "Hello Mr. Frost, sorry we need to get a scan done for Cindy, do you mind coming back in the room after it's done?"

I find my way out of the room. The familiar residents, fellows, and attendings that I usually see when I'm here greet me as they make their way through the hall.

She explains based on Cindy's latest report that she observed two possibilities for the spreading of cancer cells. She uses her notebook to draw a graph with two curves.

Flattening the curve for survival

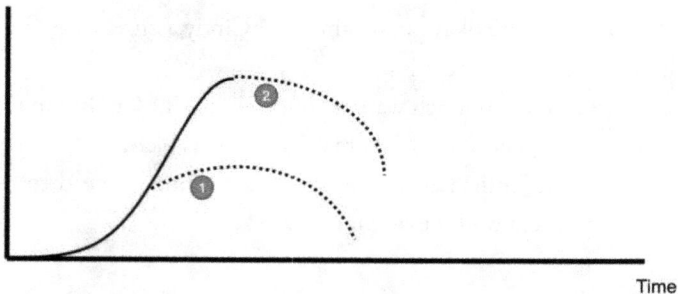

Figure 11.1 Spread of cancer

"The first curve indicates that the treatment is working well and the second indicates that the treatment is not as effective and this may require more aggressive treatment, which is more troubling. This is absolutely not something which I want to see in any of the patients." She explains.

"Mr. Frost I am sorry to say but it looks like her TNBC is getting her closer to the second curve. We need to run tests and deepen the chemotherapy."

Cindy stays in hospital and I need to return home to check on girls.

With half an hour to spare before I leave them once again with their babysitter, I am spending time resuming a previous session on cells with Tina and Ami who are being homeschooled after their school is piloting online learning with COVID-19 cases on the rise.

The girls have reminded me three times in the last weeks to continue teaching them more about cells, and I realize I cannot escape for the fourth time. I bring their chalkboard and continue to spend time with them.

"So, a British scientist, Robert Hooke named these boxes as cells, as these appear to remind him of the cells of a monastery, the simple, small, and austere rooms where monks sleep.

The cells are the basic foundations to support life. They are independent and perform end-to-end complex functions that are yet so simple and small.

Cells regulate the activity through the flow of resources and the flow of information. There are an enormous number of lessons that we can learn from our body and the inner Building Blocks, cells."

I visually explain to them.

- Due to their smaller size, cells have more surface area which makes them efficient in exchanging materials between the inside and outside of cells.
- Complex but still independent.
- Could do a variety of functions—production, power generation, packing, and maintenance.

Soon after I finish, I hit the road. I mentally try to replicate the similar logic to Walkers.

Why can't we make our teams simpler, nimbler, and independent?

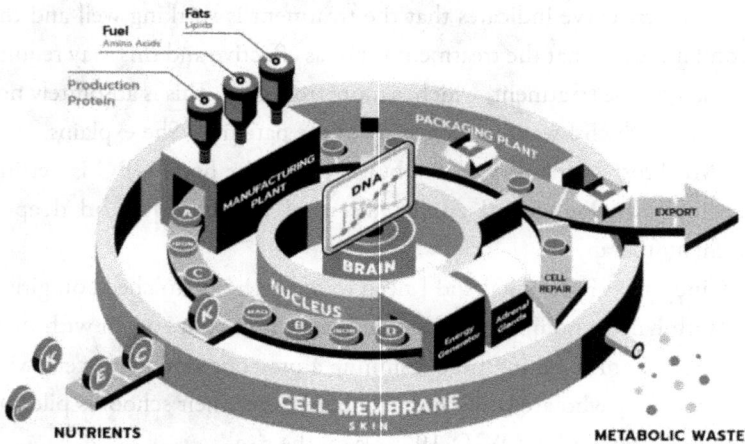

Figure 11.2 Cell-2

If the smallest Building Block in our bodies is a totally autonomous entity why can't our teams become end-to-end, truly self-sufficient? During the last holiday season of Christmas and year end back, we took special permission for Seth's team. We debossed them, as all executives were out of office. They were seamless in releasing bug fixes into the production environment.

We have a huge opportunity to make a truly end-to-end independent agile team to *reduce* interdependencies. We need to reconsider our core delivery teams to make them truly nimble and agile.

Bobby and Sid meet me for establishing the fully independent and empowered teams.

I kick off "One of the agile principles is to satisfy the customer through early and continuous delivery of valuable products. We struggle in timely developing software solutions with agile teams; their attempt toward continuous delivery, continuous integration, and production release has not been so effective."

"And the support, release tooling, and issues with DevSecOps?" I ask.

"What about those? Can you be specific?" Bobby sounds agitated, after all he leads DevSecOps.

"Bobby, the lack of stable support, delayed release management, ad hoc production operations, and bumpy delivery of software defeat the broader agility in the organization. Obviously leading to longer time to release stuff." He adds.

"A real and I mean *real* end-to-end collaboration, integrated tool landscape, and working DevSecOps tooling is what we desperately want. Right?"

We all agree to define some guiding principles for establishing truly end-to-end agile teams.

Principles to Establish End-to-End Teams

Table 11.2 Guiding principles for end-to-end teams

- **Least possible "distance" from the customer:**
  The agile teams need to have a resilient mechanism to work with continuous feedback loops with customers. They need to test and learn regularly with direct feedbacks and validate their hypothesis
- **Shared purpose and synergies:**
  When multiple teams work together to avoid a large linear collection of teams like a large program team with traditional reporting lines
- **Alignment to end-to-end value streams:**
  Adopt a holistic and systems thinking view to imagine end-to-end flow of value to engage the right groups, units/departments in the organization
- **Reduced interdependencies:**
  The dependencies create overheads in resolving underlying interdependencies. A fully independent team is a team which collectively brings business domain expertise, design, full stack development, operations, release, and support skillsets
- **Geographical locations and time zones:**
  It is helpful to have members of the team are in similar time zones. Same location provides opportunity for the team to be collocated for specific events like planning, review, retrospective, or big room planning
- **Use Flow-to-work structure:**
  Teams needing shorter-term access to expert skillsets like architecture, enterprise testing, and DevSecOps tooling are acquired with Flow-to-work structure

Organizations with siloed and hierarchical structure following *Highly Paid Person's Opinion* (HiPPO) need to shift to a newer structure enabling and encouraging objective, democratic, transparent, and data-driven decision making aligned to customer value.

To make this possible, the business structure needs to be agile, nimble, and nonhierarchical. The business structure would need transformation to support a new management approach conducive for exploiting disruptive trends and advanced digital technologies. For example, business structure could be transformed by establishing self-managed and self-organized smaller teams and using agile approach for developing new and innovative digital technology solutions.

The business will benefit from smaller cross-functional technology teams which are *independent and have end-to-end visibility* to add best value to their customers.

Optimal Size of an End-to-End Team

"What the heck is the problem in the current size of teams?" Bobby asks rhetorically.

"First, we break up large teams into smaller teams, and then we create additional overheads, practices for dependency management, scrum-of-scrum, and team-of-team synchronization to make them work together. The teams are of different sizes ranging from 3 to 4 and sometimes 12 to 14 team members. Depending on the nature of the product, there is no right or wrong number." I continue.

"But having too small teams like three or four people might create overhead in terms of coordination and managing backlog, running ceremonies, and providing statuses to the leadership. Right?" Bobby inquires with a bizarre look.

"Additionally, there is an extra effort needed for dependency management. Very small teams are generally dependent on other teams and other functions: for example, on central teams such as risk and compliance enterprise architecture, information security, and release management. Due to a large number of dependencies to the other groups and supporting functions, they lack agility in the business outcomes." Seth adds.

"Hmmm but on the other hand, if the teams are really too large with 15 or more individuals in one team, there is a real possibility of chaos and communication gaps in the team, resulting in confusion, complexity, and lower than expected performance. You see a large number of team members find that they do not have visibility of the big picture and make their own silos." Bobby looks reluctant and sounds indisposed.

Sid rationalizes "All great points and so it is very important to constantly review the team size with the intent to making the teams truly independent, high performing, and empowered to make changes happen without multiple friction points and conflicts with other groups."

Sid has a name for the teams "DOZen" which stands for a *self-organized team of total 12 persons from Development and Operations grounded in Zen values.*

"In the DOZen construct, the size of the teams generally varies from half to a full dozen (6-12) with an intent to make teams highly self-sufficient and empowered to adopt newer ways of working and making meaningful releases to the production system for maximum impact to customers. DOZen is designed for six to nine core team members and up to three part-time who Flow-to-work. The shared services including architecture, security, risk, compliance, DevSecOps, tools and automation, and other specialized skills become part of Flow-to-work pools."

DOZen teams have a maximum size of 12 people. They are primarily engaged in Development and Operations grounded in Zen values, as we see on Sid's visual illustration.

1. Developing or building something
2. Operations or support of something
3. Self-organized and grounded in Zen values

Every year, a DOZen reflects, repurposes, and actively reviews in retrospect of what the focus is and what the priorities and changes are.

How does the team see itself more than 12 months into existence? The DOZen can surely exist for more than a year, but a clearly defined purpose and confidence expressed by the team members rests in the team delivering value for stakeholders and serving customers in in a year.

DOZen is always a good number to look for as the largest size of the team, anything beyond that would require launching a new DOZen.

"We could have seen five members of scrum teams and then one in on leave or PTO and the fourth one is late, and you have two or three not so engaged members in a scrum event. The team members could be wondering *why the hell are we here?* They may feel disengaged and indifferent at times." Sid points at his visual.

Construct of a DOZen team

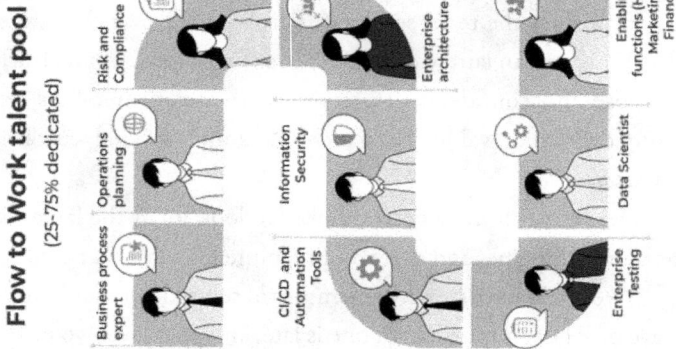

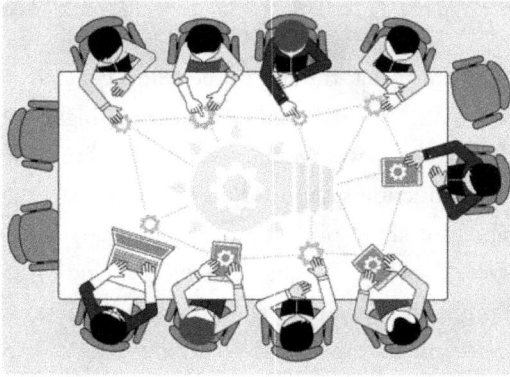

Flow to Work talent pool
(25-75% dedicated)

Business process expert

Operations planning

Risk and Compliance

CI/CD and Automation Tools

Information Security

Enterprise architecture

Enterprise Testing

Data Scientist

Enabling functions (HR, Marketing, Finance)

Up to 3 Subject Matter Experts become part of DOZen

DOZen is the truly independent Dev and Ops team of 12 or less members embracing the Zen mindset

Figure 11.3 DOZen

DOZen: The Self-Organizing Team

Approximately 40 Percent Development

Team members engage in the hands-on solution, architecture, development, testing, and building for new innovative features. The team is focused on development of solution to provide the new and upgraded functionalities for the customers or users to perform their tasks efficiently and smoothly.

Approximately 40 Percent Operations

The team members support operations, release to production, bug fixes, tooling and continuous automation. They are not just focusing on support tasks but working toward end-to-end automation. They focus on automation of operations. For example, actually writing code to automate for solving the recurring problems and reduce recurring support needs. The operations team constantly fulfills the team's obligation to WAR. For example, they resolve Toil. *Toil* are the tasks which could be termed manual, repetitive, tactical, and non-value-adding. These could be automated and eliminated from the process.

Approximately 20 Percent Zen *in Mindset, Self-Organization, and Experience Design*

The team members are committed to integrity, strong work ethics, and upright value system. Constantly self-managing for a purpose, co-creating from the lens of customer, establishing feedback loops by design prototypes, wireframes with user experience (UX) and user interface (UI), and relentlessly putting customers at the center.

(l) **DOZen (Independent teams of 12 for Development and Operations)**

(m) **Horizontal organization**

(n) **Competency-based Chapters with Flow-to-work**

"Does that work?" Sid asks.

"Perhaps. But I am indecisive. DOZen is unique but still is not completely different from a scrum team. Does that make us horizontal? What are the other components of a horizontal organization? I confront Sid.

Table 11.3 DOZen practices

DOZen practices
• **Operates in a cadence:** Defining a lightweight sprint to collaborate and establish feedback loops helps bring structure. The timebox like the two-week sprint rhythm (mainly lightweight planning, refinement, review, retro) helps improve accountability and brings systematic way of working
• **Records sprint reviews/demo for offline use:** Participating live or viewing offline sprint reviews of teams helps to provide valuable and actionable feedbacks during products development. The feedback could be in person or offline. This also makes it possible for a boarder audience and leadership to get access to what is being built
• **Reflects on opportunities:** Retrospectives at the end of sprint to reflect on improvement opportunities. Core team votes collectively for a guest, someone external to the core team, to be invited. This ensures retrospective is a psychologically safe environment
• **Celebrates wins and shout-outs:** At least monthly, the team spends 15 minutes in celebrating small and big wins and recognizing each other. This helps the team to stay positive, engaged, and motivated

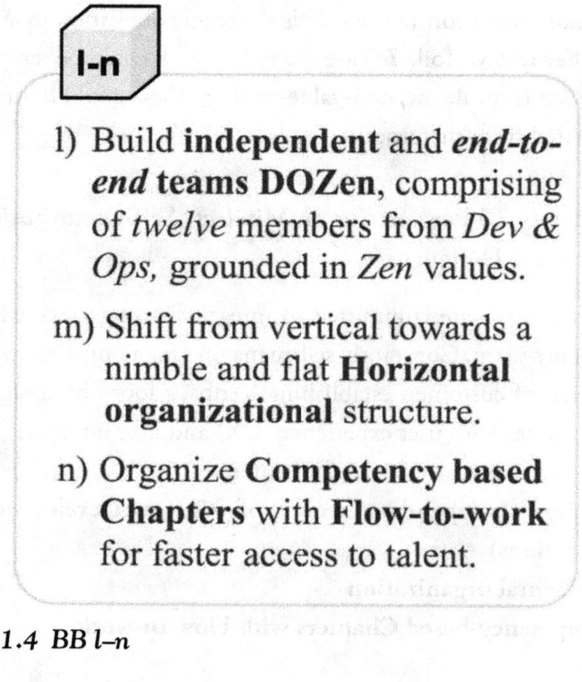

l-n

l) Build **independent** and *end-to-end* **teams DOZen**, comprising of *twelve* members from *Dev & Ops*, grounded in *Zen* values.

m) Shift from vertical towards a nimble and flat **Horizontal organizational** structure.

n) Organize **Competency based Chapters** with **Flow-to-work** for faster access to talent.

Figure 11.4 BB l–n

"Agree. And that is why DOZen alone cannot make you flat." Sid reaches for the whiteboard.

Define a Horizontal Organization

Horizontal organization is one which is aligned to the horizontal flow of value to relentlessly serve customers creating a nonhierarchical, flat, and nimble structure.

Unlike a vertical organization, the decision making is fast and efficient. The focus is primarily on the customer and not on the internal management layers.

We all look at each other with uncertainty written all over our faces.

"Sounds great ... but tactically how could you create a horizontal organization? I challenge.

"Horizontal organization revolves around end-to-end teams like DOZen, competency-based Chapters, Flow-to-work structure, and a C-suite with servant leadership." Sid double clicks.

Competency-Based Chapters

Walkers will need to embrace agile career paths for the talent across the organization. We decide to move away from siloed departments to establish skillset-based Chapters.

Chapters help to reorganize how to operate internally like a horizontal organization. It's designed to be flat to boost productivity, boost Time-to-Market, and build better products for the customer.

Talent with the similar skillsets or competencies (e.g., UI/UX designers or iOS engineers) is organized in what is called Chapters.

Chapters have deep skillsets in certain areas, but still a T-shaped skillset is encouraged by enabling teams to contribute effectively across other areas.

- A Chapter is a community of expert/career professionals with quarterly rotating responsibilities for chapter leads:
  - Product owners
  - Domain SMEs
  - Technology experts (front-end, back-end, and full stack development)
  - Agile coaches and scrum masters
  - Designers (UX/UI)
  - Risk and compliance and information security

The Horizontal Organization

CUSTOMERS

Servant Leadership	Chapters	Independent Teams

Product 1 — Team 1, Team 2, Team 3, Team 4, Team 5

Product 2 — Team 6, Team 7, Team 8

Product 3 — Team 9, Team 10, Team 11, Team 12

DOZen

Dojo

KAIZEN

Servant Leadership

CEO

CFO

CDO (Chief Digital Officer)

CLO (Chief Learning Officer)

CEXO (Chief Experience Officer)

CHO (Chief Happiness Officer)

CIO

CDIO (Chief Diversity & Inclusion Officer)

COO (Chief Operations Officer)

Chapters

Product Owner

Scrum Master

Architecture

Design

Front-end Dev

Testing

iOS and Android

Security

Risk and Compliance

Flow to work pools

Tools and Automation

Senior Leadership team empowers and serves the organization to enable uninterrupted flow of value to customers

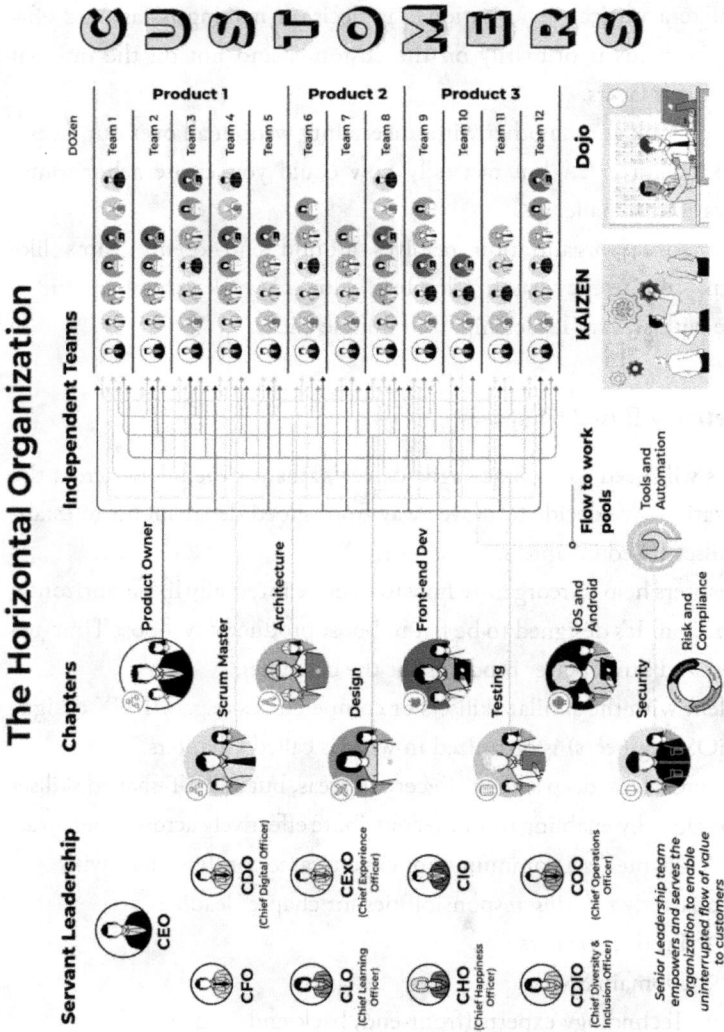

Figure 11.5 Horizontal organization

Each Chapter has about ideally 12 and in some cases up to 15 team members. Chapters help identify and assign suitable talent to the independent teams.

Extreme caution is required to ensure that the Chapters do not revert to vertical silos or top-down departments. They are lightly governed with a Chapter scrum master and a Chapter product owner. Both these roles for the Chapter are part-time, up to 33 percent allocation and rotate for senior and seasoned professionals with the required subject matter expertise.

Flow-to-work structure

Chapters generally become effective by adoption of a Flow-to-work approach.

Based on the needs of DOZen, the Chapters help talent in Flow-to-work pools to move fast and get embedded to support value being released to customers. If they are sluggish, they could get left out and the required talent could be temporarily secured from outside through continuous talent. Scrum masters are empowered to orchestrate efforts to use talent across teams and Chapters with the Flow-to-work model.

Teams that have suitable expertise must 'flow' to work and support a set of sprints. This helps to efficiently get access to skillsets and competency groups like enterprise architecture, tooling, risk management, regulatory compliance, marketing, enterprise testing/QA, and other shared services or corporate functions.

Servant Leadership

Our C-suite team is now called servant leadership to ensure their role is clear. It is to get out of the way for teams to create wow products from the customers. The focus of leaders needs to be on removing the constraints, resolving enterprise-wide blockers, and nurturing a culture of innovation. The Servant leadership keeps them honest to focus on their accountability:

- Enable Chapters to stay relevant using the Flow-to-work construct.
- Launch and nurture new Chapters, when needed.

- Empower Dojo, Kaizen, and foster independent teams (DOZen) to get optimum level of support.
- Always think of better ways to relentlessly serve customers.

To conclude, we all decide to align with the boarder set of stakeholders and to initiate a journey to flatten the organization by reducing redundant middle management layers. In the coming quarters, the direction will be to merge pure managerial roles with agile career streams.

Table 11.4 Kanban board

To-do	In progress	Done	
		• Optimal size of an end-to-end team defined as a 12 • Least "distance" from the customer, alignment to value streams, and least dependencies are the hallmarks of end-to-end team	
			The latest Building Blocks: l) DOZen (Independent teams of 12 for Development and Operations) m) Horizontal organization n) Competency-based Chapters with Flow-to-work construct

CHAPTER 12

Vultures of the CULTURE

Critical Role of Leaders in Mindset Shift

Tuesday, March 10, 2020

Table 12.1 Kanban board

To-do	In progress	Done
• Limitations of RACI matrix • IT and digital sync-up meeting • Resolution for wasteful meetings • Introspection of company's culture		

It's a warmer but muggy morning, and I decide to practice my own inner agility as I as wake up. I turn up the volume in my car as I listen to my daily podcast.

"Mindfulness means that we keep our minds from wandering and going astray. During the meditation we must sincerely attempt thoughtlessness by liberating ourselves from any thoughts that pop into our minds. We need to essentially think about nothing."

As I am driving a bit fast, I notice that my speed was about 35 mph in a residential zone which had a limit of 25 mph. I slow down as I notice a school bus with the stop sign.

How can you stop just like that in the middle of the road with all the cars on the other side of the road as the kids board the bus? I feel annoyed at the bus driver.

Every car ahead of me follows suit by stopping in the most cautious and effective way, without any harsh braking or hesitation. I start to think, *well why is this so seamless, so easy, and so regular for everyone to stop on a blinking school bus with the stop sign on?*

This has to do with something more than the fear of getting a traffic fine, a ticket or the fear of something else. What is it? Is it always fear? Is this not a culture?

Everyone knows they need to stop, and everyone also knows that the school bus is full of children, who are innocent, and a bus driver, who wants to keep them safe. Why do we not have a similar degree of empathy for our colleagues, especially those who are less tenured, less experienced, the freshers, and junior colleagues?

I make a mental note of three things so important to this culture:

1. *Leadership must exemplify the right culture,* mindset, and behaviors (e.g., the first driver who leads and stops first).
2. People need to be *educated on the right behaviors* (e.g., a driving course/manual).
3. There needs to be a deterrent—a *fine/penalty* which deters them! (e.g., a traffic ticket).

Limitations of RACI Matrix

As I reach the office, I notice an upcoming meeting. There is a follow-up action item coming out of the Gemba Walk that Sid and I had planned to review for the RACI matrix of four groups. The RACI is the widely known acronym, which is Responsible, Accountable, Consulted, and Informed.

Many consulting companies stress on it so that their clients get clarity on internal decision making. It is popular among hardcore believers of classical project management and governance.

"You know, I find it extremely intriguing that the companies become vertical and siloed, and then they spend enormous time and energy to define a RACI matrix to work together." Sid adds.

I nod, agreeing with him. "Most of us spent weeks and even months last year to define our company's multiple RACI matrices. Perhaps, a few are using a wee better than others, though the majority hardly looks back and use their RACI!"

"The RACI matrix, especially when not updated and not used regularly, becomes restrictive and even dilutes responsibilities and accountabilities. It makes people narrow-minded, confined to doing what is in their rows or columns, and in this process avoiding a sincere and collective ownership for outcomes … .

… Everyone wanted to be consulted and informed, but no one wanted the responsibility." He argues.

Sid wants to plan a follow-up Gemba Walk right away, but this time focusing on organization silos and RACI. But I push back.

"No, no. First things first, I am drafting the communication and I need to show the draft to Richie. Our last Gemba Walk had created some controversy. I had to individually placate Riche, Tim, and then Gus. Gus had an uncanny choice of some swear words for us that evening when he came to know about our walks. I did not want to bother you."

Sid looks surprised to hear this.

"Folks are too protective of their teams and culture, and they would not like to see any external guy walking in and changing things. That's the culture we have here buddy!" I make things clear.

"Why do we need to get it vetted all the way from the CIO?" Sid curiously asks.

I try to explain. "I have been burnt before. Richie wants to see every damn e-mail I send to teams and his peers, and most importantly, he will make a huge scene if any e-mail is sent to Charles without him reviewing it."

"Informal communication is okay, but you see we are just visiting digital team space and nothing more than that."

"I need to keep Charlie in loop on this one too. He needs to know what we're doing and what I'm doing to work with you." I further add, trying to get Sid to understand.

"Blah blah blah!" Sid rolls his eyes, pacing the room.

I chuckle in an attempt to ignore his remarks, but he stops in front of me with a smile on his face.

"Do you know why I said blah blah blah?"

At this point, I am now irritated by his nonstop nagging. I just want to get on with our work.

"It means *Boot licking across hierarchy!*" Sid exclaims.

"There's too much formality in doing things which are relatively normal business and harmless. For this effort, we're not firing or hiring anyone or blowing up the budget. We're just going to observe some meetings, ask questions, and observe respectfully!" Sid puts it simply.

"I'm trying to play it safe by making formal communications to teams, their managers, their managers' managers, all while trying to please my boss who expects me to review with him as well. But we're spending hours doing what will actually have no value for our customers."

I sigh, realizing the endless cycle I am accustomed to.

We do so much Blah Blah Blah ... Boot licking across hierarchy.

As I take a coffee break, I see an e-mail from Gus in my inbox. He has pushed back on my decision to pivot the roadmap and update the backlog. His reservation came from the fact that those changes would require changes in IT plans too.

With his e-mail, it seems he won't budge. I waste no time in calling him.

IT and Digital Sync-Up Meeting

All are still there with *Gus-the-Pus*. I realize I am late to the meeting.

As I walk into the corner meeting room, I see Gus sitting with Saira and two of her other team members from the master data management project.

I see Gus has both hands thrown in air, raising his voice and staring at Saira. She looks uncomfortable. I wait outside to let the heated exchange pass. All of them are looking at a presentation deck. As I enter the room, he stops talking and looks somewhat indignantly at me.

"Sorry to for being late." I raise a hand, apologizing as I walk into the room.

Gus makes a bizarre face. He turns back toward Saira and resumes the conversation,

"Hey, *listen*." He stresses.

"I'm the VP of IT, so I get to decide." Gus yells, reminding them who is the boss.

"I want two hours on my calendar on this topic. End of discussion."

He mentions without much emotion, clearly indicating that this is nonnegotiable. What he wants to do in those two hours is unclear.

"Please ensure you use my time super effectively when we meet." He looks and expects the team to nod their heads and the intensity of their nodding leaves him reassured.

As he talks, he looks at the e-mail forwarded by Saira just as a terse FYI, and he doesn't like it. "It's not that I don't trust you, but you need to copy me on these e-mails?" He gives Saira a hard look.

"It's essential to provide all the status stuff to the review committee. You can't beat around the bush, so here is what we should be doing."

Gus takes the charge on the flow of presentation.

"The first page is the history of the program. Second shows the last sprint velocity."

"So, I wanted those four pages in the presentation." He squeals.

He rambles and rambles looking at his phone several times as Richie is sending one e-mail after the other. By the time it comes to fourth slide, Gus forgets the point that he is trying to make.

Saira and the team are struggling to compare their notes and identify what the fourth slide is. I want them to push back but they don't. They are not conditioned to ask too many questions to a big boss.

It appears that Gus insisted this team produce exactly four pages, but they don't know what's on the fourth page or what it included.

Gus scratches his head and avoids engaging further. This was typical of Gus asking his team overbearingly to do things which he himself did not completely understand.

Saira speaks up, in an effort to resume the conversation while Gus gathers his thoughts.

"Gus, you know I'll be away on vacation for the next few days. Can I get back to you on this presentation on Monday?" She asks.

"So, this means you're not going to be in for the rest of the week?"

He frowns, as if it was unlawful for her to take deserved time off for work, whether it was for personal reasons or for leisure.

There is a sour mood in the room.

"Why don't you complete it right away or over weekend?" Gus demands, crossing his arms.

Saira almost laughs at his unreasonable request, with wrinkles forming around her lips as she looks at him, hoping he is joking.

"And the quality better be good. You should know, you are managing it."

Gus brusquely walks out as he gets called to another meeting by Richie. Another firefighting!

I mutter to myself, *boot licking across hierarchy at its finest and Gus is obviously no exception!*

Gus abruptly leaves Saira and the team hanging from the edge with a deadline and unclear requirements for presentations.

One of the team members speaks up. "We don't know what to do. He is impossible and such a pain in the backside!"

Saira smiles, before she breaks out in laughter, amused by Gus' requests.

"So, Neil, now you know why they call him what they do."

She avoids mentioning his nickname, but I quickly complete the politically incorrect sentence in a rage.

"You mean *Gus-the-Pus*" my trivial effort to make them feel psychologically safe!

On my back, I am thinking Saira needs to be a scrum master serving agile teams and not a project manager making presentations for Gus-the-Pus. I schedule a time to have an open conversation on her role.

I am back, adding to the *WALL, along with Sid and Seth* I share the two things.

Firstly, this meeting was a pure waste of time, and furthermore, it indisputably again reminds that the *dysfunctional Culture is all around us.* It's like the air we breathe. How guys like Gus and even our other senior management team, including Richie and Tim ask for meetings, assign random presentations and ad hoc tasks to our people, sometimes just a way to "keep them busy."

"Come on Neil, bragging about the meetings and presentations is a nice way to please your bosses, the Blab-blah thingy!" Sid says sarcastically.

Resolution for Wasteful Meetings

We spend at least 8 to 10 hours every week in sync-up meetings and it's not the best use of everyone's time. These meetings are without an agenda. People are asked to set up for meetings for everything under the sun!

A measure of how important and how busy people are is determined by their calendars. For example, Tim Woods is known to ask for a *meeting to plan another meeting resulting in a follow-up meeting,* as he loves to talk. And his favorite ask is "block some time in my calendar."

"A number of meetings Tim hosts and sets up are to review the reports, documents, and e-mails before anything goes to Richie. We have a broken meeting culture.

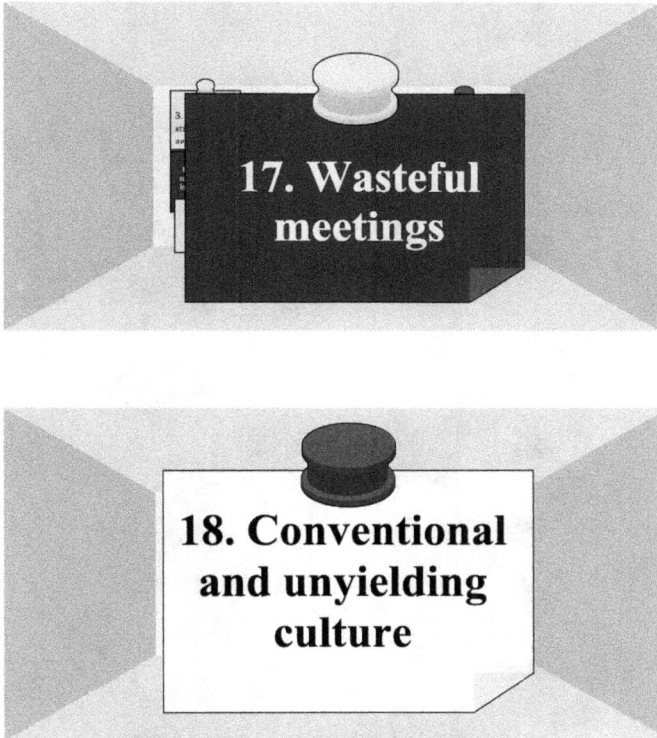

Figure 12.1 WALL No. 17 and 18

Meetings are where we *make minutes and waste hours!*" I forcefully say.

(o) Optimum meetings with APT and AID

The teams are now suggested that meetings should be for 30 minutes and in some cases up to 45 minutes. They are encouraged to cut down on meetings altogether by using our online messaging and chats for crisp and real-time communications when urgent.

Fortunately, we have the next session focused on the same problem.

Figure 12.2 Meetings

Table 12.2 *The Writing on the WALL No. 17*

17. Wasteful meetings	

What does it mean?	• Too many meetings without a clear agenda, or more than required number of people fills up calendars and capacities without many outcomes
	• Many wasteful activities could exist throughout the whole day and they can range from anything to do like:
	  o Attending meetings which are not the best use of our time
	  o Sitting in sessions with a large number of audiences without clear outcomes

What are its effects?	• Loss of productivity, demoralization, and boredom • Skills, expertise, and intellect waste • Opportunity costs of deferring more impactful work

Table 12.3 *The Writing on the WALL No. 18*

18. Conventional and unyielding culture	
What does it mean?	• Lack of psychological safety—top leadership becomes complacent to let executives, senior, and even middle managers create an atmosphere of subservience, insecurity, and fear among the workforce • A culture of avoiding accountability, skirting issues, and hiding problems in front of bosses discourages timely course corrections • Sycophancy and conformity are required for promotions, career progression, and other growth opportunities
What are its effects?	• Sluggish, risk averse, and slow-moving pace of change • Discourages self-organization and collaboration

Introspection of Company's Culture

We have an upcoming session with Richie and Charlie to agree on a plan for cultural renewal. Both have conflicts but have agreed to join after their meeting with the board. We have an open conversation without any judgment for the next 45 minutes.

Sid starts the session with some storytelling. "One of my old friend working in a large IT company admitted to me that he intentionally includes a large number of colleagues mostly senior to him in the cc field, and sometimes even those who are junior to him, just to emphasize how important his e-mail is so that he can elicit a timely response."

Meet for outcomes! Plan "APT" meetings with outcomes "AID".

APT: Agenda, Participants, Timebox
AID: Action, Information, Decision

Figure 12.3 BB o

Table 12.4 APT and AID meetings

	APT
	• *Agenda*: Stop meetings where no agenda exists in the initial five minutes
	• *Participants*: Plan meetings with a maximum of 12 people
	• *Timebox*: Suggest options for duration—15/30/45 minutes or give back time
	AID
	• *Action*: A next step, a task, or a follow-up if needed with an owner
	• *Information*: That cannot be shared using email, slack or team chats
	• *Decision*: That which considerably impacts steps, tasks, and activities
Dos	• Come prepared in meetings • Anything more than 45 minutes is a town hall or all hands meeting • Only attend meetings with a meaningful agenda or a clear intention
Donts	• Assume amount of work based on meetings on calendar • Continue meetings not leading to action/information/decisions • Set up meetings for everything—instead of online chats • Push for more meetings and instead let meetings PULL people, if really needed!

"Executives and managers in most large companies not only get paid more than others but also enjoy people's attention and their praise. In general, it is widely seen that when individuals are put in positions of power, they start talking more and listening less."

"Managers assume that workers are not passionate about their work. Managers in Walkers also think that their teams are not intrinsically motivated and are not interested in work. Most supervisors and managers are conditioned to be demanding. They don't hesitate to create fear and insecurity as ways of getting things done." Hana shares the ground realities.

This is ironical coming from her. I wonder if she is talking of her own GRC team.

"The people have fewer incentives to work when micromanaged and consequently need to be motivated by extrinsic rewards to achieve goals." Paris adds.

At this point, Charlie and Richie enter the room.

She continues and doesn't hold back. "The performance measurement of our company has a number of opportunities. I've been told that the parameters and metrics which we use to evaluate our people are not well aligned to the work they do. We unintentionally make them order takers."

Charles and Richie take a seat, listening carefully.

"We stress way too much in measuring each employee as an individual, and not their teamwork."

Sid has a provocative question.

"So, the current system of performance appraisals makes the people sycophant and self-centric?"

"Bosses, on the other hand, become selfish, even narcissist, and keep emphasizing their own agenda. When they talk, they often stress on what they want for themselves." He circles the room.

We can clearly see that Charles and Richie look surprised and almost ambushed.

"They start their sentences with *I want* and choosing to ignore the *we*. This in turn also means that they easily ignore what *less powerful* people say. Overall, their mindset, behavior, and actions neglect the desires and aspirations of less powerful people, and they end up treating any situation or person as a means for satisfying their own needs."

Charlie jumps in the conversation.

"Walkers' executives tend to be more like those who generally adopt a hopeless and pessimistic view of our people. In fact, when I say this, I am doing it too!"

Charlie openly admits and laughs.

Paris brings us back to the main topic after a few minutes.

"Our organizational culture is prejudiced by the hierarchy, influence, internal politics, and other vested interests. This easily and consciously gets reflected in our day-to-day thinking, habits, actions, and behavior."

She shows a few e-mails to illustrate this.

"Most of us will have a different level of attention, mindshare, and response to a request based on one or more of the following:

- Pay grade, title, or designation of the individual
- Unit, function, or the department of the individual
- Number of persons in the cc field of the e-mails
- Influence of the persons in the cc field of the e-mails"

"Our lesser tenured colleagues also copy a number of the managers in their e-mails, to get the timely response from concerned individuals." I add.

"We don't really work, as we are in the midst of an intense barrage of meetings and e-mails." Richie jokes to our surprise, as he is the master-mind behind most of those.

"There is a kind of 'management by fear' culture. This is counterpro-ductive for a number of reasons. Whenever people meet high-handed bosses, they feel oppressed or inferior about themselves. You see these bad bosses don't hesitate to target people who are less influential and powerful than them." Sid explains.

Paris concurs "Unfortunately, HR systems, policies, and processes surrounding the roles of scrum master, product owner, and project man-ager roles continue to be blurry."

"The HR group in most cases remains a bystander in boarder trans-formation and continues to preoccupy itself in hiring and firing, or sup-porting administrative tasks."

Charlie apologizes and gets up with speed.

"Team I have to prepare for my next meeting with a board member. I am fully supportive of this conversation. I believe this effort is crucial to resuscitate the company, and we must invite other colleagues to create the pillars for cultural renewal!"

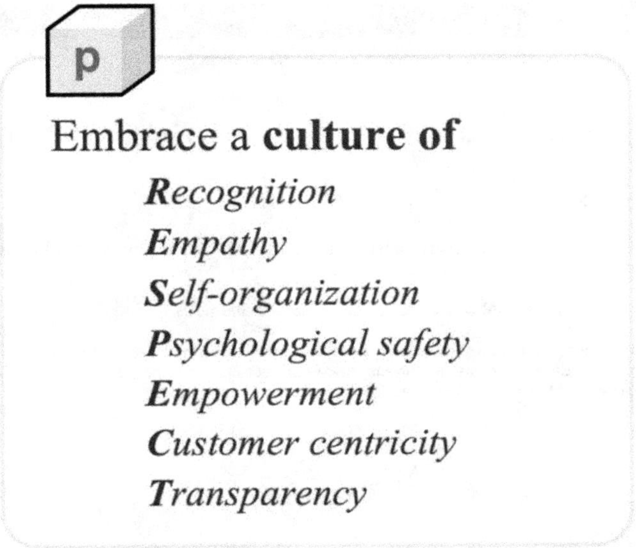

Embrace a **culture of**

Recognition

Empathy

Self-organization

Psychological safety

Empowerment

Customer centricity

Transparency

Figure 12.4 BB þ

He leaves after a CLAP. Our modest symbol is now embraced by the CEO.

(p) **Culture of RESPECT**

- **R**ecognition for all deserving colleagues in a timely manner.
- **E**mpathy for ALL (customers, colleagues, contractors).
- **S**elf-organization within the teams and Flow-to-work pools.
- **P**sychological safety to respectfully challenge anyone.
- **E**mpowerment for teams and team members.
- **C**ustomer centricity in products, services and experiences.
- **T**ransparency based on mutual trust and integrity

The euphoria about the new mindset and cultural renewal gets a reality check the very next day. Richie continues to conveniently send the ball in my court.

Wow! He has effectively delegated the talent problem of the company to me with his e-mail. The rest of my week gets consumed chasing recruiters, both inside and outside the company.

Urgent – A new digital-agile team

Richard Parker
To: Neil Frost

Thursday, March 12, 2020 at 9:42 AM

Hi Neil,

I understand that the curbside pick-up features team is getting blocked due to talent crunch.

I strongly suggest that you launch another back-up team ASAP.

The budget is getting approved as I write this, so focus on mobilizing the designers, engineers, data scientists, architects, and whatever else that they may need.
Could you get the ball rolling please? And please keep me posted tomorrow.

Thanks,
Richie

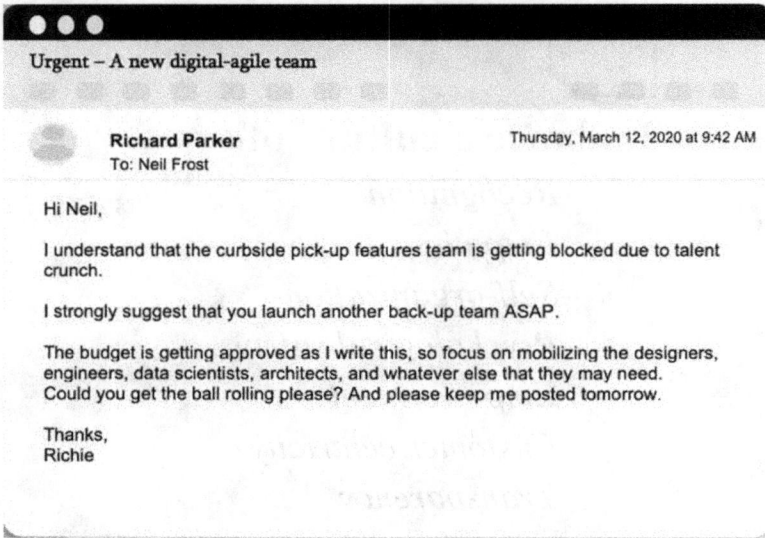

Figure 12.5 E-mail—a new team

Table 12.5 Kanban board

To-do	In progress	Done	
		• The RACI matrix leads to narrow-minded focus and is counterproductive to a collective ownership for outcomes • The decay in organizational culture is mainly due to undue hierarchy, influence, internal politics, and vested interests	
		The latest Writings on the WALL: 17. Wasteful meetings 18. Conventional and unyielding culture	The latest Building Blocks: o) Optimized meetings with APT and AID structures p) Culture of RESPECT

CHAPTER 13

TALENT Escalator

Establishing the Continuous Flow of Capabilities

Monday, March 16, 2020

Table 13.1 Kanban board

To-do	In progress	Done
• Agility for vendor processes • Time-consuming onboarding process • Assess the current talent strategy • Developing T-shaped talent • Sprint review and retrospective	• Recalibrate roles for scrum masters, product owners, and team	

After a quick mindfulness exercise, I put capsules in my coffee machine. I hear a ding in the process from my phone. It's a text from Tim. *This is a surprise.*

He is not much of a text guy. He prefers sending long e-mails.

It seems like he is becoming more active every day, trying to integrate himself with all. I put my espresso down to check.

Figure 13.1 Text—Tim and Neil

I digest the news for the next few minutes and wondering if it's true indeed. Gus is no lightweight. He is the one who fires people that he doesn't like. *How can he get fired?*

Tim must have found out about this from Richie. Is Sid behind this?

"Man, Gus was really fired!" I say it loud enough for Cindy to hear. She looks at me curiously.

I need to soon login to a virtual session with vendor partners. Traditionally, vendors joining meetings about vendor management with CIO and with GRC is not a common sight. It was forbidden. But we cannot be a horizontal organization and have access to Continuous Talent if we are not inclusive of our vendor partners.

Agility for Vendor Processes

Hana, Richie, and I are joined by two consultants from PMAG. I start the virtual meeting by writing two questions on the interactive whiteboard.

How do we *accelerate flow of talent from our vendor partners?*

How do we adopt the agile manifesto value, *customer collaboration over contract negotiation?*

Our consulting colleagues have conducted a series of analysis and created a presentation. It is insightful and something which intrigues all.

"Technology and product complexity require an ecosystem of different internal, external, and third-party vendors, contractors, and consultants. The key challenge is how to integrate the different external entities in such a way which enables agility instead of adversely impacting it."

I am glad to see Hana taking notes.

Centralized supplier management and procurement departments are not very conducive to end-to-end agility. I listen to the lead consultant's recommendation.

"Most organizations are old-fashioned in the procurement decisions. The procurement department is highly bureaucratic. Most midlevel managers are not empowered to make independent suppliers or contracting decisions, and they need to get approval to get the services of an external partner or supplier."

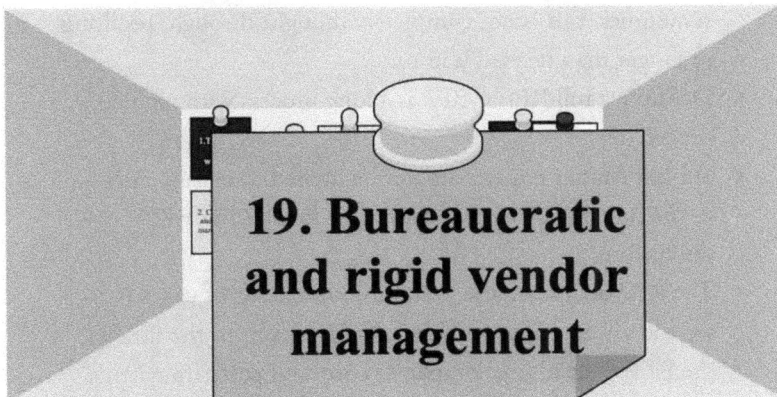

19. Bureaucratic and rigid vendor management

Figure 13.2 WALL No. 19

Table 13.2 The Writing on the WALL No. 19

19. Bureaucratic and rigid vendor management	
What does it mean?	• Complexity and siloed structures lead to convoluted and complicated webs of vendors, contractors, and suppliers of services, products, and materials • The fixed price and fixed scope SoWs contractually bind vendors with a rigid list of deliverables. There is a sharp contrast between agile principles and fixed scope, fixed plan, and fixed services
What are its effects?	• Increases rework, cost overrun, and schedule overrun • Raises efforts in effective collaboration and communication

"Moreover, the procurement departments' whole process could take three to five months."

"We are all really surprised, and we are keen to understand why the timelines are so long.

How so? Care to say more. Why do we have such long timelines?" Hana wants to deep dive.

The lead consultant from PMAG explains their average process steps from the previous four proposals, using presentation slides which we are all able to see on our screens.

- Managers establish initial contact with vendor managers with a set of meetings.
- The next conversation starts with how to fund the efforts, and sometimes, this is not completely thought through, resulting in longer than needed lead times.
- Defining a full RFI or RFP is a long process with many procedures.
- Subject Matter Experts are not be invited to engage early in the process. Only sales people are involved in RFP discussions.
- The RFP documentations run into hundreds of pages if we add all the paperwork and documents from the time of the RFP. Consulting companies copy and paste from other proposals that are not needed. The number of documents generated by vendors is hard to read and time consuming.

- The talent mobilization process does not start until the agreement or contract has been signed alongside documentation approvals.
- The talent onboarding process is lengthy with a number of formalities for three to four weeks.

The PMAG guy is fearless in raising his concerns. "Vendor teams do not have visibility, influence, and skillsets to impact the success of boarder product? We are treated as second-class citizens despite of knowing a lot about the product and underlying technologies. Delays in mobilization and onboarding reduce the excitement of people in the initial days."

Hana highlights the key wastes in the process.

Time-Consuming Onboarding Process

Table 13.3 Waste analysis in onboarding process

• *Overdocumentation*: The proposal and RFP documentations are long. The number of documents generated by vendors is time consuming
• *Waiting and Transportation*: The talent mobilization process does not start until the agreement or contract has been signed by multiple parties and by finance and legal teams
• *Overprocessing, Skills and Intellect*: The talent onboarding process is extremely lengthy, confusing, and ambiguous, and compliance training is needed
• *Inventory, Waiting and Movement*: The process to activate physical and virtual access takes another three to four weeks. The steps in e-mail creation, access badges, and access to enterprise systems like agile tools are lengthy and could consume three to four weeks

(q) **Vendor and supply chain agility**

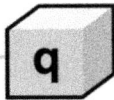

q

Nurture **vendor and supply chain agility** to accelerate end-to-end flow of value.

Figure 13.3 BB q

Hana and the two consultants from PMAG begin to discuss and define the guiding principles.

We all pay attention for the next 45 minutes.

Keep the vendor management department truly lean and nimble as they impact downstream time to value. Build strategic partnerships with vendors and suppliers for maximizing tangible value across the value streams.

Suppliers need to be clearly aligned to where their product/service fits in the broader value stream so they can continually improve. It provides them with long-term visibility as their role does not get limited to specific staffing requests. The key changes we agree to implement:

- *Key success factors for vendor partners:* Traditionally, the key success factor for vendors is narrow batch of services for which they have been contracted, without linkage to a broader mission. It is in the interest of companies that their vendors and contractors fit in organically with the bigger picture and are naturally integrated with overall roadmap to get best value. This, in turn, provides vendor partners with transparency of their roles and potential duration of their engagements.
- *Outcomes in place of rigid deliverables:* The deliverables should not be rigidly included as fixed in SoWs or contractual purchase orders. Instead, the deliverables in a contract need to be tightly coupled with the business value and a product roadmap. It helps to maximize time and material contracts with flexible SoWs.
- *Dynamic work packages:* There needs to be quarterly reprioritization and course corrections in assignments to respond to changes. The vendor work packages must evolve in close relation to the evolving product.
- *Continuity of teams:* Reduce temporary or ad hoc staffing of contractors focused on tactical, overly short-term, and minor tasks. Most complex programs are executed with staffing from multiple internal groups and external contractors. Reassignment, exit, and separation of team members are common due

to higher demand of this talent. It is important to define ways to have the same team continue for at least a quarter.

- *Cultural integration and respect:* We must shift away from the way we differentiate between colleagues and contractors. It should never be a case of "us versus them" as both full-time colleagues and consultants within the organization are critical to instill a sense of belongingness and to have a meaningful collaboration. All good faith efforts must be taken for suppliers to get paid on time for the products and services they provide.
- *Productive from day one:* The agility in the vendor processes and onboarding refers to reduced administrative efforts in SoW process. Umbrella processes and comprehensive document like signed confidentiality agreements to protect company information could be key to reduce redundant transactional checks balances and access related delays.

It's a productive conversation. I feel hopeful but soon get interrupted by my phone's vibration. It is none other than Daisy calling about our slower rate to hire newer talent.

Assess the Current Talent Strategy

"Neil, why did we not hire the product owner? We both had interviewed her in the last quarter and she was amazing."

"Hmmm …" I pause to remind myself about that specific interview.

"Wasn't she?" Daisy, as always, sounds forceful and wants a quick answer.

I explain it's not the problem with the candidate.

"The company process remains unbelievably protracted. After many rounds of interviews and approvals, and by the time we make employment offers, folks get other opportunities. It is too late."

She wants analysis of the long-drawn-out hiring process, and I share the process mapping which Paris and Seth had developed soon after their own Gemba Walk on the talent acquisition value stream.

My phone vibrates. We get stood up at the last minute. Coronavirus concerns already are increasing and leading to people missing their professional commitments.

"So ... your babysitter is unable to come. Tina and Ami, you both need to come with us to the hospital. Get ready girls!"

"Yay"

"I like it ..." they both are animated thinking it's an outing.

As soon as we reach, Dr. Anu fortunately shares some encouraging news "Scientists have recently discovered a cancer treatment based on T cells. It is awaiting FDA emergency use authorization. This improves prospects now for Cindy's treatment."

After meeting with Dr. Anu, the three of us are on the hospital ground floor trying to kill an hour of our time before Cindy's scans and the chemotherapy.

I try to make the most out of it without the girls getting too bored. I grab a coffee and start walking a bit aimlessly with the girls as time passes.

We notice a number of people standing and waiting for the elevator. Some of them had really large bulky bags and some of them had children with strollers. There are three ways to get to the highest floor. There is obviously the elevator, the escalator, and then there are stairs. All three are modes of elevation that we could end up taking.

The elevators go up and down, each coming back after six to eight minutes. The escalators are a continuous flow and stairs are manual. From a flow perspective, I contemplate whether escalators could be preferred by most people.

Ami walks up to the elevator, Tina runs to the stairs, and I go close to the escalator.

"Let's go up the stairs," Tina suggests.

"No, the elevator is faster," Ami argues.

"The escalator is the best way up." I attempt to persuade our girls.

"How?" Ami folds her arms, demanding an answer.

"Yeah dad, why and how is it the best way up?" Tina adds to the question.

"Ami, when you press the elevator button, you have to wait right? Then you go up, to the next floor but waiting is never good."

I stand in front of the elevator, illustrating my point.

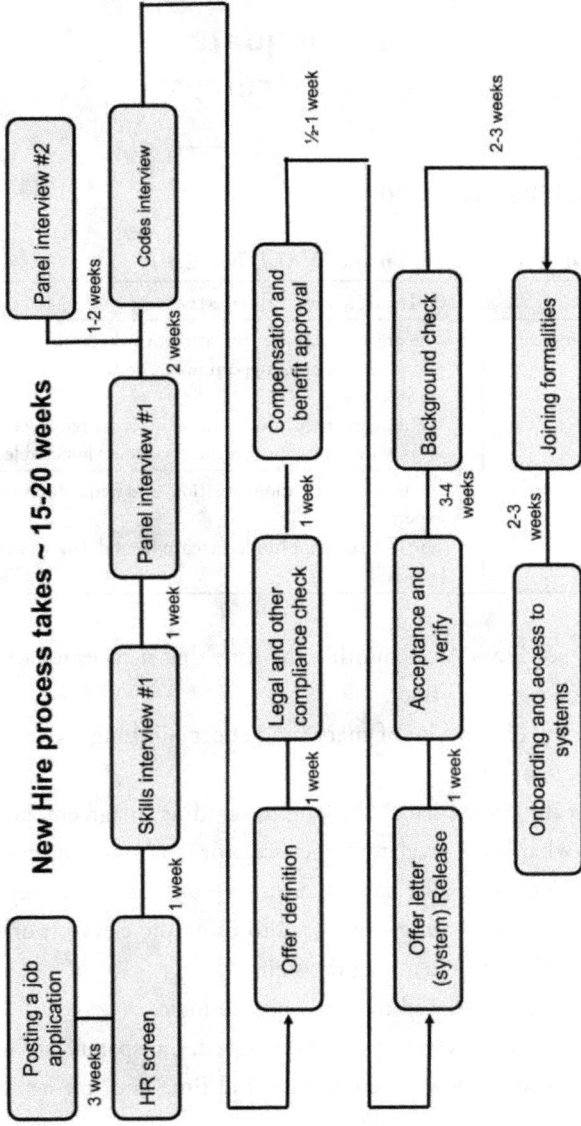

New Hire process takes ~ 15-20 weeks

Posting a job application → HR screen (3 weeks) → Skills interview #1 (1 week) → Panel interview #1 (1 week) → Panel interview #2 / Codes interview (1-2 weeks) (2 weeks)

Offer definition (1 week) → Legal and other compliance check (1 week) → Compensation and benefit approval (½-1 week)

Offer letter (system) Release (1 week) → Acceptance and verify (3-4 weeks) → Background check (2-3 weeks)

Onboarding and access to systems (2-3 weeks) → Joining formalities

Figure 13.4 New hire process

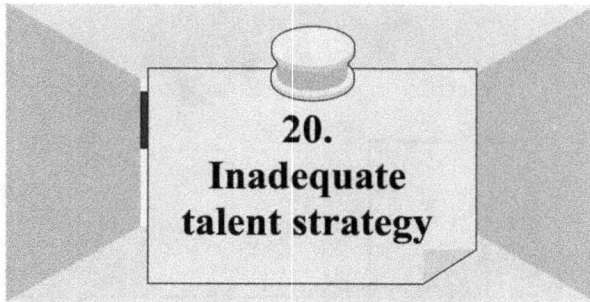

Figure 13.5 WALL No. 20

Table 13.4 The Writing on the WALL No. 20

20. Inadequate talent strategy	
What does it mean?	• The organization does not attract the best talent, overlooks talent development opportunities, and compromises with meritocracy • Building the best-in-class and start-of-art products and services without the best people is virtually impossible
What are its effects?	• Leads to demotivation, attrition, and frequent churn of experts • The lack of talent hinders creativity and delays product launches

"Oh, I see," says Ami counting the time that it takes for the elevator to come down to their floor.

"Tina, you use up a lot of energy and effort climbing the stairs, right?" I ask with open arms.

"Oh, yeah, I know dad." She laughs, nodding in agreement.

"Now, what is the escalator? The escalator is a bunch of moving stairs that never stop. Now all I have to do is step on them and they will take me up. I don't take as long, compared to using the elevator; or spending energy and wasting time taking the stairs."

I smile, as the girls nod that they get my logic.

"The escalator provides a predictable speed, transparency of where you are, and a constant flow by combining full-time and free-agents. Faster talent sourcing" I look at them both.

I am using rather complex words for my kids and remind myself.

Tina smiles, agreeing.

I call Paris but she does not pick. I keep calling Paris a few times.

Both girls know it's a work call with my demeanor. "I am looking to solve a similar problem where I could use a constant flow." I assure it will be quick.

"Sorry for missing calls. Like other colleagues in Europe and Asia-Pacific, I am working remote for a few days. I am struggling to get into the rhythm with all these issues in connectivity, devices, and so on." Paris explains.

I sensitize her about the idea of building the *Continuous Talent*.

"Paris, I think that if we can get a constant flow of talent just like an escalator, then we can build a talent escalator for continuous pool of talent—leveraging experts from the crowd and using the gig economy to build proactive, background checked, and ready to be onboarded talent exchange."

"Very exciting, would love to collaborate. Ohhh wait a minute … ." She pauses.

She is receptive and is willing to partner on the next steps but knows better than me that nothing is easy at Walkers.

Her silence for the next few minutes makes me nervous. I hold my breath, as I hear her typing at the background.

"… So, you see this requires changes in company's HR policies. This needs modifications in our performance management approach. I need approvals from our CEO."

I quickly reach out to Richie and ask about sending an e-mail to the CEO to get his approval for. He agrees almost immediately.

I start to notice gradual change in his behavior after committing to Inner Agility Manifesto (I AM) in the last couple of weeks.

I send the e-mail directly to our CEO without a line-by-line review from Richie, a move that was unheard earlier in the IT organization.

I get a thumbs up response from Charlie in about 30 minutes, "thank you for taking the lead" message from Richie soon after. Shortly after, Paris loops in her team who are ready to draft specifics of the policy.

I smile at the sheer speed of this decision making. What could have been a quarter long process is now feasible in three hours. Walkers is really changing!

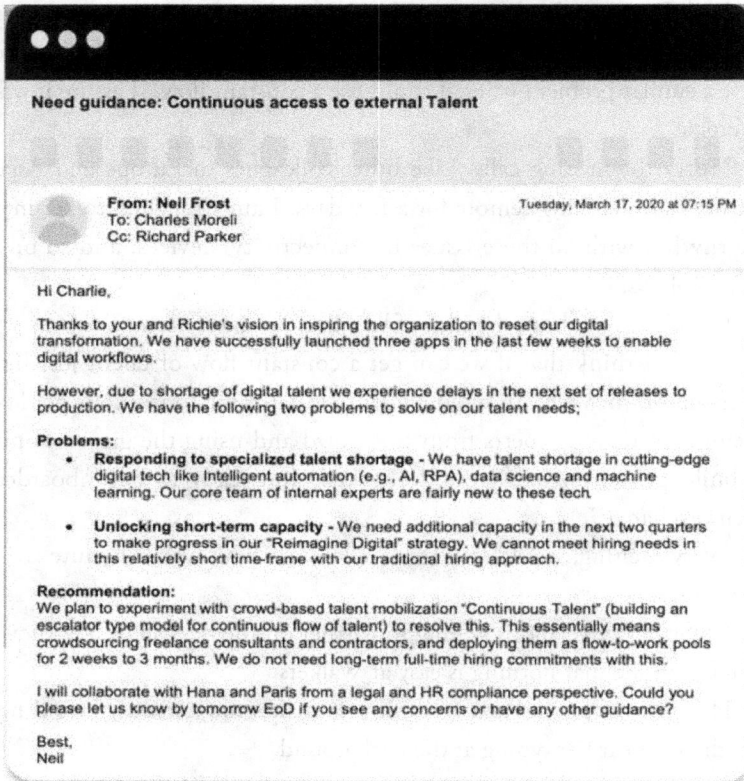

Need guidance: Continuous access to external Talent

From: Neil Frost   Tuesday, March 17, 2020 at 07:15 PM
To: Charles Moreli
Cc: Richard Parker

Hi Charlie,

Thanks to your and Richie's vision in inspiring the organization to reset our digital transformation. We have successfully launched three apps in the last few weeks to enable digital workflows.

However, due to shortage of digital talent we experience delays in the next set of releases to production. We have the following two problems to solve on our talent needs;

Problems:
- **Responding to specialized talent shortage** - We have talent shortage in cutting-edge digital tech like Intelligent automation (e.g., AI, RPA), data science and machine learning. Our core team of internal experts are fairly new to these tech.

- **Unlocking short-term capacity** - We need additional capacity in the next two quarters to make progress in our "Reimagine Digital" strategy. We cannot meet hiring needs in this relatively short time-frame with our traditional hiring approach.

Recommendation:
We plan to experiment with crowd-based talent mobilization "Continuous Talent" (building an escalator type model for continuous flow of talent) to resolve this. This essentially means crowdsourcing freelance consultants and contractors, and deploying them as flow-to-work pools for 2 weeks to 3 months. We do not need long-term full-time hiring commitments with this.

I will collaborate with Hana and Paris from a legal and HR compliance perspective. Could you please let us know by tomorrow EoD if you see any concerns or have any other guidance?

Best,
Neil

Figure 13.6 E-mail—continuous talent

(r) **Continuous Talent**
(s) **Developing T-shaped talent**

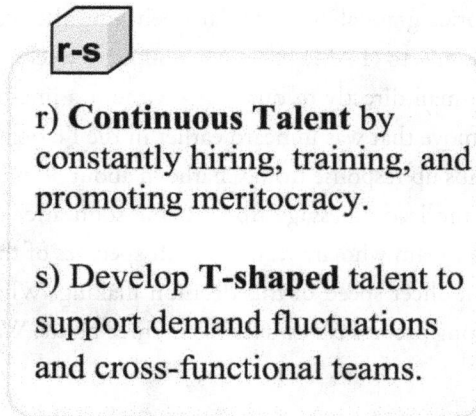

r-s

r) **Continuous Talent** by constantly hiring, training, and promoting meritocracy.

s) Develop **T-shaped** talent to support demand fluctuations and cross-functional teams.

Figure 13.7 BB r and s

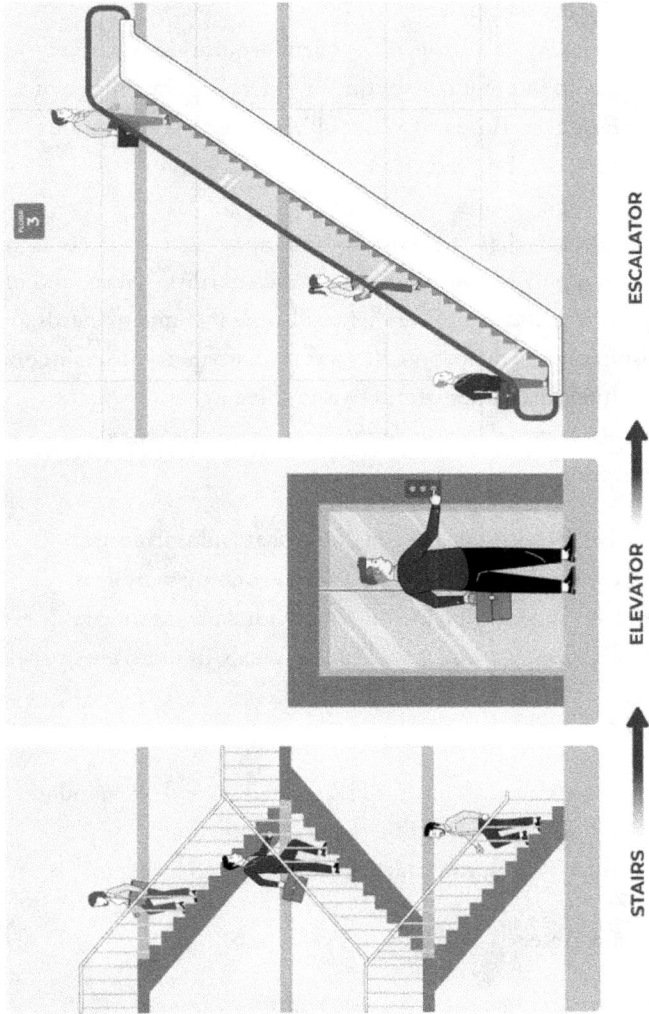

Figure 13.8 SEE: continuous talent

The SEE model and ways to establish continuous flow of talent:

- *Stairs*: This is when hiring and onboarding talent is effort-intensive, slower paced involving manual processes, and lack of clear transparency.
- *Elevator*: This is when the talent acquisition is partially automated but requires waiting at different points of the process.
- *Escalator*: This is when mobilizing talent is continuous, smooth, and predictable.

We decide that the existing and new talent will be continuously invited to apply for positions. We could shortlist, screen, and offer them temporary contracts or hire them full-time if company needs aligns with the aspiration of the people. It gives a transparency in maintaining pipeline to hire capabilities within two to three weeks.

Escalator model helps to build the continuum of talent.
Selection

- Tie-up with freelance marketplaces and universities
- Daily job advertisements in gig economy platforms
- Continuous pipeline building with daily interviews
- Colleagues spend 1 to 2 hours weekly in interviews panels

Onboarding

- Three-day guideline for HR formalities and background checks
- Two-day guideline to fast-track onboarding
- Three-week sprint cadence for end-to-end hiring for urgent roles

Steady state

- Cross pollination with the crowdsourced talent
- Build unified teams of 12 with external and internal talent
- Designate a relevant Chapter as the primary home of the freelance talent
- Make the Chapters "one-stop shop" for the Flow-to-work assignments

Our website gets updated with our new talent strategy.

Walkers believes in the *Continuous Talent* which refers to spotting, hiring, training, developing, and promoting meritocracy every day—constantly to attract the brightest and the best and no less! We are committed to building a pipeline of world-class talent for *staffing-on-demand*.

- Collaborator: Team players and discourage self-serving, directive, high-handed individuals.
- Protean: Lean–agile practitioners who are T-shaped by being a life-long learner, adaptable, and versatile. Life is a learning until you learn it!
- Hacker: Creators who spend 10 percent of their time to reflect, explore, learn, and experiment new possibilities and build prototypes outside their day jobs.
- Soldier: Fighters who affirm obligation to WAR by contributing to Kaizen and A3.
- Troublemaker: Challengers who fearlessly but respectfully challenge status quo and boldly ask questions to manager, peers, and superiors.
- Steward: Protectors who live by, spread, and preserve company values with deep integrity, dedication, and commitment.

Developing T-Shaped Talent

We decide to prioritize the T-shaped persons in our hiring. The letter T is also a reminder of the skills we need to constantly inculcate in our talent.

There are a number of benefits that a T-shaped person has as a result of both specialization and generalization. A T-shaped person avoids the constraints common to people who are specialists in only one field or generalists in many other fields but are not an expert in any of these fields.

T-shaped people easily adapt to varying demands, domains, and situations.

This is because a T-shaped person is capable of many things and is an expert in at least one of them. For example, a product owner is a T-shaped person, because they have deep knowledge and strong skills in the area of business domain, and they also have a broad skillset in areas like digital technologies, software development, and user acceptance.

Overall, T-shaped people tend to be more attractive to employers not only because they meet the criteria of the job description but because they add value to the firm as key players driving and influencing business objectives and outcomes.

I walk to the board, marking the letter T, and asking them to look at the second page of the document I received from PMAG's talent development expert.

The vertical bar of T represents the depth of skills and expertise in a primary field, whereas the horizontal bar is the ability to meaningfully collaborate across a set of capabilities and disciplines with experts in other areas.

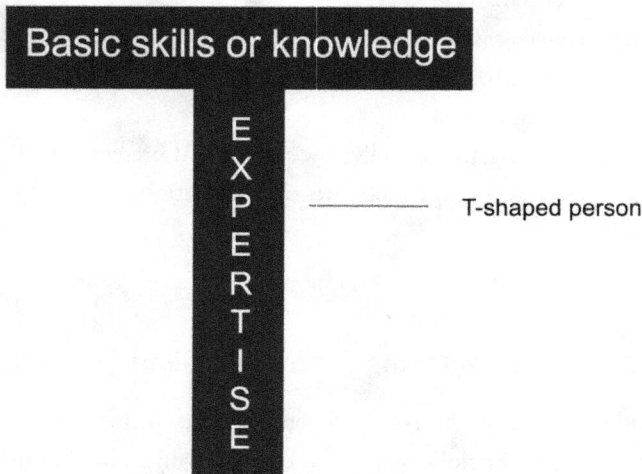

Figure 13.9 T-shaped people

The horizontal aspect includes empathy, redefining problem form an independent perspective of which someone is not an expert and passion about new knowledge domains and disciplines. It is about contributing to the innovative pursuits and creative processes.

Mobilizing T-shaped talent in the company is important as there are the two main benefits of being a T-shaped person include:

Having strong engagements and collaborative networks: T-shaped people are team players who are skilled in collaboratively working with people across a wide range of networks. Their broad knowledge and skills help them to have the basic knowledge that is required to communicate meaningfully with specialists in a variety of fields. This basic understanding of many fields or areas enables them to have strong engagements and collaborative networks with a range of experts. For example, a data scientist with a basic understanding of the health care industry will be able to assist health insurance professionals with visualizing data charts and analytics.

Having transferrable skills and knowledge: While specialists are restricted to one field, T-shaped people have the flexibility to move across different areas, as their skillset can be easily transferred and applied to other fields. For example, an English Literature graduate's expertise in written and communication skills, like the ability to frame arguments and critically assess complex topics, can be useful to dip into technical writing and copywriting. T-shaped people learn new things as they cross over to different disciplines.

Objective: We will attract best-in-class digitally fluent talent through meritocracy, values, and culture of inclusion. We will develop a vibrant T-shaped talent pool with Dojo and Continuous Talent Escalator to accelerate an atmosphere of rapid learning and implementation.

Key Results:

- People Net Promoter Score 85+ percent promoters
- All-round talent development by investing at least 10 percent time in training and development
- Meaningful people policies to address the pay equity gap, health care, paid time off, work–life balance, and overall wellbeing
- Establish diverse interview panels for hiring and promotions within two years for top performers

Recalibrate Roles for Scrum Masters, Product Owners, and Team

Sid and I invite Saira and Keisha for a candid conversation.

"Saira was a project manager for the last seven years. She was in the core team of project managers who had established a project management center of excellence with Tim's sponsorship. Despite working closely with agile teams, Saira still considered her primarily role to be a project management expert."

Saira joins us first.

"Hey Saira as you know we wanted resolve confusion in your roles." I cut to the chase.

"Certainly, there is confusion. I am the project manager, but I am not sure if I could be scrum master?" Saira says, unsure.

"What do you think is the difference between the roles?" Sid raises the question.

Saira knows this is a tricky question. She looks a bit perplexed, realizing it has been a topic of politics in the company.

"Sorry Sid, what do you mean?" She says with an artificial smile.

"How do you think these roles are distinct? What makes them different?" I persist.

Saira discerns that there is no way she could avoid this conversation anymore.

"So, project managers focus on the project plan, ensuring schedules are met, and costs are kept down." Saira explains.

"The scrum master coordinates with the team, runs the ceremonies, and ensures adherence to agile processes."

Saira looks worried, not knowing what to expect after she candidly shares her thoughts.

"So, which role are *you* passionate about?" I ask swiftly.

"Could I be frank with you folks?" Saira continues.

"Project managers are spending way too much time reporting and doing internal stuff. I don't like to remain a PM forever, but with what I know, even the scrum masters do PM tasks themselves. So, I guess what you are called hardly makes a difference."

"It should not matter what you are called, but actually what you do, always matters. I believe the role of scrum master and product owner is not well-defined and is loosely practiced. We need to clearly express roles and sensitize our people. Let's make it easy to remember!" Sid circles the room.

"However, we cannot just continue to have misunderstandings and vagueness. We need to distinguish project manager and scrum master. And even Product owner" Keisha joins now.

"Let's take a step back to recalibrate some of the basic roles and set up Dojo to improve training."

Action: I take the action to loop in Tim Woods, describing the nature of the work where Saira could be best suited and more effective to act as scrum master and not as project manager.

Information: Need to clarify the three roles in an agile team to avoid confusion.

Decision: Saira agrees to take on the role of a scrum master.

I call Paris immediately after.

"Can we prioritize to accelerate launch of Dojo?" I plead her.

"You're kidding. How early?" She sounds nervous.

"If you could help it stand up in the next one to two days, please? Parallelly we also need to upgrade the performance appraisal. I have a few ideas."

She is noncommittal but agrees to help.

Optimize titles and roles: Eliminate fancy titles which worsen power play and hierarchy. Simplify roles and titles around three main role streams—scrum master, product owner, and team. All groups could also leverage the similar structure of roles.

- Business analyst, product owner, product coach
- Agile team member, scrum master, agile coach
- Engineer, system architect, enterprise architect

We all decide to clarify the three roles in an A3-sized paper to avoid confusion, myths, and misunderstanding.

(t) **Institutionalize roles of scrum master, product owner, and team and no fancy titles**

(u) **360° performance evaluation**

Change "performance appraisal" system to "performance enablement" guidance.

Understanding the 3 key Roles

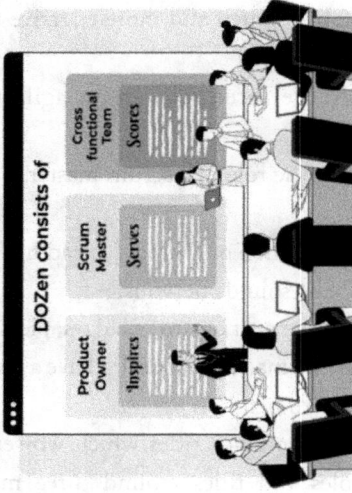

DOZen consists of

Product Owner	Scrum Master	Cross functional Team
Inspires	Serves	Scores

The Product Owner INSPIRES the team

INnovates with an abundance mindset

Socializes with key stakeholders

Prioritizes Epics and Stories

Invites customers to co-create

Reviews feedbacks and feasibilities

Engages team to experiment

Spreads best practices with Dojo

The Scrum Master SERVES the team

Schedules sprint events

Enables the team culture

Removes impediment with the team

Visualizes the key artifacts in Obeya

Expedites progress towards sprint goals

Spreads best practices with Dojo

The Team SCORES sprint goal

Self organizes with responsibility

Collaborates within and across the teams

Obligation to WAR (waste avoidance and removal)

Reviews with PO at continuous intervals

Expedites progress towards sprint goals

Spreads best practices with Dojo

Figure 13.10 SM, PO, and team

- *No weekend work policy*: Encourage scrum masters to avoid teams working during weekends or holidays.
- *Holistic 360-degree performance* reviews to encourage all-round performance and inclusiveness. Our performance reviews need to be open, and two-way conversations should be used to improve the performance, and not demotivate or discourage anyone.
- *No smart-ass policy:* Mechanisms to strongly penalize show-offs, "know-it all" "bad bosses," retaliatory bullying, aggressive and combative behaviors.
- *Frequent feedback cycles:* Encourage continuous, informal, and constructive feedbacks with half yearly performance reviews in place of time-consuming formal review cycles.
- *Manager to coaches:* Instead of management heavy (project and people managers), embrace roles that focus on coaching and are better aligned to specific disciplines, domains, and competency areas.
- *Four-day weeks*: Experiment with four-day work weeks at least once a month.

Table 13.5 The agile roles

The product owner INSPIRES the team	The scrum master SERVES the team	Team SCORES sprint goals
INnovates with the team. Socializes with key stake-holders. Prioritizes the Epic and Stories. Invites customers to co-create. Reviews feedbacks and feasibilities. Engages team to continuously improve. Spreads best practices with Dojo.	Schedules and orchestrates sprint events. Engages the team in mindfulness. Removes impediments and organizes Kaizen. Visualizes key artifacts using an Obeya. Expedites progress toward sprint goals. Spreads best practices with Dojo.	Self organizes with responsibility. Collaborates within and across the teams. Obligation to WAR (waste avoidance and removal). Reviews with PO at continuous intervals. Expedites sprint progress with mindfulness. Spreads best practices with Dojo.

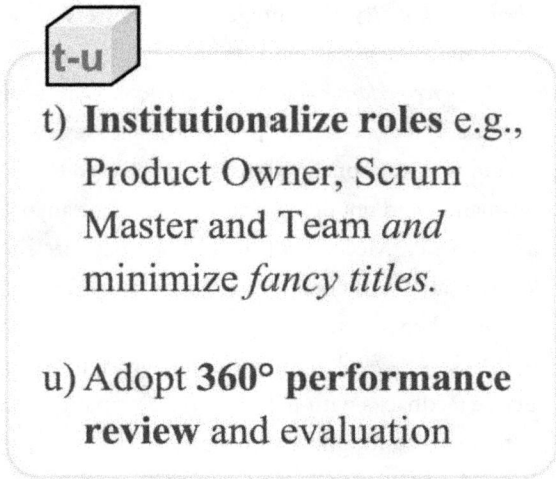

t) **Institutionalize roles** e.g., Product Owner, Scrum Master and Team *and* minimize *fancy titles*.

u) Adopt **360° performance review** and evaluation

Figure 13.11 BB t and u

Table 13.6 Kanban board

To-do	In progress	Done	
	• Set up the Dojo	The latest Writings on the WALL: 19. Bureaucratic and rigid vendor management 20. Inadequate talent strategy	The latest Building Blocks: q) Vendor and supply chain agility r) Continuous talent s) T-shaped people t) Institutionalized roles (SM, PO, and team) and no fancy titles u) 360° performance review

Sprint Review

The key lessons learned during the sprint include the following:

- The organizations are organized vertically, while the value flows horizontally.
- The scaling framework when implemented without context becomes too complex.
- Leaders have a critical role to lead by example in cultural renewal and mindset shift.

- It is critical to shift from vertical to horizontal organization to realize true agility.
- It is crucial to establish continuous flow of talent to have agility in proactively embracing change in product development.
- People need to be developed as T-shaped so they could adapt to varying skillset requirements.

Sprint Retrospective

What is working well?

- The HR to champion rejuvenation of policies, including 360° performance systems and recalibration of roles to ensure product owner *INSPIRES*, scrum master *SERVES,* and team *SCORES* sprint goals.

What could improve?

- Sustaining productivity in a hybrid operating model.
- Continuous learning and development of the talent.
- Adoption of agile in the strategic planning.

The problems, Writings on the WALL, identified during the Sprint 3:

11. Fragile scaling frameworks
12. Ineffective learning and development
13. Redundant roles and inflexible HR policies
14. Rift between agile and nonagile factions
15. Communication gaps due to silos
16. Heavily hierarchical structure
17. Wasteful meetings
18. Conventional and unyielding culture
19. Bureaucratic and rigid vendor management
20. Inadequate talent strategy

SPRINT 4

Rebuilding and Recovery

Sprint Goal

- Embrace life-long learning to be the vanguard of digital talent.
- Expand agility from execution to strategy to restore and sustain progress.
- Experiment with a hybrid operating model to minimize pandemic-related disruptions.

CHAPTER 14

DOJO

A Place for Experiential and Immersive Learning

Wednesday, March 18, 2020

Table 14.1 Kanban board

To-do	In progress	Done
• What is the Dojo? • Uniqueness of a Dojo • Benefits of Dojo • How is Dojo set up? • Day in the life of Dojo: Performance measurement of agile teams		

Paris and Seth have organized a session with two digital teams to launch our first Dojo. I had tentatively accepted, hoping I could join in person, but I decide to stay with Cindy at home and attend via video call.

Paris, along with the learning experts, shares a brief presentation for the overview.

Strategically investing in talent building and people development without a disproportionate fear of losing talent to attrition improves the quality of talent.

What Is the Dojo?

Dojo is set up for accelerated learning. It enables learning by doing and learning by examples.

Learning by doing is an innovative pedagogical practice which is useful for both trainers and coaches to improve learning outcomes. It is a dedicated space where teams from all over the company come for a devoted one or two weeks of intensive skills building.

Dojo is a Japanese word that means *place of the way*; it means that it's both a physical and mental space. The word Dojo actually comes from martial arts or karate. It is indeed the dedicated place of learning and meditation. The concept of a professional Dojo is similar. It is also used for a dedicated place for learning, and they do things in a more practical way.

This is where teams can come to learn lean–agile and design concepts and can learn newer methods and techniques. The function of Dojo is as follows:

- Develop passionate change agents, servant leaders, and catalysts, who can help relentlessly train, upskill, and spread agile talent across enterprise.
- Adopt focused coach-the coaches and train-the-trainers' initiatives to accelerate talent development and cultural change.
- Pragmatic, hands-on, and articulate lean–agile experts and coaches are equally essential to develop agile practitioners to build best-in-class products.
- Develop T-shaped that will have expert skillsets, deep knowledge, and robust capabilities in specific areas and a broader general knowledge/skillset for supporting a number of other competency areas.

In a nutshell, Dojo promotes the idea of experiential learning, which is developing new skills, knowledge, and values from direct experiences in contrast to a traditional classroom environment, lecture, or an academic setting.

We decide to articulate benefits and e-mail to get faster funding for Dojo from the acting CFO.

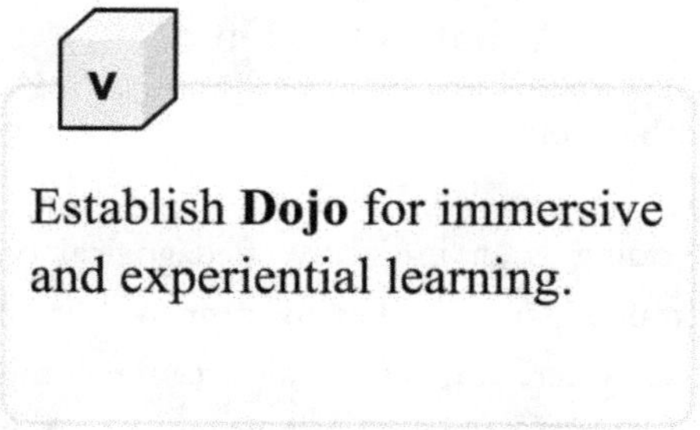

Establish **Dojo** for immersive and experiential learning.

Figure 14.1 BB v

(v) **Dojo for immersive and experiential learning**

Uniqueness of Dojo

What makes Dojo a unique experience? Dojo is not about sitting in a classroom. Passively sitting in the classroom setting makes people dull, sleepy, and lethargic. People yawn a lot especially after lunch and in afternoons.

Also, one major problem with the trainers standing, and with students sitting, is it reinforces the cultural flaws of our hierarchical organizations. Faculty or a trainer who is standing commands the students who are sitting in a "controllable" position. This diminishes the thought processes and critical thinking, finally reducing the intensity of probing questions of the participants.

The learning in Dojo is not unidirectional. It is multidirectional, meaning it is not one-way flow of information from teacher to student but participants learning from each other as well.

Some of the training and knowledge content is co-created and codified as part of Dojo.

Dojo is fast-tracked learning like a drive-thru or passing through an automated car wash through its e-construct and deliberate design, making it a place for immersive, engaging and thorough learning which is practical and applied.

The whiteboards, big visual indicators, and other visual management aids are everywhere.

The energy and excitement are pervasive—this is a place and time set aside for an intense and collaborative effort.

The knowledge and vibes in Dojo are contagious! The setting is highly conducive for experimentation, collaboration, and building meaningful learning partnerships. It is about building intellectual, creative, cultural, social, and emotional connections.

In a nutshell, it makes learning fast, focused, and fun!

- Dojo provides an atmosphere of rapid learning and an immediate focus on team areas. It establishes an immersive environment, where teams receive the support they need to grow and learn at an accelerated pace, including coaching, gamification, experimentation, and more.

- This enhances efficiencies, helps develop talent across broader skillsets, and enhances competencies while aligning with strategic business priorities.
- Dojo is effective in not only building conceptual skills in design, software engineering, technology, and production operations but also a cradle for cultural renewal, mindset shift, and behavioral change.
- Dojo provides an abundance of possibilities of accelerated learning, deep reflection, critical thinking, and synthesis of holistic concepts by direct sharing of experiences, successes, and failures.
- It establishes a fast feedback loop between learning and applying in context of work. It is an incubator to accelerate and deepen learning by experience, sharing, and hands-on experimentation.

How Is Dojo Set up?

A team expresses desire to learn a specific skillset or requests help to solve a critical problem impacting its progress. It fills a form and shares it with one of the coaches in Dojo.

This flows into the Dojo's backlog. A brief 15-minute alignment and consultation between scrum master, product owner, and coaches helps confirm the Dojo participation. Coaches sync-up and plan their capacity to support teams twice a day and confirm start dates for teams to get invited to Dojo.

Dojo is the starting point in running Shibumi sprints, especially when the team is newly formed or in the storming and forming stages of the team formation life cycle. Dojo helps to provide the ability to build muscle for teams to independently run subsequent Shibumi sprints.

Depending on the needs and current state of a team which comes to the Dojo, four lightweight steps, each lasting for one and quarter days, are followed for one-week Shibumi sprints launched in the Dojo:

- *Empathize*
- *Engage*
- *Enable*
- *Empower*

The Dojo : A dedicated place of Learning

Learning by Doing

Learning by Example

System mapping and Visualization

Empirical and Experiential setting

Experimentation and Test & Learn

Gamification and Group Reflection

Figure 14.2 The Dojo

Dojo is a dedicated place of learning and can be used by teams and coaches to work together. Coaches are basically helping the team learn better and understand in an empirical and experiential manner. It provides an opportunity for hands-on and practical learning.

The teams could spend anywhere between two hours and two weeks—an entire sprint to learn new capabilities or hone their existing skillsets to exponentially improve the performance. Coaches help the team learn and apply concepts better and faster.

For example, lets plan to have four types of coaches in Walkers' Dojo.

- Design coach help to better understand the mindset of Zen design and facilitate Shibumi sprint to design better experiences, products, and services.
- Business domain coach help teams better understand the business processes.
- Technology coach help improve their technological skills.
- Lean–agile or product coach help adopt relevant principles.

Sid, Keisha, the GOD, and two technology coaches from PMAG are identified for the first week as coaches for Walkers' Dojo. Coaches nurture teams to build products, experiences, and accelerate accomplishments of the team. Working closely with a coach, the team sets OKRs (Objective and Key Results).

A Day in the Life of Dojo

Performance measurement of agile teams

Teams learn from Zen mindfulness, experience design, front-end and back-end technologies, data sciences, analytics, lean thinking, agile ways of working, and DevSecOps tooling.

The teams learn fresh ways to resolve challenges and troubleshoot issues independently before waiting to get support from helpdesks and other teams. This could range from a specific business process (mis)step, an error in business logic, software bug, a production defect, an erroneous test case, or an architectural issue.

All the key stakeholders and leaders are invited to join and spend time in the Dojo with the teams and take up some coaching responsibilities for areas they are comfortable with. They are also encouraging to look for opportunities to engage teams and organize celebration whenever teams accomplish anything.

The next day

Lately, we have had lots of conversations on the ways we have been tracking the tasks to generate reports, calculate productivity, and compare velocities of teams. One of the first focus of the Dojo is to solve the confusion around measuring performance and velocity of agile teams.

"Could we still continue to compare the productivity and velocity of teams with a simple structure for our reports to Richie?" Saira asks looking inquisitively at Tim.

Week in Life of a Dojo – Practice areas

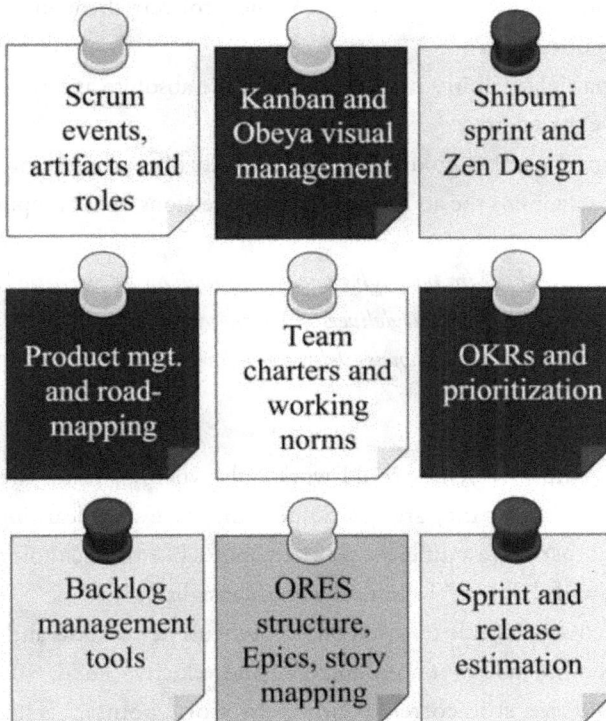

Figure 14.3 Life in Dojo

"The agile teams under PMO use relative estimation, meaning story points based on Fibonacci series, and we calculate velocities for each sprint. My team then correlates story points and days for reporting to Richie. We also show comparative performance of team's velocities." Tim explains his side of process.

"You see Richie had asked for measuring productivity and velocities to compare the performance of the teams." Tim insists on comparing performance of teams.

"Why do we need to compare productivity and velocities across teams?" I ask.

"I *think to fire the lesser performing teams.*" Seth jumps in with a smile on his face.

We all have a good laugh for a minute.

We've been using story points for our estimations. We have a table that provides with a number of days a particular story is going to need. You know the story points are based on the Fibonacci series. We first estimate the relative story points and then convert them into absolute estimates or days.

Keisha rightly points out "But you see the absolute and relative both cannot be mixed up.

Comparing teams' productivity and velocities offer diminishing returns."

Seth enlightens the audience with two questions he is grappling with:

- *What if the team has high velocity and high on a "synthetic" productivity score but delivers mediocre products?*
- *What if interdependencies delay work and reduce velocity? Is it team's fault?*

"Comparing velocities could work only when all teams are exactly the same. We know they are not. Some teams have steep learning curves. Team members have a different set of attributes like the technology, backgrounds, and skill sets." Keisha adds more insights.

"We could dissuade teams in trying out with newer ideas and spikes if there is too much focus on productivity and velocity." I add.

"Could we still correlate hours to story points?" Tim is still visibly confused.

"Absolute estimation is in terms of hours, days, or months and it is absolute number. While the relative estimation is a number relative to others items. The absolute and relative both cannot be mixed up as this doesn't make much sense." I explain.

Key Takeaways on the Performance Measurement

- There is no "best" measure for measuring the productivity of agile teams.
- Using productivity (and velocity) is not a fair "apple to apple" comparison because each team has:
  ○ Unique level of product and backlog complexities
  ○ Different level of experiences within the team
  ○ Varied business process complexity
  ○ Different technologies and architectural complexities

The teams should commit to aspirational OKRs, continue to have a well-articulated roadmap linked to OKRs and showcase progress during the sprint reviews, and regularly celebrate wins along with lessons learned.

Later in the night, I see two missed calls from Sid. My phone was on silent.

Table 14.2 Kanban board

To-do	In progress	Done
		• Dojo to disseminate knowledge and foster learning • Dojo acting as the cradle of the cultural change • Each team is unique, and productivity (or velocity) is not a fair "apple to apple" comparison
		The latest Building Block: v) Dojo for immersive and experiential learning

CHAPTER 15

Platform as a Strategy

The Roadmap to STRATEGIC Agility

Wednesday, March 25, 2020

Table 15.1 Kanban board

To-do	In progress	Done
• What is a digital platform? • Difference between products and platforms • The case for the platform • Value proposition for the participants • Key attributes of a digital platform • Strategic agility roadmap		

I wake up late in the morning, and I hear the beeping sound of Ami's alarm clock. On my way to the living room after a quick shower, I hear Ami groaning next door in her bedroom, she hated waking up early.

I have a worried start with the all the news of coronavirus across TV channels. Seemed like a D-day of sorts is fast approaching.

The girls join us downstairs shortly after and are surprised to find Cindy making their pie topped with caramelized fruits.

"Yay!" The girls jump excitedly.

"Good morning girls! Can you go get your dad?"

"We are eating pies for breakfast!" Tina yells. We smile seeing the joy on everyone's face.

We gather around the dining table and dig into our pies … there is lemon, apple, and peach. We barely exchange words, as we munch away and savor every bite. "Mmm those pies taste so delicious."

"Slow down sweetie."

Tina is eating fast so she could stake her claim on the last peach pie.

It reminds me of the pie analogy in our recent conversations with CEO. Charlie has been asking us to guard against our "fixed pie" mentality—implying we cannot afford to limit our ingenuities in just fighting competitors to get a measly share of the revenue pie. We must craft *newer revenue streams with platforms*!

He is truly visionary. With preliminary success of the *FLOW*, we have a lot of interest from our vendors and third parties. This becomes an ideal time for us to think in terms of a wider digital platform and establishing a marketplace. We decide that the platform businesses could have an integral role in Walkers' business value creation.

My apple pie is delectable but I eat fast when I notice an upcoming session "Platform as a strategy."

As I open the meeting a few minutes late, I hear Daisy "So, where's Sid?"

"Actually, I haven't heard from him in the last couple of days." I admit.

Tim interjects with his presentation on the shared screen. He knows that PMO is not going to remain a full-blown department, as he had made it out to be.

I have invited him to collaborate on the topic. He even volunteers to facilitate the session.

What Is a Digital Platform?

Platforms foster communities and interactions. Platforms are environments and ecosystems which aid building communities that, in turn, benefit from the interactions of their participants and co-create value though collaboration. They foster the consumer-to-consumer and business-to-consumer sales with better marketplace interactions and vibrant ecosystem.

Platforms allow easy user access to, rather than ownership of products, goods, and services. That is why they are also called sharing economy platforms, gig economy or collaborative consumption. Uber, Netflix, and LinkedIn are platforms.[*]

Businesses until a couple of decades ago used to be largely pipelines supplying goods and services leveraging manufacturing supply chains.

---

[*] Uber is a trademark of Uber Technologies, Inc., Netflix is of Netflix Inc., LinkedIn is of LinkedIn Corp.

But there are some examples of partial platforms from the brick-and-mortar world.

"You see, our nation's Freeways system is a type of platform." Tim proposes.

"And how so? Tim, is that not your next slide?" Daisy pulls his legs.

"Daisy, actually my example was moved by Neil to the appendix." He smiles.

Tim scrolls to relevant parts.

- You can *connect* to the freeways from multiple entrance freeways.
- The higher speeds permitted on freeways *pull* the driver to them.
- Design of lanes and its maintenance supports continuous *flow* of traffic.
- People use and *reuse* them on a regular basis over a lifetime.
- The businesses can utilize proximity to freeways to gain *economic* advantage.
- People *trust* freeways to be safe and secure despite higher speeds.

The platforms have similar six characteristics to become useful as a strategy. These include:

i. *Connectivity:* Ease of plugging into the platform to participate and interact seamlessly.

ii. *Pull:* An attractive proposition for multisided participants to join, for example, producers, consumers, end users, and relevant third parties.

iii. *Flow:* Conducive for uninterrupted flow of interactions and exchanges.

iv. *Reusability:* Designed to reuse processes, policies, and technological infrastructure.

v. *Economics:* Fertile to increase revenues through business, trade, and commerce.

vi. *Trust:* Dependability to gain trust of participants to fearlessly collaborate and innovate.

"Even stock exchanges could be viewed as examples of platform." Tim adds.

"Are platforms not the same as products?" Bobby looks puzzled.

"And that is my next slide." Tim flicks to next one.

Difference Between Products and Platforms

- Products and platforms are fundamentally different. For example, products could be essentially an application for a specific purpose to solve a specific problem.
- Platforms help us to move away from selling products to establishing ecosystems to solve problems.
- Platforms shift value from products and services to community interactions (and not just individual volumes).

"Incisive indeed. Someone has done lots of research," Daisy smiles.

The Case for the Platform

Walkers cannot own all value and asset creation.

Walkers cannot own all infrastructure across the value chain.

The company needs to foster open interactions and innovation.

- A platform serves as a common technology infrastructure and ecosystem with reusable technologies which can be used to connect multiple stakeholders like original equipment manufacturers, third-party suppliers, third-party providers, consumers, and users.
- Platforms could give us strategic agility in the long term. They provide us with access to multiple segments of customers, where we can connect with different sets of suppliers through an integrated and self-organizing marketplace.
- A platform is the core of an ecosystem, which enables the participants to meet and build connections, and a place where trade is conducted.
- It requires companies to *orchestrate* and *facilitate* the aspirations and behaviors of multiple parties.

"But how so? I am still on the edge. Platforms only work with a critical mass of participants? Right?" Bobby looks puzzled.

"That's right!" I affirm.

"So, where do we start? You know that we don't have any platform at this stage? We don't have any users?" Bobby further asks.

"We need to build trust. And we need to sell platforms to potential participants with a unique selling proposition."

"And what would that value be for participants?" Daisy asks.

Value Proposition for the Participants

- Platforms will provide them with long-term and constant growth opportunities without investing in infrastructure to serve many more customers than they do today.
- It will lift them up and they could decide what and how much you want to do with it. They can walk or run, or perhaps build another sub community.
- They can start new ventures, test, and learn their potential by making use of platforms.

"How do we control this so that our competitors don't benefit at our expense?" Bobby asks.

"Lightweight 'just enough rules', protocols, privacy policies, and some elementary but strict governance. We must not control, manage, or govern the platform. We could create mechanisms to orchestrate and balance its interactions to achieve mutual trust, collective value creation, and shared growth." Tim explains.

Key Attributes of a Digital Platform

(a) *Network:* The overall value proposition of a platform is directly proportional to the number of people who use it. There is a multiplicative effect of platforms when users, consumers, providers, and third-party suppliers connect with each other. It becomes one stop-shop for a number of interconnected needs.

(b) *Adaptability:* The platform provides flexibility by acting as a cradle for multiple unique possibilities, customers, market segments, and geographies. A product supports practically fixed business scenarios

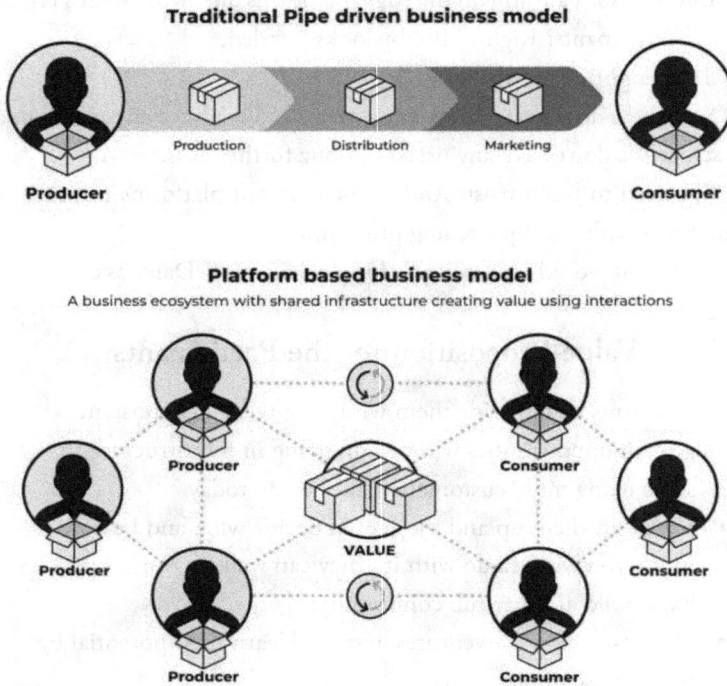

Figure 15.1 Platform

and use cases. The platform is open-ended from the beginning. Platforms provide a plethora of opportunities to different firms to try for their (often very different) scenarios, creating a much wider market segment.

(c) *Durability*: The products have a life cycle. They are used by consumers for specific durations and timeframes. The platforms become an integral part of the overall business ecosystem. The companies make considerable investment in building APIs, interfaces, and integrations with platforms. They also contribute toward widening the reach of the platforms. Platforms become connected to processes and are sticky.

This platform will provide more choices and better experiences for our customers without significantly impacting our revenues. This improves efficiency and experience for consumers in getting what they need without searching too much.

"This is fantastic. I am *so* excited with the insights and passion." Daisy exclaims.

"What are the immediate next steps for business launch?"

- *E-commerce ecosystem:* Create an integrated marketplace for the mutual benefit of customers (who get more product variety) and third-party vendors (who get increased sales revenue).
- *Phase 1 (0–4 months):* Provide free access and free delivery to local businesses to sell their products. In some cases, this obviously means that Walkers must subsidize products of local businesses who tend to have slightly higher pricing due to lower economies of scales than us.
  - *Complementary business model:* Customers buying certain products could be offered discounted and recurring monthly subscriptions for refills and supplies creating complementary business models with "one-click and hassle-free" products (e.g., printer and ink cartridges, vacuum cleaner and cleaning supplies, water purification systems, and replacement filters).
- *Phase 2 (5–10 months):* Assuming that our platform has built a network of at least a third of local businesses in a region, a commission could be charged to local businesses when selling products on the platform. During this phase, we could look at tie-ups with financial institutions to offer branded credit cards and other financial services to best-selling local providers, creating newer revenue models.
  - Connecting customers to vetted and certified local service providers and installers: for example, handymen, plumbers, and electricians in a few product categories where an installation, professional setup, and regular maintenance are required for home improvement products, furniture, and electrical or electronic products.
  - *Network of local mom-pop stores*: We could establish and use a network of stores and delivery and logistics providers to fulfill orders of those products for which we have lower inventory in certain geographical areas.

(w) **Platform as a strategy**
(x) **Strategic agility roadmap**

w) Leverage **Platform as a strategy** to develop novel ecosystems and interactions.

x) Implement **strategic agility roadmap.**

Figure 15.2 BB w and x

We have largely confined agility in the execution. It helped us get out of woods, and now, we are exploring to broaden agility into our strategic planning and direction. I open the last notes on the topic to refresh my memory. Keisha and a community of product owners have created a Strategic agility roadmap.

Strategic Agility Roadmap

- Consistently and frequently delivering value in the short term but keep everything on the table in the longer term.
- Revisit and reconfirm strategic priorities every quarter. For example, 30/60/90-day release plans or a reasonable number of sprints or iterations could be defined to enable the next immediate quarterly outcomes instead of too lengthy roadmaps.

Strategic agility roadmap primarily focuses on objectives and epics.

- *Objectives* remain constant for at least one quarter and up to four quarters.
  - *Results* are for one quarter and targets are redefined/reset every quarter.

- *Epics* are defined and completed for one or two quarters.
  - *Stories* underlying within Epics are defined usually for one to three sprints.

Shorter Term

- Establish a convergence of ideas, priorities, and solutions.
- Focus narrowly for implementation within a set of sprints and release to customers to use regularly (ideally within a quarter).
- Have higher clarity, confidence, and focus of what needs to be accomplished in shorter terms.

Medium to Longer Term

- Divergent thinking is to generate creative newer ideas in a spontaneous, free-flowing, nonlinear ways.
- Keep apertures wide-open with a variety of strategic alternatives and opportunities for the future.
- Develop the Abundance map to identify the ideas, opportunities, and prospects.
- Explore techniques like Ethnography to identify customer behaviors.

Ethnography is qualitative research that involves immersing in cultures, communities, or organizations to closely observe their behavior and interactions to better understand how they live their lives and how they behave.

By the time I have wrapped up all my calls, it's almost 7:15 p.m. The girls have just finished their homework, and I find them in the living room.

"Dad!" Ami and Tina scream as they run toward me, so happy to see me back in the living room earlier than they are used to.

Our evening is spent watching TV and eating burritos and nachos.

I've been working remotely from home for last few weeks. It was initially supposed to be for two weeks, but this might be our new norm for a while.

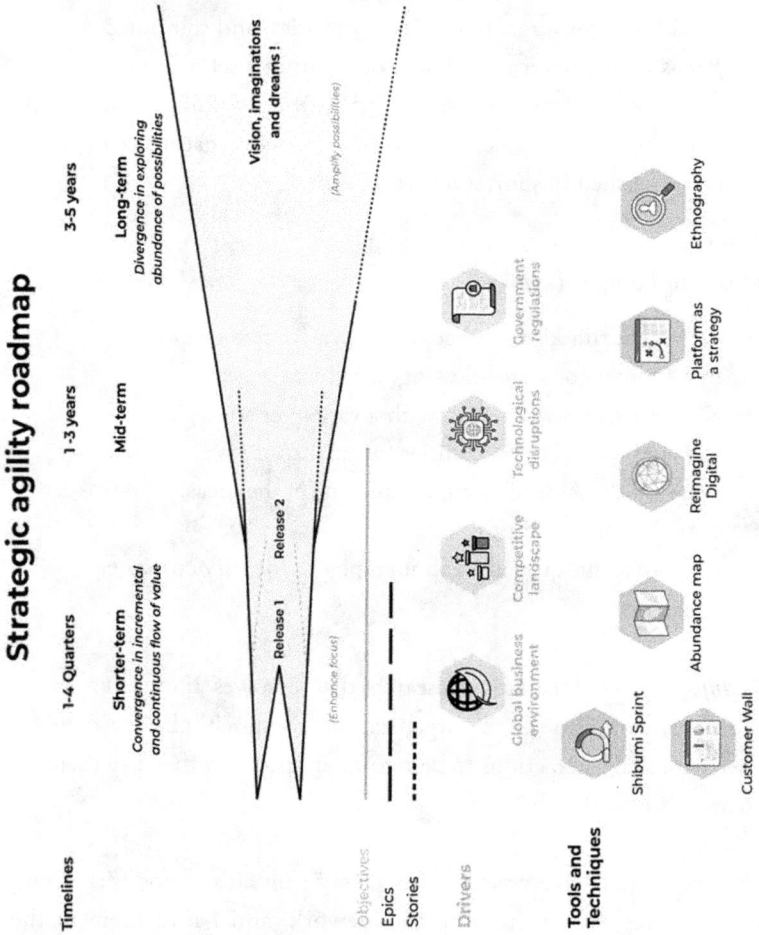

Strategic agility roadmap

Timelines	1-4 Quarters	1-3 years	3-5 years

Shorter-term
Convergence in incremental and continuous flow of value

Mid-term

Long-term
Divergence in exploring abundance of possibilities

Vision, imaginations and dreams !

(Enhance focus)

(Amplify possibilities)

Release 1

Release 2

Objectives
Epics
Stories

Drivers

Global business environment

Competitive landscape

Technological disruptions

Government regulations

Tools and Techniques

Shibumi Sprint

Customer Wall

Abundance map

Reimagine Digital

Platform as a strategy

Ethnography

Figure 15.3 Strategic agility roadmap

Ninety-two percent employees are in favor of hybrid model as compared to pre-COVID-19 model.

The board wants more clarity on what exactly this change means.

Charlie has asked Richie and I to prepare our response to the unescapable question:

What will be the future of work in this new reality?

Table 15.2 Kanban board

To-do	In progress	Done
	• Future of work: the hybrid model	• Platforms help build ecosystems • Products are applications for a specific purpose, while platforms are for community interactions • Key attributes of a platform: network, adaptability, durability • Strategic agility roadmap and platforms as a strategy improve the agility in longer term
		The latest Building Blocks: w) Platform as a strategy x) Strategic agility roadmap

CHAPTER 16

HOME–Agility

Hybrid Operating Model for Enterprise–Agility

Saturday, April 4, 2020

I cannot just continue working from my dining table or kitchen island, so I am setting up my home office in the basement.

… grrriiizzz … rat-a-tat … strange loud sound !!!

Early in the morning on Saturday, I am vacuuming the basement to set up my remote workstation. "Dad, keep it down. It's too loud!" Ami screams from upstairs.

Our basement is seldom used; it's dusty, dull, and dark. I am cleaning hard, dusting, sanitizing, and brushing surfaces to make it ready. I choose to change the lighting to LED daylight bulbs, and I set up my desk. It gets bright and lively.

But something is lacking?

I have got so used to the visual aid blocks, stickies, and charts in my office. *How will I manage to be productive and creative here?* I need my own Obeya, a big room information radiator and visual management.

I pick up my phone to see if Sid called me back. I had missed his call last night and tried calling back but got no response.

Sid has been coaching our teams in the last few days on ways to set up an Obeya in a hybrid mode and avoid too much churn in reporting and document searching. Seth and Keisha have compiled lessons learned from our Asia-Pacific, Europe, and U.S. colleagues. Some have been working in hybrid for 10 weeks. I wrap my head around the hybrid model in my to-do list.

A hybrid model is to sustain and grow enterprise agility with a balanced and well-oiled combination of remote and in-person teams working in synergy. It's not just work from home ... but a hybrid model will be the future of work.

Future of Work: The Hybrid Model

Table 16.1 The elements of HOME–Agility

1. Practices	Technology	
	2. Internal collaboration	3. Customer collaboration
• Obeya, a collaborative visual space • Team norms • Hybrid cadence	• Hybrid Floor • Telepresence robots • Digital Org-wide Obeya Room (DOOR)	• Digital Customer Wall • Visual Customer Support
4. Workspace	5. Organization policies	6. People
• Redesigned workspace to inspire creativity and innovation	• Location and remote work • Business travel • Digital devices stipend • Dress code • Talent acquisition	• Perks and benefits • Work–life balance • Ecofriendly ways of working

I scan the playbook on Obeya from last week. I feel guilty that I haven't even opened it until now. I also rearrange our older 40-inch smart TV set and the abandoned turntable on the mahogany wooden shelf in the corner of my basement. I clean the dust and turn on the TV to test it.

It's now 10:15 a.m. and both Tina and Ami are awake. They run down to me, eager to see my new workstation.

"Dad, you can't work on a weekend! Can we all play tag?" Ami protests.

My children remind me that I have been so excited and engaged in my work lately, to a point where I'm working over the weekend.

Practices

Obeya: A collaborative visual management space

In Japanese, Obeya means "big room" or a "war room," where you can get a clear understanding of the team's purpose, roadmap, definition of success, sprint cadence, and the amazing people who build it.

An Obeya can be imagined as a *dedicated physical or a digital room* with a slew of intuitive tools. It helps to create a central place, a team room to share progress, discuss key problems or impediments, and conduct problem-solving exercises. It reduces the barriers that could prevent teams to interact and helps to raise concerns candidly in the psychological safety of the room and collectively make fast decisions.

An Obeya provides a safe and open environment for interactive and creative dialog, and it helps teams, colleagues, and stakeholders to stay present, *here and now*, while retaining an abundance mindset for future possibilities.

We could schedule daily stand-ups, sprint planning, and sprint review/demos, and we could utilize an Obeya for impromptu progress sharing with leadership.

A well-maintained Obeya will enable to easily avoid the habit of sending lengthy, scripted, and formatted status reports. Instead, we invite all the concerned to the Obeya. This helps them to learn through compelling visual aids, asking questions in real time, respectfully challenging the approach, and providing guidance, suggestions, and newer ideas to the team.

As I navigate my way through the intranet after placing my order, I find guidance for setting up the Obeya for remote work from home.

I turn on my laptop to create an order for supplies from the company's own IT store.

"Post-it dry erase whiteboard film, sharpies, boards, easels, and two monitors. For expenses exceeding $500, there is a mandatory expense justification field." I read the guideline out loud as I scan the checkout options. I enter the detailed descriptions to justify the business case for my expenses in building a Obeya before scrolling down further.

Benefits of Obeya

- *Here and now:* helps concentrate effectively and focus on the most important problems to solve and right things to do.
- *Engagement, collaboration, and creativity:* fosters an environment for engaging conversations and teamwork.
- *Faster decision making:* enables fast problem-solving and decision making by synthesizing required information,

visual management aids, and other important team resources together in one place.

- *Elimination of lengthy reports*: eliminates hours of traditional status reporting.
- *Productivity improvement:* exponentially enhances productivity, reduces costs of delays, increases efficiency, and drastically streamlines communication.

Reduce status reporting and improve collaboration with a visual management space, an *Obeya*. I open the image from the Obeya, the first one which Seth has set up in one of his teams and shared that day. The Obeya has actually eliminated hours of effort per sprint for traditional reporting that normally requires 24 people's effort. An Obeya is a welcoming place with open doors for all to come—especially all relevant colleagues and stakeholders.

OBEYA - The Visual Room

Figure 16.1 Obeya

Elements of an Obeya

Establish big visual information radiators in physical or electronic forms, A3 Thinking, problem solving, and collaborative tools.

- ○ Big visual chart.
- ○ Information radiator.
- ○ Charts, images, maps, graphs, and drawings.

- *Roadmap and epics*: Displaying the roadmap and epics helps bring clarity, focus, relevance, and objective linkage between strategy and execution.
- *Customer Wall*: Creating a Customer Wall helps us to transparently visualize customer testimonials, feedbacks, complaints, and key challenges, where we can continuously listen to the voice of customers.
- *Kanban boards*: Using a visual management with a Kanban board including key tasks with owners, along with a board for blockers and risks, could be useful in most situations.
- *Alignment timeline*: Updating an Obeya in alignment with sprint cadence like a two-week rhythm will keep visuals up-to-date and improve a team's accountability.
- *Showcase*: The team defines "open house" hours to demo Obeya to anyone in the company. The physical "Walk-in-Walkers" timeslot is also open for anyone two hours twice a week Tuesdays and Fridays.

Table 16.2 Artifacts of an Obeya

Customer artifacts	Team artifacts	Design artifacts
• Voices and vibes of customers • Customer Wall • Quotes and/or complaints	• Objectives and key results • Team norms • Roadmap and epics of where we are • Team blockers • Upcoming 1–2 sprints • Risks and interdependencies	• Empathy maps • Design alternatives • ARTISTS Zen design • Personas • Customer journey maps

Team Norms

Internal gigging required locational and departmental restrictions. The guardrail is established by HR that people do not need to be in the office every day of the week and every week of the year. Every team could decide to work hybrid ranging from three days per week to three days per month in-person at office.

Teams establish specific days for meetings and collaboration and other days for remote work.

Democracy prevails! The team votes on the days and session which they meet in person. The work hours become more flexible, predictable, and planned. Life–work balance is improved significantly due to less time on road for long-distance commute.

- Every team to work hybrid ranging from two days per week in-person at office.
- Every team gets up to two fully remote weeks every quarter.
- Team votes on a three-hour slot when everyone is expected to be available in virtual office: 10:30 to 11:30 a.m.|3:00 to 5:00 p.m.
- No camera timeslots.
  - Monday to Thursday: before 9:30 a.m. and after 6 p.m.
  - Friday: after 2 p.m.
- Mindful and stretching exercises three times a week for 10 minutes.

Hybrid Cadence

Table 16.3 The cadence of a hybrid team

Event	In person	Remote
Shibumi sprints	Highly recommended	
Dojo days	Highly recommended	
Kickoff and Obeya set up	Highly recommended	
Objectives and Key Results workshop		Recommended
Stand-up and team huddles		Highly recommended
Backlog refinement		Highly recommended
Sprint planning		Recommended
Sprint review	Recommended	
Retrospective	Recommended	
Operations, support, and heads-down task		Highly recommended
Monthly team lunch—learn and town halls	Highly recommended	
1:1 meetings		Highly recommended

Technology: Internal Collaboration

Bridging the digital divide! The company has embraced multiple communication and collaboration systems.

Hybrid Floor is established for unified digital workspace of remote and in-person in one view. This provides a uniform and homogeneous digital work-space of remote and in-person in a single visual platform. Anyone can login to this digital workspace and visualize the team members, teams, and even search anyone else in the entire company. They can ping and connect anyone available regardless of where the person is working, for example, home, in-person at office, or heads-down on a beach.

Almost everyone across the entire organization is "seen and reached" by connecting on exactly one single virtual floor exponentially increases the communication and collaboration. As long as someone is online, they can be seen on the virtual floor. There are lesser obstructions in communication leading to better interactions and free flow of ideas. Ability to see everyone across the entire company on exactly the same virtual floor tremendously enriches interactions and conversations. There are lesser barriers in free exchange of ideas with a horizontal structure which is not bolstered with the Hybrid Floor. The new unified Walkers could be drastically more equitable workplace.

There are no remote-in-person divides, no corporate-regional divides, and no corner office-desk divide. Everyone, including executives, are in Hybrid Floor and work in redesigned layout even when working out of office.

Telepresence robots enable an instant presence wherever someone wants to do a virtual walk on the physical floor. The company procures over 60 robots. People can attend meetings by steering the robots from their computers to actually walk inside the building floors and hallways. They can enter physically into the meeting rooms by steering the robot safely with a remote presence. It becomes popular with remote teams and helps alleviate the lack of physical hallway conversations.

The digital and IT groups have already prototyped a smart enterprise-wide Obeya for location independence in our Digital Org-wide Obeya Room. It is called the *Walkers Situation Room.* It is one of our first company wide collaborative efforts between digital teams connecting their Obeya and Innovation Hub building the back end with the now fully functional *FLOW system.* All of the displays could be accessed remotely from anywhere.

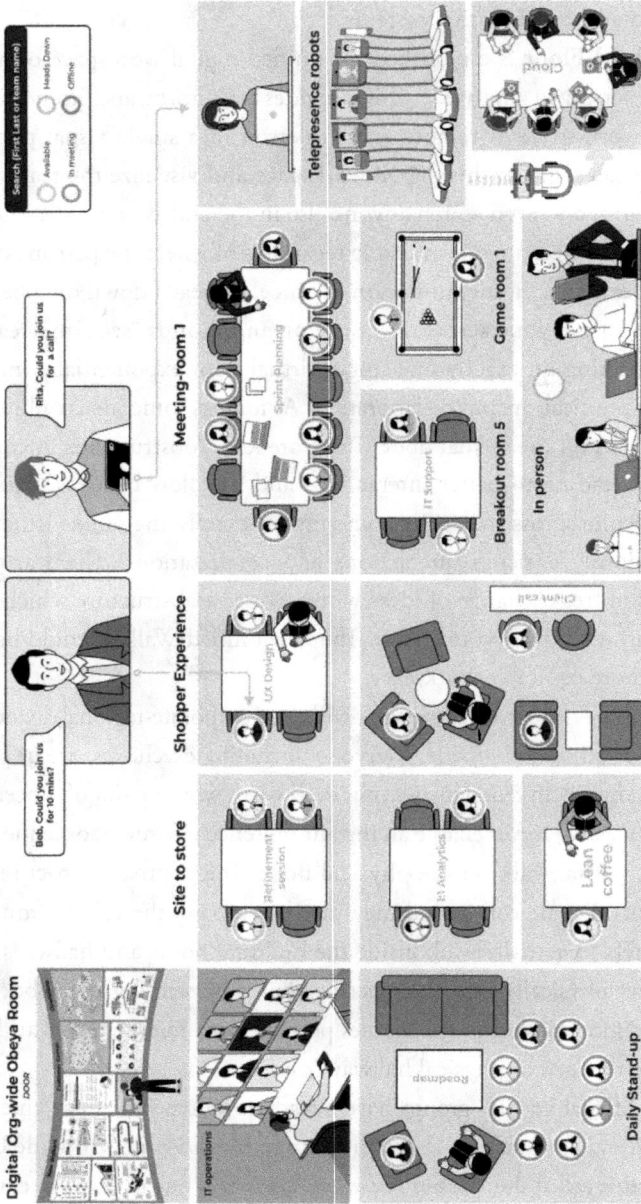

Figure 16.2 Hybrid Floor

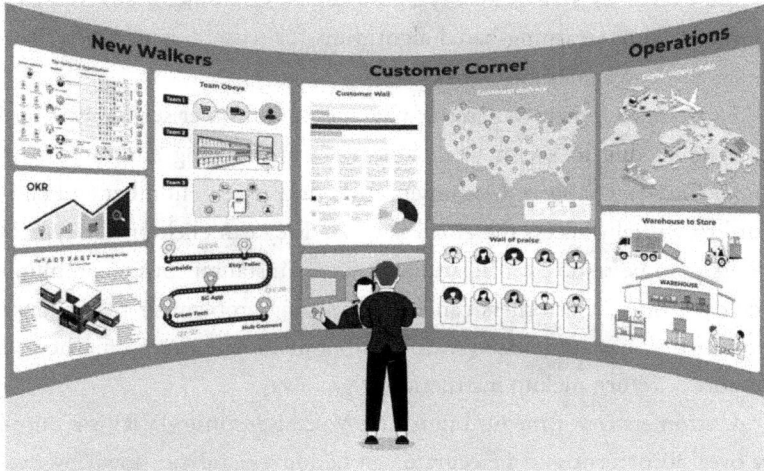

Figure 16.3 DOOR

(y) **Collaborative and visual workspace with Obeya**
(z) **Visual Customer Support**

y) Establish **collaborative and visual workspaces with Obeya**.

z) **Visual Customer Support** to enhance customer experience and reduce efforts.

Figure 16.4 BB y and z

Technology: *Customer Collaboration*

Digital Customer Wall: A near real-time digital Customer Wall leveraging AI and machine learning-based algorithms for pattern recognition, synthesis, and consolidation.

Customer support gets visual: Changes in customer service desk and store hours due to stay-at-home restrictions are being addressed with *Visual Customer Support*. Customers enter their loyalty number and password to virtually access the *visual support*. They can click on the type of the issue to be resolved. The available agents instantaneously communicate over video. Customers can verbalize their problem or may show a product they have purchased with their phone camera to return. They get support or return pickup instructions right away.

Customers wait time on Interactive Voice Response (IVR) is reduced by over 30 percent and inaccurate call handovers are cut down by over 50 percent.

I read two customer reviews on the Customer Wall already set up by Seth.

"The GPS-based curbside pick-up … is GOAT!"

"App looks better. They folks are getting their sh** together."

Visual Customer Support

Customer see available agents and connect over video call for real-time resolution

Figure 16.5 Visual Customer Support

Workspace

Daisy has been one of the leaders who had reservations about the hybrid work. I call her and ask about her understanding of a workplace,

"What is an office?"

"It's a place to sit, work, and get better connectivity." She says with a hint of smug.

"But we all have that in our homes too, right?" I push her thinking with my explanation and craft an argument.

"Generally, offices are seen in terms of objects precisely the way you said, or the *CDC, the chair, desk, and compute*r. It is essential to debunk the myth that offices are merely a bunch of physical objects. The impression of office should need not be limited to materials or things. Those things are in our homes too.

We must use this opportunity to reinvent workspaces and shift the meaning of *CDC* in offices, from chair, desk, and computer to *Collaboration, Design thinking and Creativity*. We must rediscover offices and transform them as a physical space providing a set of objects to a vibrant and inspiring environment to accomplish our objectives.

We must rediscover the very idea of office: *from objects to objectives.*

Due to more flexibility and variety in choosing the place to work from, the office cannot be boring or monotonous as it used to be. Office gatherings must be fun, exciting, and animated. *Thanks to new workspace designs.* Everyone would want to be in office at the least for designated days. The workspace and offices are much more than objects. There is much more natural collaboration, inspiration, and innovation when teams are co-located. It is about creating those *Shibumi moments.*"

Daisy is now more open to looking at the prototypes and experimenting with them.

Organizational Policies

A number of corporate policies are being adapted to support the hybrid model.

Redesigned Workspace
Collaboration, Design thinking, and Creativity

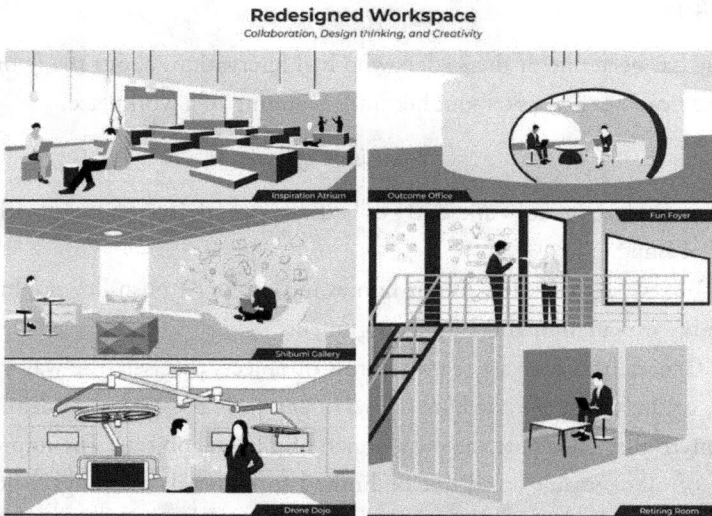

Figure 16.6 Redesigned workspace

Hoteling concept is to aid team members to dynamically schedule their use of workspaces such as offices, desks, and closed cubicles.

The smaller office hubs were created so that colleagues don't have to travel all the way to the city center office. They could collocate to a nearby and easily accessible suburbs mini hubs to attend the office two or three days a week with an option to work from anywhere for two months once every year. Both domestic and international business travels are supported only for customer meetings.

Digital connectivity policy and additional device for remote work is published and dress code policy now strongly recommends smart casuals and fun Friday dressing.

Talent escalator accelerates the flow of capabilities. Location is no longer important for hiring new talent. The requirement for candidates to be physically present during hiring is a thing of past. The continuous pipeline of candidates generated with talent escalator are hired within two weeks as full-time or free agents. It enables more in person and face-to-face time for those who require coaching, mentoring, and apprenticeship.

People

Perks and benefits: Reduced facilities budget and office space meant more savings. The savings are being passed on to employees in form of meal vouchers, reimbursement for health-fitness subscriptions, and home connectivity-related expenses.

Co-location is not physical but mental: Adoption of agile has far too long stressed heavily on physical colocation. However, people can be in the same office, same floor, and even sitting in close proximity, but it may not translate into collaboration. Especially, when there is lack of genuine motivation and purpose, colocation does not mean meaningful cooperation. People tend to collaborate better when they get flexibility and leeway. They feel empowered, excited, and engaged making them better team players.

Asynchronous and continuous communication: Asynchronous communication is when message is sent and the recipient processes the information and responds immediately. For example, chat messages could need immediate response. In contrast, the asynchronous communication is when message is sent without expecting an immediate response like an e-mail which can be responded hours later.

More asynchronous communication enables team members to work within multiple time zones, so they have more predictability in their workflow. Thoughtful and planned conversations reduce surprises and stress and improve time-zone equality. Reduce commute is environmentally friendly and with 30 percent less carbon footprint.

Scrum masters and product owners could work with smaller cohorts of developers, testers when feasible and productive instead of the entire team. The smaller subgroups or clusters within agile teams help team members, who are working on similar set of tasks, to interact more often.

More collaboration by flattening the curve: The company's culture had revolved round climbing the ladder. Higher the floor of ones' office, more the influence. The C-suites had corner offices in topmost sixth floor. The communication did not flow as company had long remained siloed because of multiple tiers of separation, for example, office, floor, location, function, time zone, and ways of working (agile or nonagile).

What Will Change With Hybrid Model?

Table 16.4 Before and after in the hybrid model

Category	*From* Normal operating model before the pandemic	*To* Hybrid Operating Model for Enterprise *Agility*
Workspace	*Objects* Office is construed in terms of CDC, Chair, Desk and Computer	*Objectives* CDC now symbolizes Collaboration, Design thinking, and Creativity
	Fixed Desk, office is assigned to everyone	*Flexible* spaces to get inspired and co-create
	Physical presence in office in working hours	*Predictability* for quicker and consistent availability
People	*Costly* driving, commute, and child care	*Cost-effective* combination of remote and in-person
	Guilt or fear of missing out when remote	*Guidance* and guardrails from HR policies
	Commute increasing the carbon footprint	*Carbon neutrality* becomes possible with remote days
	Chitchats sometimes even cause distractions	*Communication* is both continuous and asynchronous
	Work takes priority over life events	*Work–life balance* by reducing travel time and commute
Technology	*Communication gaps* due to location and building silos	*Collaboration* as teams are connected and reachable on the Hybrid Floor
	Hallway conversations are erratic, random, and by chance	*Hallway robots* spark frequent serendipitous chats
Organization practices	*Location* of work is firm and nonnegotiable	*Leeway* to work from anywhere for a period
	Travel across cities vital for key meetings	*Technology* preferred for out-of-town meetings
	Employees hired with 3–6 months long process	*Escalator* for continuous flow of talent

Category	From Normal operating model before the pandemic	To Hybrid Operating Model for Enterprise *Agility*
Culture	*Headquarter* is the power center of the company	*Homes and hubs* aid in decentralization
	Higher floor offices imply influence and clout	*Hybrid Floor* epitomizes a horizontal organization
	Visibility in office is performance parameter	*Value* and outcomes are what really matters!
	Suits or pantsuits characterize executives, managers	*Smart casuals* aid equitable and inclusive culture
Customer	*Customer complaints* due to queue and long support time	*Customer support* gets visual, self-guided, and faster

What Are the Expected Benefits of Hybrid?

Table 16.5 Benefits of hybrid model

Category	Expected benefits
Workspace	↓ 30% real estate costs over a period of 5 years ↓ 45% travel, administrative, utilities, and facilities costs
People	↓ 65% commute and other non-value-adding driving time ↑ $125 monthly stipends for devices and connectivity ↑ 350% faster crowd sourcing talents for gigs ↑ $100 monthly meal voucher ↓ 30% auto insurance premium ↑ 30% improvement in people satisfaction scores
Organization	↓ Sick leave 20% (less commute-related fatigue, flu, common cold, and other transmissible infections) ↓ 25% costs from attrition and turnover ↓ 35% carbon footprint of the company
Customer	↑ 20% Time-to-Market due to improved collaboration ↑ 35% first time right resolution of customer tickets ↓ 25% customer wait time in support tickets

Table 16.6 Kanban board

To-do	In progress	Done
		• Hybrid model for a blend of in-person and remote work • Hybrid Floor, digital Obeya, and telepresence robots to create a unified digital workspace • Team norms and official polices adjusted for hybrid model • Redesigned office spaces become fun, creative, and inspiring
		The latest Building Blocks: y) Collaborative and visual workspace with Obeya z) Visual Customer Support

CHAPTER 17

The *ACT FAST* Building

Codifying the Company's Experiments

Sunday, August 2, 2020
Four months later

I look at Cindy, who is wearing a denim jumpsuit and a floral kimono. She is still reading her book on mindfulness, while nibbling on our fruit salad.

The few months have been particularly harsh with a raging pandemic and ever since Cindy was diagnosed with cancer. She still is not completely out of the woods, but steadily making progress and recovering gradually.

We spend most of the weekend afternoon at the park, enjoying each other's company after what feels like years. The girls are riding their bikes not too far from us on the lawn.

There is a cool breeze in the air, as the sun sets. I take a second to absorb the moment, looking out at the view of the park.

Nature never looked this beautiful, I think with a smile on my face.

I feel content to be out together with the family and reflect on how so much has changed since we visited this park six months back.

Walkers is now upbeat and is looking forward to a very busy future. We have a jump in customer traffic of over 500 percent and 92 percent of this figure can be attributed to online shoppers. Premium customers have grown to 3.7 million, representing a 400 percent growth in one and a half quarters.

Our last quarter results have been promising as our Q2 earnings have soared by 28 percent. Our online sales have skyrocketed by almost 280 percent. The decision to close stores in January was rescinded by the Board in Q2.

All layoffs have been suspended for now. In fact, some who lost jobs recently have been recalled as contractors. We are making progress to have over 600 new hires. There is more hiring and upskilling in our warehouses with more drivers and operators.

The " A C T F A S T " Building Blocks

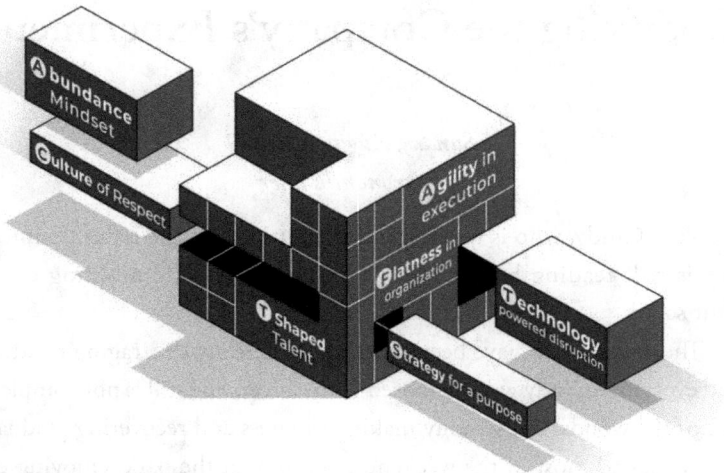

Figure 17.1 **ACT FAST-1**

Our office building's seven sections are renamed to one of the letters in "ACT FAST." FA@ST is gone, and *ACT FAST* is used to systemically embrace the inner Building Blocks.

Our approach is winning compliments both within and outside the company. We have organized virtual tours for others to learn from our Dojos and Obeyas. Nearly a hundred other company executives and practitioners have registered to visit our Dojos.

The *American Digital Business Review* journal is working on a two-series article about Walkers in its upcoming issue for September and October. It is partially also due to the Board's smart outreach and shrewd attempt to quickly regain status as an attractive destination for investors.

I draft the article describing our experiments of last few months.

Sprint 1: Current State Assessment

We leverage a comprehensive approach to define problems. This includes building a *WALL, Walkers Agile Lean Lessons Learned,* and enabling an inclusive enterprise-wide retrospective to make the problems transparent for all. Anyone could add items to the WALL, even anonymously. It helps to identify problems and challenges by creating a psychologically safe environment—one of the key foundational pillars for a true change.

The command-and-control management style diminishes honest conversations on areas of strategic importance like the purpose of transformation. On the other hand, the Net Promoter Score (NPS) offer a valuable insight into the customer perceptions and revamping product development.

The obligation to WAR (Waste Avoidance and Removal) affirms the relentless focus on value. A commitment toward WAR aids in eliminating non-value-adding activities. The eight lean wastes *TIM WOODS* raises the barriers to embrace agility. This includes efforts spent on internal reporting and unwarranted documentation.

In the agile ways of working unlike the traditional approach, the cost and time is fixed and scope of requirements is allowed to vary centered around the prioritization. Companies continue with traditional budgeting, funding, and estimation practices delaying the start of critical initiatives. The value of unused, mismanaged, and underutilized funding for customers is zero.

The Gemba Walk led value stream diagnostics galvanizes to challenge status quo and identify opportunities for cross-pollination, reuse, and innovation across teams. The servant leaders conduct Gemba Walks to observe value creation, struggles, and impediments. The Gemba Walks pinpoint wastes across the value stream across four categories: (a) processes and practices, (b) organizational and team structures, (c) tools and technologies, and (d) people and roles. The value stream mapping and survey quantified the waste in the company of over 30 percent and estimated Cost of Wastes (CoW) to be up to $0.25 billion.

Sprint 2: Reflection and Reimagination

We reimagined *organization as a living organism and imbibed system thinking to rebuild the enterprise.* Organizations are made of people, and it must be treated as a living entity and not as a machine. Living creatures must adapt as the environment changes in order to survive.

Just like cells, the basic Building Blocks define our bodies' ability to fight viruses, we define the inner Building Blocks of our organization to strengthen agility to adapt and combat external threats quickly and efficiently. Our approach is to generate solutions to identified problems centers around a number of experiments to define and test hypotheses.

The Writing on the WALL = Problem
Building Block = Solution

Clarity of purpose with objectives and key results helps companies to measure outcomes and make regular course corrections in their transformation journeys. A combination of top-down, document-driven, and overly long-term planning reduces adaptability in strategic interventions.

The pandemic is tragic for the entire world but has made us avantgarde in revamping digital strategy and growing the degree of agility. A new definition to reimagine digital embodies a totally unique way of looking at everything and reimagining digital disruption for everything around us! It needs to be inclusive (for everyone, by everyone, and from everywhere), cost-effective, scalable, and greener. It needs to adaptable to our behaviors (and not the other way around!). That includes democratization of technology, Internet of behavior, green technology, intelligent automation, total experience, Anything as a Service (XaaS), and location independence.

The Inner Agility is about the power of pause and mindfulness. Zen principles help nurture Inner Agility including *Here and Now* existing in the present moment; *Beginners' minds* with full of possibilities; *Experiential learning* from experiences; and *Continuous flow* to establish an unbroken rhythm in processes, practices, structures, and technologies. The learning becomes impactful by continuous hands-on experiences and regular reflection by stepping back to look at the larger picture. Practicing mindfulness helps to open the mind to newer possibilities.

The Shibumi sprint is an advanced Design (re)Thinking cadence with seven *Zen design* principles of ARTISTS, user personas, and customer journey mapping. A *Shibumi is a moment when one has natural, elegant, effortless, and authentic experiences.* It fosters customer centricity, best-in-class experiences, and products. The quality of Shibumi evolves out of a process of complexity, though none of this complexity is manifested in final product.

Sprint 3: Analysis and Improvements

Agile framework turns fragile when the focus is just to emulate scaling frameworks. A formulaic and prescriptive agile by following a scaling framework leads to artificial standardization efforts without rationale. Adhering to a "fixed and static" scaling framework cannot make an organization agile and nimble. The teams need to move away from dogmatic focus on terminologies to real outcomes. The uncontrolled spread of forms, templates, policies, procedures, and documentation and siloed departments adversely impact agility.

There are multiple shortcomings in a hierarchical organization including heavy bureaucracy, rift between functional departments, funding-related complications, and longer Time-to-Market. The organizations are organized vertically, while the value flows horizontally. Undue centralization and bureaucracy slow down communications. The decision making is slow due to review and approval required across the multiple layers.

CLAP, Common-minimum Lean Agile Practices, adopts elementary values, principles, and mindset in both agile and nonagile teams. Lightweight rules of engagement are essential for robust collaboration with agile teams with GRC and other functions.

Flattening the curve means shifting from vertical to horizontal organization. This fundamental shift is vital in realizing a nimble, leaner, and flatter structure. The guiding principles to establish end-to-end teams must focus on shared purpose, reduced interdependencies, and Flow-to-work structure, to ultimately reduce distance from the customer.

The self-organizing team, DOZen, comprises 12 members. They are primarily engaged in Development and Operations, and are grounded in *Zen values.* A Chapter is a community of expert professionals with quarterly rotating responsibilities for chapter leads, for example, product owners, developers, scrum masters, and designers. Chapters have deep skillsets in certain areas, but still a T-shaped skillset is encouraged. Each Chapter has ideally 12 team members and in some cases up to 15 team members.

The servant leadership style of executives is recommended, but when it is adopted without a clear purpose, it dilutes the accountability. Leaders have a critical role in cultural renewal and mindset shift. Challenging the status quo including processes and practices is vital for a vibrant culture. As an example, the RACI matrix confines people to their rows or columns and deters the collective ownership of outcomes. A conventional and unyielding culture, wasteful meetings, and disengaged workforce proliferate intellect waste and deter innovation.

It is essential to strike a right balance between the leadership accountability and empowerment for teams by nurturing a *culture of RESPECT* centered around Recognition, Empathy, Self-organization, Psychological safety, Empowerment, Customer centricity, and Transparency.

Talent Escalator helps to establish a continuous flow of capabilities. This model helps in constantly hiring contractors, leveraging our continuous talent escalator model. The model helps to shortlist, screen, and offer talented people temporary contracts immediately or hire them full time if company needs aligns. Escalator model based on hiring gig workers and freelance experts is momentous in making talent availability fast, smooth, and predictable. A nonstop flow of T-shaped and digitally fluent talent pool becomes a reality.

Sprint 4: Rebuilding and Recovery

Dojo is a place for experiential and immersive learning. Dojo is about lifelong learning with pragmatic mindsets which impart hands-on understanding of concepts and foster cultural renewal. This enhances efficiencies and helps develop talent across broader skillsets and competencies to inculcate an atmosphere of rapid learning and experimentation. Dojo is effective not just in building capabilities in design, software engineering, technology, and operations but also is a cradle for cultural renewal and mindset shift. Dojo includes technical skill development, applied lean–agile trainings, Design *re*Thinking with Shibumi, and softer aspects of cultural resurgence.

Smooth flow of value with an integrative structure

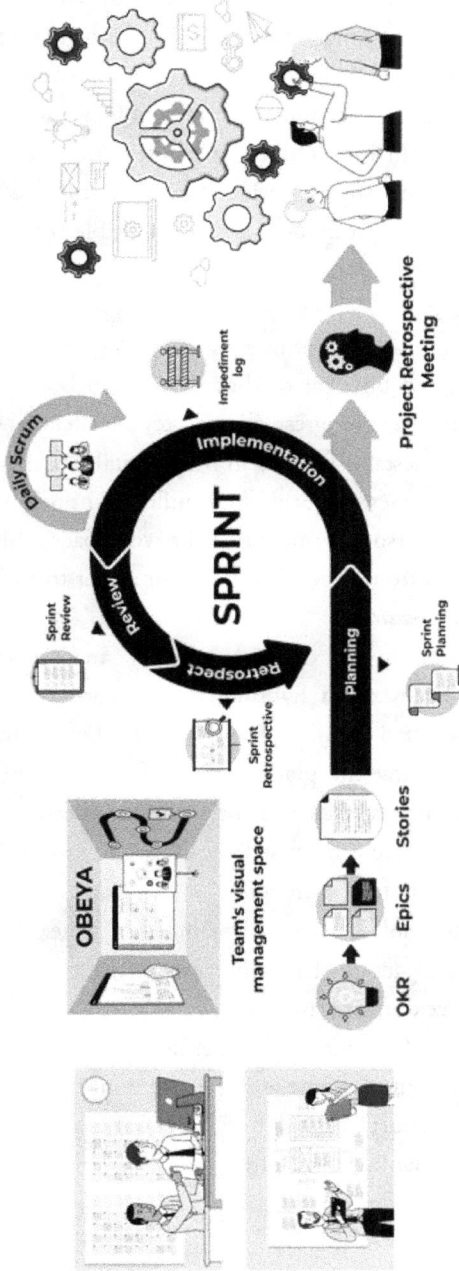

Dojo
Coaching

OBEYA
Team's visual management space

OKR   Epics   Stories

SPRINT
Implementation
Daily Scrum
Impediment log
Review
Sprint Review
Retrospect
Sprint Retrospective
Planning
Sprint Planning

Project Retrospective Meeting

DOZen
Dev and Ops

KAIZEN
Continuous Improvement

Figure 17.2 Integrative view

Platform as a strategy is adopted for strategic agility. The strategic agility is about tactfully delivering value in the short term while keeping options open in the longer term. Strategic priorities need to be revisited and reconfirmed every quarter. In shorter term, this establishes a convergence of ideas, priorities, and solutions and focusing on execution within a set of sprints. In longer term, it helps to explore a variety of strategic alternatives and opportunities. Platforms promote strategic agility in the longer term. It promotes access to multiple segments of customers, through an integrated marketplace.

HOME–Agility, Hybrid Operating Model for Enterprise–Agility, establishes an optimum blend of in-person and remote work. An Obeya provides a dedicated physical or digital room to boost collaboration and helps teams to share progress, discuss key blockers, and solve problems. Hybrid Floor is established for unified digital workspace of remote and in-person in one view. Hybrid Floor builds a unified digital workspace of remote and in-person in one view. The workspaces shift the meaning of *CDC* in offices, from chair, desk, and computer to *Collaboration, Design Thinking and Creativity.*

Team norms, hybrid cadence, hoteling, and asynchronous communication model establish hybrid ways of working. The organizational policies are adjusted to advance hybrid work. Due to more flexibility and variety in choosing the place to work from, the office is not boring and monotonous as it used to be. Office gatherings are fun, exciting, and animated. There is more self-organization, innovation, and creativity creating more Shibumi moments.

Due to the holiday season starting in the next coming weeks, the company has suggested that senior executives spend at least one day in office every week on a rotational basis.

Corporate HQ is now called the home office, and regional staff are more than welcome to come and they are no longer looked down upon.

As I make a short trip back to the office after months, I notice a brown envelope with thank you card from Sid.

The cumulative effect of Solutions is vital to solve the Problems

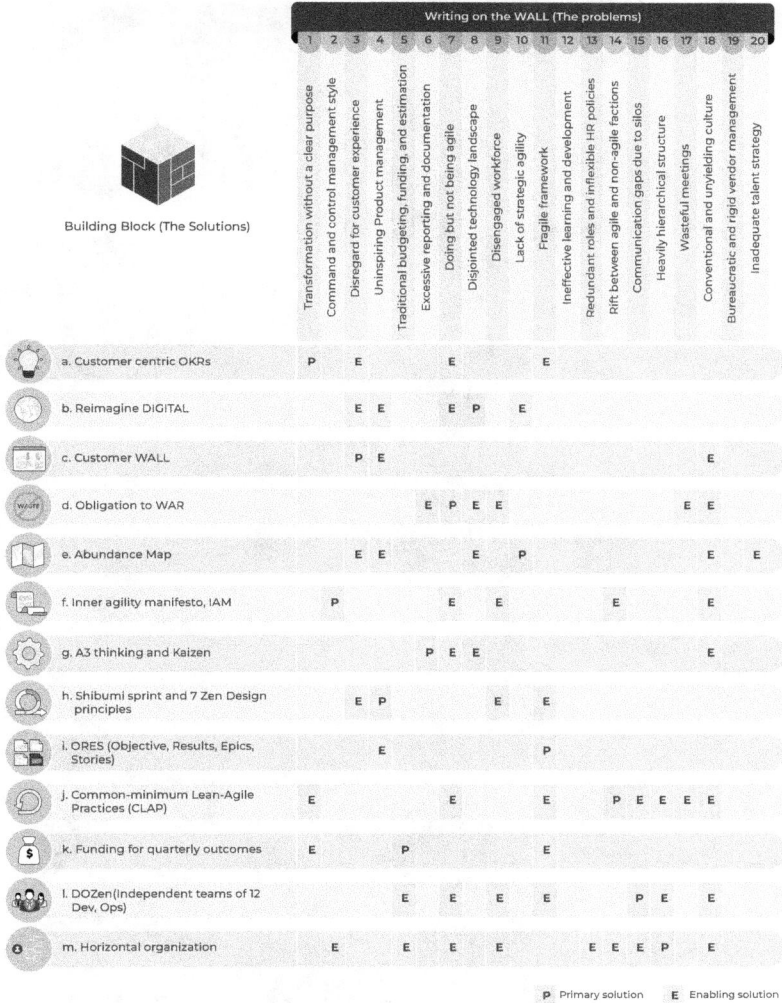

Writing on the WALL (The problems)

Building Block (The Solutions)

Solution \ Problem	1. Transformation without a clear purpose	2. Command and control management style	3. Disregard for customer experience	4. Uninspiring Product management	5. Traditional budgeting, funding, and estimation	6. Excessive reporting and documentation	7. Doing but not being agile	8. Disjointed technology landscape	9. Disengaged workforce	10. Lack of strategic agility	11. Fragile framework	12. Ineffective learning and development	13. Redundant roles and inflexible HR policies	14. Rift between agile and non-agile factions	15. Communication gaps due to silos	16. Heavily hierarchical structure	17. Wasteful meetings	18. Conventional and unyielding culture	19. Bureaucratic and rigid vendor management	20. Inadequate talent strategy
a. Customer centric OKRs	P	E				E					E									
b. Reimagine DIGITAL		E	E			E	P		E											
c. Customer WALL		P	E														E			
d. Obligation to WAR						E	P	E	E								E	E		
e. Abundance Map		E	E			E			P								E			E
f. Inner agility manifesto, IAM		P				E			E					E			E			
g. A3 thinking and Kaizen						P	E	E									E			
h. Shibumi sprint and 7 Zen Design principles			E	P					E		E									
i. ORES (Objective, Results, Epics, Stories)			E								P									
j. Common-minimum Lean-Agile Practices (CLAP)	E					E					E			P	E	E	E	E		
k. Funding for quarterly outcomes	E			P							E									
l. DOZen (independent teams of 12 Dev, Ops)			E			E			E		E				P	E		E		
m. Horizontal organization	E					E		E	E				E	E	E	P		E		

P Primary solution   E Enabling solution

Figure 17.3-1 Problem Solution Matrix-1

The cumulative effect of Solutions is vital to solve the Problems

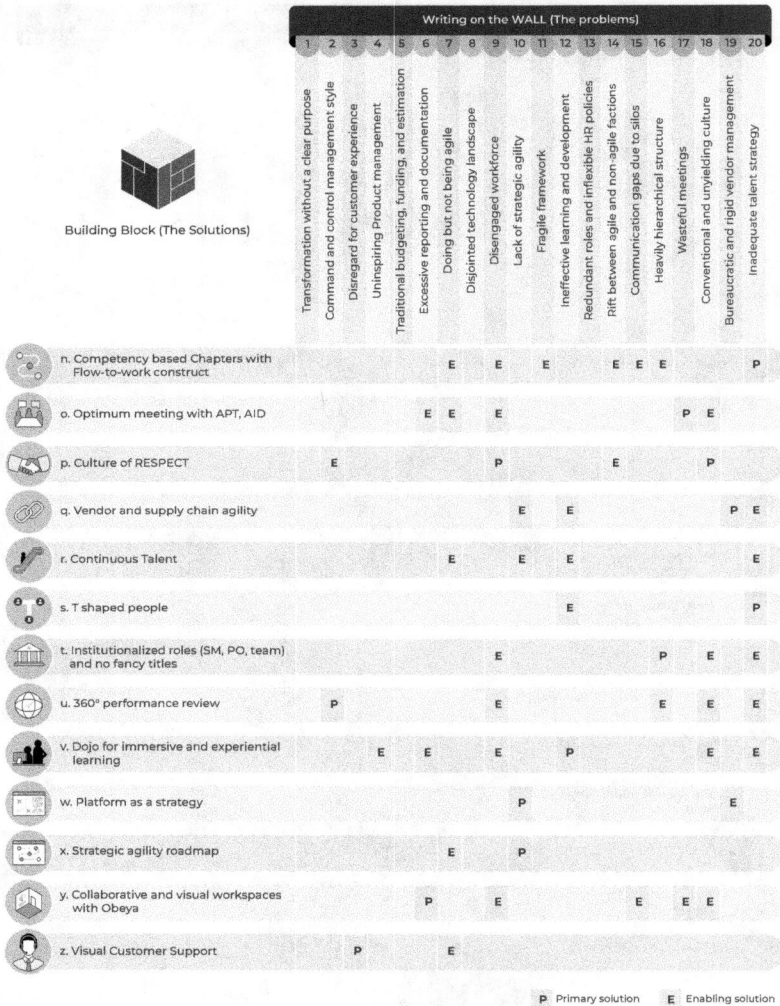

Writing on the WALL (The problems)

Building Block (The Solutions)	1. Transformation without a clear purpose	2. Command and control management style	3. Disregard for customer experience	4. Uninspiring Product management	5. Traditional budgeting, funding, and estimation	6. Excessive reporting and documentation	7. Doing but not being agile	8. Disjointed technology landscape	9. Disengaged workforce	10. Lack of strategic agility	11. Fragile framework	12. Ineffective learning and development	13. Redundant roles and inflexible HR policies	14. Rift between agile and non-agile factions	15. Communication gaps due to silos	16. Heavily hierarchical structure	17. Wasteful meetings	18. Conventional and unyielding culture	19. Bureaucratic and rigid vendor management	20. Inadequate talent strategy
n. Competency based Chapters with Flow-to-work construct							E		E		E		E	E	E					P
o. Optimum meeting with APT, AID						E	E		E								P	E		
p. Culture of RESPECT	E								P				E					P		
q. Vendor and supply chain agility									E		E								P	E
r. Continuous Talent							E		E		E									E
s. T shaped people											E									P
t. Institutionalized roles (SM, PO, team) and no fancy titles									E								P	E	E	
u. 360° performance review	P								E								E	E	E	
v. Dojo for immersive and experiential learning					E		E		E				P					E	E	
w. Platform as a strategy									P									E		
x. Strategic agility roadmap							E		P											
y. Collaborative and visual workspaces with Obeya							P		E							E	E	E		
z. Visual Customer Support			P				E													

P Primary solution   E Enabling solution

Figure 17.3-2 Problem Solution Matrix-2

Table 17.1 The farewell note

Hey Neil,
Tried calling you.
I requested Charlie for an early departure! Due to the nondisclosure with Walkers, I will avoid communications as I will work for your competitor.
I will retreat in the Himalayas to nurture my own Inner Agility. I plan to take a flight before the travel restrictions.
Siddharth Bose

Sid had generously shared his lifetime of knowledge and experience in a matter of weeks but did not forget to rehash it in forms of problem-solution matrix, a cheat sheet, and the game plan.

Truly a coach indeed!

Table 17.2 The cheat sheet - An intuitive summary

ABCD	1234
Agile-lean mindsets and behaviors	1 unified Dev and Ops team
Backlog aligned to priorities	2 weeks sprint cadence
Customer-centered outcomes	3 roles: SM, PO, team
Dedicated team members	4 ceremonies: stand-up, sprint planning, review, retrospective

Gus has started a small digital delivery startup. He has quickly mobilized a team of over 20 professionals, but all of his former direct reports from Walkers turned down his offer to join him! I have heard Gus has contracted Sid to coach him in embracing the new mindset.

I think about the day I met Sid and how wrong I was to think he wanted to steal my position.

He exited the scene without much fanfare.

I am appointed as the new chief digital officer, and I officially took over the role of product owner for advancing *TTT* efforts.

Richie has opted for early retirement from full-time work and is moving to Florida.

Bobby is being positioned to become the next CIO. Seth will be an agile coach and will work with me in setting up DOZen and Obeya across Walkers.

Saira will finally become a scrum master. She will take Zen design and Shibumi sprints to the broader design community with meetups.

Keisha is running two Chapters: product owners and business process SMEs. Hana will continue to lead the GRC but now runs it like a Chapter, along with an Obeya.

Tim now leads Chapters for program and project managers, helping them to transition to agile practitioners, obviously learning himself in his new role. Tim had always laughed a bit louder to show he is okay, but his face routinely turns pale with the term *Tim Woods*. His first request in new role is to use his full name. Both his e-mail display and signature now reads "Timothy Woods."

Paris is excited to be in her new role of chief happiness officer. Daisy will be the chief experience officer (CXO) with primary responsibility of digital shopping. She will continue to focus on increasing revenues, but her group OKRs now are purely customer centric and includes NPSs.

Doug Dicky focuses on running Kaizen throughout the company.

Dr. Anu and Cindy are now best friends chatting every week. Both are planning to incubate a support group for breast cancer survivors. Ami and Tina are getting naughtier while staying at home for months.

The *American Digital Business Review* journal has sent the copy which has the preview of their upcoming series on Walkers. A few lines mesmerize me,

"*A transformation reimagined* …

The company was seriously making preparations in early Q1 of this year for filing for chapter 11 bankruptcy. No, not anymore. This Midwest-based retail chain is not only beating the acute slowdown but also growing its e-commerce business by leaps and bounds.

The company executives have attributed its turnaround to its innovative and unique lean–agile and design thinking approach to renew its digital transformation, which they passionately call 'The Inner Building Blocks'

… to be continued."

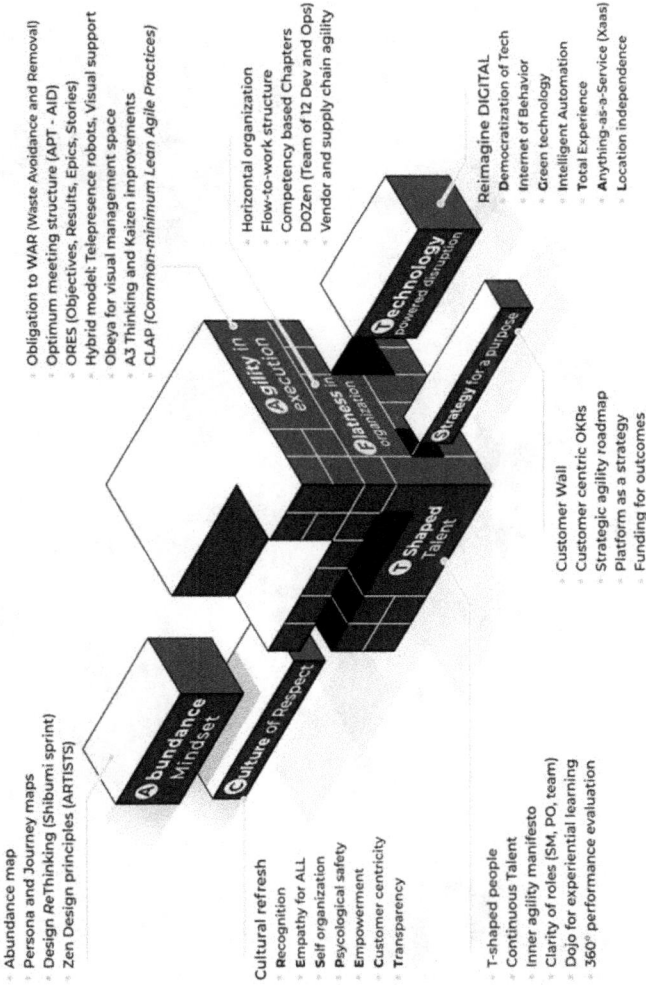

The " A C T F A S T " **Building Blocks**

The Game Plan

Abundance MindSet
» Abundance map
» Persona and Journey maps
» Design *Re*Thinking (Shibumi sprint)
» Zen Design principles (ARTISTS)

Culture of Respect
» Cultural refresh
» Recognition
» Empathy for ALL
» Self organization
» Psycological safety
» Empowerment
» Customer centricity
» Transparency

T-shaped Talent
» T-shaped people
» Continuous Talent
» Inner agility manifesto
» Clarity of roles (SM, PO, team)
» Dojo for experiential learning
» 360° performance evaluation

Agility in execution
» Obligation to WAR (Waste Avoidance and Removal)
» Optimum meeting structure (APT - AID)
» ORES (Objectives, Results, Epics, Stories)
» Hybrid model: Telepresence robots, Visual support
» Obeya for visual management space
» A3 Thinking and Kaizen improvements
» CLAP (Common-minimum Lean Agile Practices)

Flatness in organization
» Horizontal organization
» Flow-to-work structure
» Competency based Chapters
» DOZen (Team of 12 Dev and Ops)
» Vendor and supply chain agility

Strategy for a purpose
» Customer Wall
» Customer centric OKRs
» Strategic agility roadmap
» Platform as a strategy
» Funding for outcomes

Technology powered disruption
» Reimagine DIGITAL
» Democratization of Tech
» Internet of Behavior
» Green technology
» Intelligent Automation
» Total Experience
» Anything-as-a-Service (Xaas)
» Location independence

Figure 17.4 Game plan

Summary of the Chapters

1. The Discovery: Background, Key Players, and Situations: This chapter starts with the introduction, background, and struggles in the personal and professional life of the main character Neil Frost. Then, it the outlines the journey of the past few years and how the company, Walkers Mart, has been unsuccessful in its digital transformation. Finally, the chapter illustrates the approach for transforming the transformation with the sprints. The storyline is divided into four sprints, and the concepts are organized in each chapter using the visual structure of Kanban board—starting with Chapter 2.

   - Sprint 1: Current state assessment
   - Sprint 2: Reflection and reimagination
   - Sprint 3: Analysis and improvements
   - Sprint 4: Rebuilding and recovery

Sprint 1: Current State Assessment

2. Building the WALL: An Inclusive Approach to Define Problems: The chapter starts with a structure for identifying problems in the company with a comprehensive enterprise-wide retrospective. The chapter explains the limitations like a lack of clear purpose in a transformation, and command and control management styles of executives. Finally, the chapter underlines the problems of deficient customer experience and mediocre product management using the approach of Net Promoter Score (NPS) and voice of customers.

3. Obligation to *WAR* (Waste Avoidance and Removal): Relentless Focus on Value: This chapter explains lean wastes using one of the characters and articulates the implications of wastes. Then, it explains the meaning of agility and its difference from traditional ways of working. Next, it includes the illustration of value-add and non-value-add analysis. Finally, it describes problems in embracing

true agility such as traditional budgeting and excessive focus on status reporting and documentation.

4. Gemba Walk and Candid Talk: A Value Stream-Based Diagnostics: It explains the purpose, approach, and an example of Gemba Walk with an emphasis on diagnostic assessment. It includes an approach to train ourselves in observing areas of opportunities. It outlines the opportunities from ideation to implementation and illustrates the hidden Cost of Wastes in the company. The chapter concludes with newer problems identified with Gemba Walks: doing but not being agile, disjointed technology landscape, and disengaged workforce.

Sprint 2: Reflection and Reimagination

5. Organization as a Living Organism: System Thinking to Rebuild an Enterprise: This chapter illustrates that the organizations are not machines and are made of people and living creatures. An organization just like any other living organism must adapt as the environment changes in order to survive. The living organisms are as robust as their cells, and similarly the Building Blocks of the organization define its strength. A firm must leverage systems thinking to revitalize their Building Blocks to address problems. These Building Blocks are outlined in the subsequent chapters for the solutions. The chapter closes with an approach to redefine OKRs (Objective and Key Results).

6. "You Are on Mute!" A New Definition to Reimagine Digital: This chapter begins with the rationale for recalibration of digital strategy and need for unifying disjointed technology landscape systems. The chapter demonstrates a fresh approach to reimagine digital landscape to improve productivity, participation, and seamless flow of value. The chapter revolves around the seven concepts to reimagine digital strategy, democratization of technology, Internet of behavior, green technology, intelligent automation, total experience, Anything as a Service (XaaS), and location independence.

7. The Inner Agility: The Power of Pause and Mindfulness: This chapter explains the profound connections of our minds and our inner self with the ways we think and perform in our work environment. The beginning draws upon the notions of mindfulness, intrinsic agility,

and cultural renewal from Zen philosophy. The middle of the chapter is aimed to edify the four Zen values for embracing change as an ally. Then, we discuss a slew of concrete techniques of abundance map, A3 Thinking, and Kaizen. Finally, it concludes with the concept of Inner Agility Manifesto.

8. The Shibumi Sprint: The Zen Design (Re)Thinking Cadence: This chapter starts with a fresh approach to reinvent and refine Design Thinking drawing upon the idea of Shibumi. It portrays the seven Zen aesthetics principles for improving design of processes, products, and experiences. Next, we build the case for running Shibumi sprints focused on designs. The chapter ends with an illustration of tools and techniques including voice of customers, user personas, journey maps, and empathy mapping to improve designs.

Sprint 3: Analysis and Improvements

9. Fragile Framework: Limitations of Emulating Scaling Frameworks: Here we challenge the prevailing wisdom that adhering to any "fixed and static" framework makes an organization agile and nimble. We explain why frameworks could accrue more than required processes, roles, and layers in the company ultimately leading to complexities and confusions. We leverage agile manifesto and lean thinking to demonstrate a hypothesis of how a scaling framework could become heavy, prescriptive, ceremonial, and fragile, in turn adversely impacting agility, Time-to-Market, and innovation. The chapter ends with a solution for a cohesive approach of Objectives, (key) Results, Epic, and Story (ORES).

10. Structural Side Effects: Bureaucracy of a Hierarchical Organization: The chapter depicts an approach of Common-minimum Lean–Agile Practices (CLAP) to resolve conflict between lean and agile factions. It has illustrations of how complexities in organizational structures get compounded due to several other permutations and combinations in reporting structures and silos. Next, we analyze the problems due to hierarchical departments and how it reduces the agility. The chapter ends with solutions to resolve funding complexities and lightweight rules of engagement for governance, risk, and compliance (GRC).

11. Flattening the Curve: Shift From Vertical to Horizontal Organization: This chapter starts with principles to establish independent teams. Then, we explain the optimal size and composition of a truly independent team of development and operations grounded in Zen values. Finally, we illustrate a nimble organization structure using a combination of competency-based chapters, Flow-to-work, and servant leadership construct to depict a representative model of a flatter-horizontal organization.

12. Vultures of the Culture: Critical Role of Leaders in Mindset Shift: This chapter starts with the limitations of RACI matrix and then addresses the problem of wasteful meetings with solution. Then, we describe how behaviors and mindsets in an organization get influenced by the hierarchy, internal politics, and vested interests leading to a conventional and unyielding culture. We end the chapter with a solution to renew the culture using a construct of "Culture of RESPECT."

13. Talent Escalator: Establishing the Continuous Flow of Capabilities: The chapter starts with problem of bureaucratic vendor management and introduces the principles for achieving vendor and supply chain agility. Then, we explain the problems of inadequate talent strategy and time-consuming process to mobilize talent. We draw upon the continuous flow from the functioning of an escalator to showcase method to continually crowdsource talent. We discuss the importance of T-shaped talent and end with an easy-to-remember description of roles of the scrum master, product owner, and team.

Sprint 4: Rebuilding and Recovery

14. Dojo: A Place for Experiential and Immersive Learning: This chapter focuses on the concept of Dojo and its importance in *learning by doing and learning by examples*. We outline need for talent building without the disproportionate fear of losing talent to attrition. The middle of this chapter outlines the benefits and uniqueness of Dojo and ways to set up the Dojo. Finally, we illustrate a day in the life of Dojo taking an example of the performance measurement of agile teams.

15. Platform as a Strategy: The Roadmap to Strategic Agility: We explain the role of digital platforms in terms of the ecosystems, marketplace, and communities that benefit from the interactions of their participants. The middle of the chapter explains differences between products and platforms. Then, we rationalize the case for building platforms. Next, we outline the attributes of a digital platform and discuss benefits of platform as a strategy. Finally, we introduce the technique of strategic agility roadmap.

16. HOME–Agility: Hybrid Operating Model for Enterprise–Agility: We depict a hybrid model for the future of work. A thoughtful hybrid model is vital to advance enterprise agility with well-orchestrated remote and in-person teams. This starts with practices of hybrid cadence, team norms, and a visual management space, Obeya. Then, we discuss digital technologies, such as Hybrid Floor, telepresence robots, and digital Obeya for internal collaboration, and then digital Customer Wall and Visual Customer Support for customer collaboration. Finally, the focus is on redesigned workspace and organization policies to enhance people experience.

17. The ACT FAST Building: Codifying the Company's Experiments: The final chapter explains the summary of the chapters, outlines the experiments and concepts, and recapitulates the primary solutions to strengthen the inner Building Blocks of the company. Then, we demonstrate the combined effects of the four sprints in terms of the new lives and roles of the characters along with the effect on the Walkers Mart's business performance. We conclude with an integrative approach and mapping of the identified problems (Writings on the WALL) to solutions (Building Blocks) using the "Problem–Solution Matrix."

Acronyms

- ARTISTS: Austere, Refreshing, True to life, Imperfection, Simplicity, Tranquility, Subtle
- APT | AID: Agenda, Participants, Timebox | Action, Information, Decision
- Blah (- blah): Boot licking across hierarchy
- CoE: Center of Excellence
- CoW: Cost of Wastes
- CRM: Customer Relationship management
- CI/ CD: Continuous Integration/Continuous Delivery
- CLAP: Common-minimum Lean-agile practices
- CDC: chair, desk and computer; collaboration, design thinking and creativity
- DevSecOps: Development, Security and operations
- DOOR: Digital Org-wide Obeya Room
- DOZen: Development, Operation and Zen values
- FA@ST: Framework for Agile@Scale Techniques
- FLOW: Feedback Loop Orchestration Workflow
- I.AM: Inner Agility Manifesto
- IoT: Internet of Things
- IoB: Internet of Behavior
- IVR: Interactive Voice Response
- GRC: Governance, Risk Management and Compliance
- GOD: Guru of Design
- HiPPO: Highest Paid Person's Opinion
- HOME-Agility: Hybrid Operating Model for Enterprise-Agility
- MoSCoW: Must have; Should have; Could have; Won't have
- NPS: Net Promoter Score
- OKR: Objectives and Key results
- ORES: Objectives, (Key) Results, Epics and Stories
- OSAP: Office of Strategic alliances and partnerships

- PICASO: Problem, Importance, Current state, Alternatives, Success metric, Ownership
- pSAT: People Satisfaction
- RACI: Responsible, Accountable, Consulted and Informed
- RFI / RFP: Response for Information/ Response for Proposal
- RESPECT: Recognition, Empathy, Self-organization, psychological safety, Empowerment, Customer centricity and Transparency
- SEE: Stair, Elevator and Escalator
- SoW: Statement of Work
- SME: Subject Matter Expert
- TIM WOODS: Transportation, Inventory, Motion, Waiting, Over-processing, Over documentation, Defects, Skills and Intellect
- TTT: Transform-the-Transformation
- UX/UI: User Experience / User Interface
- VSM: Value Stream Mapping
- WALL: Walkers Lean-Agile Lessons learned
- WAR: Waste Avoidance and Removal

Glossary of Terms

List of Problems and Solutions

Writings on the WALL (The Problems)	Page #
1. Transformation without a clear purpose	32
2. Command and control management style	37
3. Disregard for customer experience	39
4. Uninspiring product management	40
5. Traditional budgeting, funding, and estimation	54
6. Excessive reporting and documentation	60
7. Doing but not being agile	68
8. Disjointed technology landscape	70
9. Disengaged workforce	74
10. Lack of strategic agility	97
11. Fragile framework	167
12. Ineffective learning and development	168
13. Redundant roles and inflexible HR policies	173
14. Rift between agile and nonagile factions	177
15. Communication gaps due to silos	187
16. Heavily hierarchical structure	189
17. Wasteful meetings	219
18. Conventional and unyielding culture	219
19. Bureaucratic and rigid vendor management	228
20. Inadequate talent strategy	234

Building Blocks (The Solutions)	Page #
a) Customer-centric OKRs	97
b) Reimagine DIGITAL	103
c) Customer WALL	132
d) Obligation to WAR	132
e) Abundance Map	132
f) Inner Agility Manifesto (I AM)	132
g) A3 Thinking and Kaizen	132
h) Shibumi sprint and seven Zen design principles	146
i) ORES (Objective, Results, Epics, and Stories)	169
j) Common-minimum Lean–Agile Practices (CLAP)	180
k) Funding for quarterly outcomes	192
l) DOZen (Independent teams of 12 Dev, Ops)	205
m) Horizontal organization	205
n) Competency-based Chapters with Flow-to-work	205
o) Optimum meeting with APT and AID	217
p) Culture of RESPECT	223
q) Vendor and supply chain agility	229
r) Continuous talent	236
s) T-shaped people	236
t) Institutionalized roles (SM, PO, and team) and no fancy titles	243
u) 360° performance review	243
v) Dojo for immersive and experiential learning	253
w) Platform as a strategy	268
x) Strategic agility roadmap	268
y) Collaborative and visual workspaces with Obeya	281
z) Visual Customer Support	281

Bibliography

Goldratt, Eliyahu M., and Jeff Cox. 2016. *The Goal: A Process of Ongoing Improvement*. Abingdon: Routledge Taylor and Francis Group.

Kim, Gene, Kevin Behr, and George Spafford. 2014. *The Phoenix Project: A Novel about It, Devops, and Helping Your Business Win*. Portland, OR: IT Revolution.

May, Matthew E. 2011. *The Shibumi Strategy: A Powerful Way to Create Meaningful Change*. San Francisco, CA: Jossey-Bass.

Prentiss, Chris. 2019. *Zen and the Art of Happiness*. Chatswood, NSW: New Holland Publishers.

Reynolds, Garr. n.d. *PresentationZen*. New Riders.

Suzuki, Shunryū, and Trudy Dixon. 1989. *Zen Mind: Beginner's Mind ; Informal Talks on Zen Meditation and Practice*. New York, NY: Weatherhill.

About the Author

Abhi Rai is a seasoned transformation leader and an accomplished coach. He is passionate about advancing lean thinking and agility to improve the world around us! He has trained and coached more than 1500 professionals across four continents and over three dozen organizations in 10 diverse industries. His over two decades of professional experience include senior expert positions in the prestigious management consulting and digital firms such as Accenture, BCG, Infosys, and McKinsey. He holds bachelor's degree in Engineering, master's in International Business and received MIT Executive Education in Digital Business Strategy.

www.linkedin.com/in/abhishekrai2

Index

OTHER TITLES IN THE PORTFOLIO AND PROJECT MANAGEMENT COLLECTION

Timothy J. Kloppenborg, Xavier University and
Kam Jugdev, Athabasca University, Editors

- *Greatness in Construction History* by Sherif Hashem
- *Project Profitability* by Reginald Tomas Lee
- *Lean Knowledge Management* by Forsgren Roger
- *Moving the Needle With Lean OKRs* by Bart den Haak
- *The MBA Distilled for Project & Program Professionals* by Clark Brad
- *Project Management for Banks* by Dan Bonner
- *Successfully Achieving Strategy Through Effective Portfolio Management* by Frank R. Parth
- *Be Agile Do Agile* by Vittal Anantatmula and Timothy J. Kloppenborg
- *Project-Led Strategic Management* by James Marion, John Lewis, and Tracey Richardson
- *Hybrid Project Management* by Mark Tolbert and Susan Parente
- *Design: A Business Case* by Brigitte Borja de Mozota and Steinar Valade-Amland
- *Workplace Jazz* by Gerald J. Leonard
- *Stakeholder-led Project Management, Second Edition* by Louise M. Worsley
- *A.G.I.L.E. Thinking Demystified* by Frank Forte

Concise and Applied Business Books

The Collection listed above is one of 30 business subject collections that Business Expert Press has grown to make BEP a premiere publisher of print and digital books. Our concise and applied books are for...

- Professionals and Practitioners
- Faculty who adopt our books for courses
- Librarians who know that BEP's Digital Libraries are a unique way to offer students ebooks to download, not restricted with any digital rights management
- Executive Training Course Leaders
- Business Seminar Organizers

Business Expert Press books are for anyone who needs to dig deeper on business ideas, goals, and solutions to everyday problems. Whether one print book, one ebook, or buying a digital library of 110 ebooks, we remain the affordable and smart way to be business smart. For more information, please visit www.businessexpertpress.com, or contact sales@businessexpertpress.com.

www.ingramcontent.com/pod-product-compliance
Lightning Source LLC
Chambersburg PA
CBHW061127220326
41599CB00024B/4190